The Miracle Braves, 1914–1916

1914 Boston Braves, National League and World Series champions. *From left, front row:* Joe Connolly, coach Fred Mitchell, batboy Willie Connor, Dick Rudolph, Rabbit Maranville, Dick Crutcher, Bill Martin, Johnny Evers. *Middle row:* George Whitted, Oscar Dugey, Lefty Tyler, Paul Strand, Josh Devore, Larry Gilbert, Red Smith, Herbie Moran. *Back row:* Bill James, Ted Cather, Charlie Deal, George Davis, Ensign Cottrell, Gene Cocreham, Otto Hess, Les Mann, Hank Gowdy, Butch Schmidt, Bert Whaling (National Baseball Hall of Fame Museum and Library).

The Miracle Braves, 1914–1916

CHARLES C. ALEXANDER

McFarland & Company, Inc., Publishers

Jefferson, North Carolina

LIBRARY OF CONGRESS CATALOGUING-IN-PUBLICATION DATA

Alexander, Charles C.
    The miracle Braves, 1914–1916 / Charles C. Alexander.
       p.   cm.
    Includes bibliographical references and index.

    ISBN 978-0-7864-7424-0 (softcover : acid free paper) ∞
    ISBN 978-1-4766-1964-4 (ebook)

    1. Boston Braves (Baseball team)—History.   I. Title.
GV875.B59A54 2015
796.357'64097446109041—dc23   2014047208

BRITISH LIBRARY CATALOGUING DATA ARE AVAILABLE

On the cover: Catcher Hank Gowdy of the 1914 Boston Braves
(George Grantham Bain Collection, Library of Congress)

Printed in the United States of America

McFarland & Company, Inc., Publishers
  Box 611, Jefferson, North Carolina 28640
    www.mcfarlandpub.com

To the memory of
the 1950 Beaumont Roughnecks,
whose Texas League pennant
was almost as improbable
as that of the 1914 Braves

Acknowledgments

While I was writing this book, the Society for American Baseball Research (SABR) published *The Miracle Braves of 1914: Boston's Original Worst-to-First World Series Champions*, to which thirty-eight SABR members contributed essays and collected contemporary materials on the personnel, course of the season, press commentary, and various other aspects of the 1914 champions. My book is inclusive of the 1914 Braves but also chronologically broader. Readers wishing to know even more about that remarkable team, and in particular about the careers of its players, should consult the SABR volume, which was edited by Bill Nowlin.

As always, it was a pleasure to work in the Giamatti Research Center at the National Baseball Hall of Fame in Cooperstown, New York, and to receive the prompt and efficient assistance of Tim Wiles and his staff. I also wish to thank Deb Jayne, of SABR's lending library in Phoenix, Arizona, and the staffs of the Miami University and Ohio University libraries. Special thanks to Jeff Ferrier, Lucy Conn, and Edie Luce for their help with microfilm loans from Ohio University's collections. Valerie Elliott, manager of the Smith Center for Regional History at the Oxford, Ohio, branch of the Lane Public Library, put up with my almost-daily presence in front of microfilm readers in the crowded circumstances of the Center's room. I owe special thanks to various fellow SABR members for their support and encouragement, especially Rick Huhn, Jerry Wood, Steve Steinberg, and John Thorn. Once more, I express my loving appreciation to my two best friends: my daughter, Rachel, and my wife, JoAnn.

Charles C. Alexander
Hanover Township, Butler County, Ohio, May 2014

Table of Contents

Prologue: "Its most romantic episode"

Early in 1946, on the eve of the first post–World War II baseball season, Harold Kaese, the veteran sportswriter for the *Boston Globe*, looked back on the history of the city's National League team (the subject of the book he would publish two years later). Kaese characterized the surge of the 1914 Boston Braves—who rose from last place as late as July 8 to win the pennant by ten and a half games and then sweep Connie Mack's lordly Philadelphia Athletics in the World Series—as having given baseball "its most romantic episode." Two years earlier, a national poll of Associated Press sportswriters had voted the "Miracle Braves" the all-time sports team; in 1950 another poll, this one of 361 AP writers, named the Braves' sweep of the Athletics the biggest sports upset of the past half-century. "Even Cinderella," wrote one overwrought Kansas scribe, "is no more famous than the Boston Braves of 1914. No achievement was more unexpected. It was synonymous with climbing from the depths to the topmost heights."[1]

Today few baseball fans—except the minority who take seriously the history of what, a hundred years ago, was truly the National Pastime—know anything about the 1914 Boston Braves. After all, it's been sixty-two years since the Boston National Leaguers, after winning a pennant in 1948, went into decline and moved to Milwaukee, where the franchise remained for little more than a decade before relocating again to Atlanta. In the mid–1950s, moreover, the Braves' 1914 World Series victims left Philadelphia for Kansas City, then moved on to Oakland in 1968. The landscape of major-league baseball is far different today from what it was a century ago.

Before the "Miracle Braves," Boston's National League entry had finished in the "first division" (the top four teams in a then-standard

1

eight-team league) only twice in the twentieth century. After a third-place showing in 1902, the city's National Leaguers had never made it higher than sixth; from 1903 to 1912 they compiled an aggregate record of 521–980—a cheerless .347 winning percentage. Seven different men had managed teams that finished last five times.

It hadn't always been like that. From 1891 to 1898, under the calm but shrewd direction of Frank Selee, Boston's "Beaneaters" won five National League championships, including three in a row (1891–1893).[2] But the emergence of the American League in 1901 as a rival organization under the forceful presidency of Byron Bancroft "Ban" Johnson, and its aggressive raids on National League rosters, brought most of the game's top players into the new league.

The Boston National League team, once baseball's strongest, was virtually devastated. As it went from mediocre to plain bad, most of its followers transferred their allegiance to the local American League entry, which won back-to-back pennants in 1903–1904, defeated Pittsburgh in the first "modern" World Series in 1903, and won another pennant and Series championship in 1912.[3] Whether as Beaneaters (as some older baseball writers continued to call them); "Doves" (perhaps the most unfortunate nickname in sports history), when John S. C. Dovey was its president (1907–1910); or "Rustlers," during William H. Russell's brief presidency (1911), Boston's National League teams were perennial losers.

They played the 77 home games of their 154-game schedule in the smallest ballpark in the two major leagues. South End Grounds, located at Walpole Street and Columbus Avenue, was in the same neighborhood as Huntington Avenue Grounds, where the Boston American Leaguers had played since their inception in 1901. South End Grounds was a single-deck, wooden facility that had undergone various modifications since it reopened in its third incarnation in 1894. By 1912 its seating capacity was about 11,000, and like most ballparks of the era, it had irregular outfield dimensions. Changes before the 1912 season made the distances down the left-field line a formidable 350 feet but down the right-field line only 235 feet, although the fence curved out sharply in right-center field to the deepest point in the outfield, about 400 feet from home plate. Those dimensions were ample in the so-called Dead Ball Era, when scores were usually low and home runs—particularly ones hit over fences—were rarities.

So far in the twentieth century, the South End Grounds' seating capacity had been ample as well. In 1911 only about 116,000 people paid to watch a team that won forty-four times and finished fifty-four games behind the pennant-winning New York Giants. Like the other eight major-league teams located in the eastern cities as well as Pittsburgh, the Boston team was handicapped by state and local "blue laws" prohibiting professional baseball and other commercial amusements on Sundays.

William H. Russell, Harold Kaese has written, "gave up an extensive legal practice in New York because of his health, then virtually committed suicide by buying the Doves."[4] After suffering through a year's losses both at the ticket windows and on the ball field, Russell died of a heart attack in November 1911. Yet while few suspected it at the time, Boston's National League fortunes were about to take a turn for the better. For the third time in four years, the team's ownership changed. Russell's widow was anxious to unload the franchise, and a new group of investors quickly appeared.

The man who brought off the deal was John Montgomery Ward. Fifty-one years old, Ward had been an outstanding pitcher and infielder from 1879 to 1894 and the leader of the Brotherhood of Professional Ball Players, which revolted against the owners' control and in 1890, attracting most of the top players of the day, operated the semi-socialistic, ill-fated Players' League. Ward held both political science and law degrees from Columbia University and, after he quit playing, became a successful New York attorney.

Wanting to get back into baseball, Ward paid a representative of Russell's estate $5,000 for an option to buy Russell's majority stock in the Boston franchise. Then, with the help of John Carroll, a wealthy New York friend, he enlisted James E. Gaffney, a New York contractor. The trio paid $177,000 for the 945 shares owned by Russell's widow, and assumed the $200,000 mortgage on South End Grounds the Dove brothers had taken out when they bought the franchise. Ward became the club's president and Gaffney its treasurer, although Gaffney held a majority of the stock and would clearly be the major influence in the club's affairs.

Gaffney, the son of Irish immigrants and a onetime New York City policeman, had married into a wealthy family and formed some close connections to the Tammany Hall political organization that usually controlled city hall. He was known to be particularly close to Charles F. Murphy, Tammany Hall's powerful boss. Gaffney used his connections—and occasional bribes—to obtain contracts for a number of highly lucrative construction projects, including the Grand Central railroad station. He was also not above taking bribes to use his influence on behalf of other contractors. Forty-three years old in 1911, he was already a multi-millionaire.

One of Gaffney's first acts after the purchase of the Boston franchise was to rename the team. As a "Grand Sachem" of Tammany Hall—which had as its symbol an Indian figure called "Chief Tammany"—and as one of its "Braves," he decided his team would be called the Boston Braves. The new name, said John Ward, carried a "true fighting ring that the fans [will] take to."[5] (People today who regard the nickname of the Braves' descendants in Atlanta as racist, and object strenuously to their fans' tomahawk rallying chant, might consider that the nickname originally was intended to connote a political organization.)

James Gaffney watching the Braves in spring training at Central City Park, Macon, Georgia, 1914. For Gaffney, baseball was first and last a business (George Grantham Bain Collection, Library of Congress).

On January 6, 1911, President Ward announced that Fred Tenney, who had played first base and managed the team from 1905 to 1907 and then again during the past dismal season, would be replaced as manager by Johnny Kling. A mainstay of the Chicago Cubs' four-time pennant winners and twice World Series champions (1906–1908, 1910), Kling had come to Boston the previous June in a multi-player trade. He was considered the best catcher in the league and one of the smartest players in the game. Ward signed Kling to a one-year contract as player-manager. In March, after two months in limbo, Tenney received his release and the $4,000 balance on his two-year contract.

Gaffney, Ward, and Kling looked over the South End Grounds and talked about making improvements to the little ballpark. Work began on rebuilding the rickety right-field bleachers, adding a new wing to the grandstand, and reconfiguring the playing field. But Gaffney had long-range plans for a new ballpark in a completely different location and started working to raise the capital to build it. Meanwhile the Red Sox, the city's American League team, were about to abandon Huntington Avenue Grounds, their little wooden park, for a new, mostly steel-and-concrete facility named Fenway Park.

The newly christened Braves did their spring training at Augusta, Georgia, in the local South Atlantic League team's ballpark. As he was supposed to, Kling talked optimistically, telling the press contingent at Augusta, "I have as fine players in this bunch as any manager in the league." It was, he went on, "the best the team has started out with in a long time."[6] Kling may actually have believed that, and he did have a few good ballplayers—a very few. Second-baseman and team captain Bill Sweeny had batted .314 the previous season and in 1912 would have what would later be called a "career year," batting .344, third best in the league, and driving in 100 runs. The veteran Art Devlin, purchased that winter from the Giants, was still a useful infielder.

Among a generally nondescript assortment of pitchers, two merited respect: George Tyler, a young, slender left-hander with an unusual overhand delivery in which he stepped toward first base, and Hub Perdue, a right-hander from Tennessee whose stocky build had earned him the nickname "Gallatin Squash." Both had pitched well at times in 1911, for a team that led both major leagues with 347 errors.[7]

One of Kling's pitchers at Augusta was anything but nondescript—

Denton True "Cy" Young. After being released by Cleveland late in the 1911 season, Young had caught on in the National League with Boston and won three of seven starts. He reported to the Braves the next spring with hopes of pitching one more year at the age of forty-five, but after working 7,377 innings in 906 games and winning 511 times in twenty-two major-league seasons, Young had to admit his arm was simply worn out. He went north with the team but never pitched before receiving his release late in May.

The Braves' 1912 season started promisingly on April 11 with a 7–4 win over the Philadelphia Phillies. Hub Purdue outlasted Grover Cleveland Alexander, who had won a remarkable twenty-eight games in 1911, his rookie season. But within a month the Braves had become the losers their fans had long been accustomed to, falling to the bottom of the league with a 10–18 record. They never got any higher, although they did improve on their 1911 record, finishing at 52–101, a mere fifty-two games behind the Giants, who again led the National League. Tim Murnane—baseball editor of the *Boston Globe* and a former player and part owner, as well as the current president of the Class B New England League—observed that while the team had looked good in the spring, "things have gone from worse to Worcester."[8]

Among the many indignities the Braves suffered in 1912 was a June 20 game in which the Giants stole twelve bases. Shortly thereafter, in losing to Brooklyn, the Braves somehow failed to score in an inning in which they had a base hit and drew four bases on balls. Perdue's 13–16 record was the pitching staff's best; "Lefty" Tyler led both major leagues with twenty-two defeats, although he did win eleven games. Walter Dickson managed but three wins while losing nineteen times.

On September 12, a twenty-year-old, 5'5" shortstop weighing at most 145 pounds—purchased by the Braves from the New England League's New Bedford club for $2,500—began a major-league career that would stretch over more than two decades.[9] Walter James Vincent Maranville, a policeman's son from Springfield, Massachusetts, had already gained the nickname "Rabbit," supposedly given to him by a little girl who said he jumped around on the ball field just like a rabbit. Indeed Maranville was extraordinarily quick-footed afield and fast on the bases. He made quite a lot of errors, in part because he tried for many balls other shortstops couldn't reach. At New Bedford and everywhere else he would play, he delighted spectators with his "basket" method of catching pop flies, waiting with his arms at his sides until the last second, then grabbing the ball at his belt buckle.

Rabbit didn't like for people to talk about his size. "I am not so small as you think," he protested. "I'm almost 5 feet 6 inches tall. It's because I'm playing with such big fellows that I look short."[10] (Actually the typical major-leaguer of Maranville's day—apart from pitchers—stood about 5'10" and weighed about 175 pounds, hardly big when compared to today's players.)

Maranville batted with little power, but given the prevailing batting styles of the period, few ballplayers did. He choked up on the bat about four or five inches, as did much bigger men, and sought to "place hit" the ball over the infield or between the infielders and outfielders. Home runs hit over fences were rarities; the great majority of homers were inside-the-park drives. Batters swung at balls that, after the second inning or so, were stained by grass, dirt, and tobacco juice, scuffed up, and increasingly softened. Balls remained in play until they were fouled out of the ballpark or otherwise lost—which didn't mean lost when retrieved by spectators, who were expected and often forcibly compelled to return balls to the field. In most games only two or three balls were used; in some games, only one.

Rabbit Maranville was also an excellent bunter, which every player was expected to be at a time when teams played for a run or two here and there and seldom managed a big inning. (The sacrifice bunt with a runner on first base and nobody out was virtually an automatic play.) The little New Englander would prove to be an intense, scrappy performer on the field as well as one of the game's great jesters and pranksters—an all-around colorful character. But in what remained of the 1912 season, he was less than impressive, batting only .209 in twenty-six games.

Ward and Kling didn't get along; the manager complained that the club president interfered in the running of the team. At the end of July, Ward resigned and for $50,000 sold his stock to Gaffney, who took over the president's duties. Although Gaffney declared his support for Kling, recently he had traveled to Buffalo to talk with George Stallings, manager of that city's Eastern League entry.

Buffalo was only a fourth-place team, but Gaffney had watched

**Walter "Rabbit" Maranville, merry prankster and shortstop *extraordinaire*
(George Bantham Bain Collection, Library of Congress).**

Stallings when he managed New York's American Leaguers to fifth- and
second-place finishes in 1909 and 1910 and knew him to be somebody
with a wealth of baseball experience. A couple of weeks later the two
met again in New York, where they watched the Braves lose to the Giants
at the new edition of the Polo Grounds. Afterward Stallings said, "I
always seem to get the hopeless teams, but this one is the worst I ever
saw." By then Clark Griffith, manager of the American League Washington Senators and a close friend of Gaffney, was telling the press
Stallings would manage the Braves in 1913. Stallings denied it, calling
such reports "absolutely unfounded.... I shall stay where I am for the
next few years anyhow."[11]

So much for denials. Shortly after the Boston Red Sox defeated the
Giants in a dramatic eight-game World Series, Stallings signed a three-
year contract said to pay him $12,500 per year.[12] That was generous for
the period, especially given that the Braves drew only 116,000 to South
End Grounds, while the Red Sox's home attendance at their new Fenway
Park totaled nearly 600,000. (Chicago led the American League with a
few thousand more; the Giants led the majors with 638,000.) While Tim

Murnane predicted the Braves would play "more scrappy ball" under Stallings, the new manager was quoted as saying that he wasn't encouraged by the talent he inherited, and that the Braves job was like being "sentenced."[13]

Although their faithful followers could scarcely have imagined it, the arrival of George Stallings was about to produce a remarkable turnaround in the fortunes of the downtrodden Boston Nationals. As he once described himself, Stallings had "that heart-breaking determination to win." Yet the Braves' spectacular success in 1914 has almost completely obscured what the team did in the following two seasons. In 1927 John Kieran, the *New York Times'* urbane sports columnist, dismissed the post–1914 Braves: "The Braves of 1914 were a 'one-year' team. They flashed and disappeared." Twenty-seven years later, Irving Vaughan of the *Chicago Tribune* echoed Kieran: "The Braves' pennant feat, as expected, proved a flash."[14]

But there's more to the story—much more. What I have sought to do in this book is to put the achievement of Stallings and his 1914 Braves in the context of the general revival of the Boston National League franchise in the years 1913–1916. The Braves of those years were more than a "'one-year' team" or "a flash." In fact, they gave their long-suffering fans the best baseball they would see for another three decades.

1912–1913: "The most interesting achievement in the baseball world"

George Tweedy Stallings was a true son of the South. He was one of five sons born to William Henry Stallings and Elizabeth Jane Hooper Stallings. William Henry Stallings's owned a plantation at Haddock (or Haddock Station), a community in Jones County about seventeen miles from Macon, Georgia. At some time Stallings's father suffered financial reverses that caused him to lose the property and become an itinerant building contractor, initially in Augusta, Georgia, which is where George Stallings was born.

Stallings claimed to have attended Richmond Academy in Virginia, to have graduated from Virginia Military Institute (V. M. I.), and to have completed two years at the College of Physicians and Surgeons in Baltimore. Yet Martin Kohout, in his research on Stallings, didn't find his name on V. M. I.'s alumni rolls and also found no record of his having attended medical school. Moreover, while Stallings's tombstone has his birth date as November 10, 1869, he was actually born on November 17, 1867.[1]

What is known to be factual is that in the summer of 1886, a member of the National League's Philadelphia Phillies saw Stallings playing as a catcher for a local team in Jacksonville, Florida, where his father had relocated his contracting business. Recommended to manager Harry Wright, young Stallings signed to play for the Phillies. Thus began more than four decades of travels across the landscape of professional baseball.

With the Philadelphia team, Stallings played sparingly and soon received his release. The 1887 season found him with Stockton in the

California State League; he spent the next two years in the same league with Oakland. Early in April 1889, just before leaving for Oakland, Stallings married a young Jones County woman named Bell White. They would have two sons: George Vernon Stallings, born in 1894, who became a cartoonist and eventually joined the Disney Studios, and Oliver White Stallings, born three years later, who worked for the Edison Company and later World Construction.

In 1890, with most of the game's talent having defected to the rebel Players' League, Stallings answered a solicitation for ballplayers from Nick Young, National League president, that was published in newspapers across the country. He signed with the Brooklyn team, for which he caught four games and went hitless in eleven at bats. For the next two seasons, he was back in the California League.

Having saved much of his modest baseball pay, Stallings then purchased the Augusta Southern League team, named himself manager, and also played the outfield. Although the league shut down in midseason, Stallings later claimed he made $15,000 on the sale of players to higher leagues. So when the Southern League reorganized, he bought and managed Nashville. This time he lost a lot of money and (temporarily) abandoned the ownership end of the game after the 1895 season. (When he quit playing, he managed from the bench in street clothes, which meant that under professional baseball's rules, he couldn't go onto the field once the game began.)

The next year he managed Detroit in the Western League, a top-level minors circuit headed by Byron Bancroft "Ban" Johnson, a former Cincinnati baseball reporter who was already hatching plans for bigger things. Stallings was a chronic umpire-baiter, something Johnson was loath to tolerate. After a year in Johnson's league, Stallings grabbed the chance to get back to the majors, signing to manage Philadelphia, where he had started out. He was hardly a thumping success with the Phillies, managing an eleventh-place team in 1897 in what, since 1892, had been a twelve-team National League. The next year, with the Phillies going nowhere, he was fired after forty-two games.[2]

In 1899 Stallings returned to the Western League as manager of the Detroit entry; the next year he and another investor bought the team. As of 1900, Detroit was a member of what Ban Johnson had renamed the American League, in preparation for challenging the Nationals in

1901 as a second major league.[3] Stallings's team finished a strong third that season, but Stallings and Johnson still didn't get along. He had a nasty run-in with one of Johnson's umpires, followed by a shouting match with the league president. After the season he sold his interest in the Detroit franchise for $20,000 and deposited the money in a local bank, which failed the next day.[4]

Somehow Stallings always came up with money to invest in another baseball franchise. In 1902 he became part owner and manager of the Buffalo Eastern League team and led it to two pennants and three runner-up finishes, becoming a fairly wealthy man in the process. So wealthy that he was able to buy back the 2,200-acre plantation at Haddock his father had lost, rename it the "Meadows," and eventually expand it to 4,582½ acres. In 1906, Bell White Stallings, perhaps wearying of her unsettled life with her peripatetic baseball husband, obtained a divorce.

Stallings had some kind of surgery that was serious enough to keep him out of baseball in 1907. Having sold his interests in Buffalo, he bought a half-interest in the Eastern League's Newark team, in partnership with Frank Farrell, who was also president of the New York American League team. After Stallings directed Newark to a strong runner-up showing, Farrell and William S. "Big Bill" Devery, Farrell's co-owner, hired him to manage their team in 1909.

Stallings was back in the big leagues, but he was also working for a couple of very shady characters. The diminutive Farrell was a bookmaker, controlled a poolroom syndicate, and was part owner of a Manhattan gambling house. Devery, a former chief of police, had earned a reputation as "probably the most notorious police officer in New York City's history."[5] Working for "Boss" Tim Sullivan's vice syndicate, he had become wealthy in a variety of nefarious ways. Neither Farrell nor Devery fit the image of honesty and respectability Ban Johnson had trumpeted would be hallmarks of the American League.

Nor did New York first-baseman Hal Chase. "Prince Hal" was an exceptionally talented fielder—hailed as the best ever at the position—as well as a solid batter and outstanding baserunner. Chase was one of baseball's top performers when he was playing honestly, which he didn't always do. Neither Ban Johnson nor anybody else was willing to do anything about Chase's consorting with gamblers, and widely held suspicions that he bet against his own team—and sometimes failed to play his best when he had money on the outcome. For a player much admired for his wide range and fielding grace, Chase made an unusually high number of errors.

New York's American League teams had lost the pennant on the season's last day in 1904 and had run a good second in 1906, but since then had steadily declined, reaching the bottom in 1908 with a 51-103 record. They played in a hastily built wooden park on northern Manhattan Island seating only about 15,000. The "Yankees," as they were usually called in the baseball press, were the "other" team in New York City, perpetually overshadowed by the rich and consistently successful Giants.

Stallings's largely re-built 1909 team surprised nearly everybody by rising to fifth place, at 74-77. The next year the Yankees surprised again, finishing second, although they were still fourteen and a half games behind the Philadelphia Athletics. Stallings, though, wasn't their manager when the season ended. Chase worked steadily to undermine his authority, insisting to club president Farrell that he could do a better job. With two weeks left in the season, Stallings put it up to Farrell: Either he or Chase was running the team. Farrell backed Chase; Stallings quit. Long afterward, Jimmy Austin, Stallings's third baseman at New York, observed disgustedly, "God, what a way to run a ball club."[6]

Stallings returned to the Eastern League and to Buffalo, where his teams were less successful than during his earlier tenure in the city, finishing fourth in 1911 and fifth the next year. Meanwhile the 1911 Yankees dropped to sixth place under Chase and last in 1912 under Harry Wolverton, who also had to contend with Chase's troublemaking.

When Jim Gaffney hired Stallings to manage his Boston Braves, the Georgian had been in professional baseball for twenty-five years; had managed and/or played for teams in seven cities in six different leagues; and had formed contacts with club owners and managers nearly everywhere, especially in the top-level minor leagues. Yet he was still about a month shy of his forty-sixth birthday.

Although his hairline had begun to retreat, Stallings was still a handsome man: 6'1" tall and a trim 190 pounds or so, dark-complexioned and black-haired with perfect white teeth. A fastidious dresser, he favored bow ties and expensive fedoras from autumn to spring, straw boaters in summer. In 1910, while he was in his second year as New York manager, Stallings had married for the second time, to a Buffalo woman named Eunice Davis.

Although away from the ballpark Stallings exhibited such courtly behavior that he was called "Gentleman George," he was also inordinately high-strung and one of baseball's sorest losers—a manager who railed at umpires and berated his players in language that would put a muleskinner to shame. "It was an art with him," Hank Gowdy, his catcher on the Braves, remarked of Stallings's sulfurous invective. Hub Perdue, who pitched for Stallings in 1913 and part of 1914, called him "the meanest man in the world. When he starts to 'ride' you he can tell you things about yourself that you never knew." "Talk about cussing!" remembered Jimmy Austin. "Golly, he had 'em all beat. He cussed something awful." Yet as Austin and many others who played for Stallings also remembered, after the game he often apologized for his abusive language, explaining it was just that he wanted so badly to win.[7]

Nearly all managers and players in Stallings's day followed such common superstitions as not walking under ladders, avoiding black cats, carrying rabbits' feet, or, before a time at bat, rubbing the head of a team's black "mascot," as batboys were called in those days. (The Philadelphia Athletics' batboy was a deformed young white man named Louis Von Zeldt; players would rub the hump on his back before going to the plate.)

But Stallings carried superstition to an extreme. In a period before bat racks, batboys lined up bats side-by-side in front of the dugout. Stallings insisted that once the bats were in place, their order must never be disturbed. During the game, he fidgeted and slid up and down on the bench; baseball writers joked that he wore out a dozen pair of pants in the course of a season. But if his team had a rally going, he remained motionless, even keeping the same leg crossed until the side was retired. If a bird happened to fly near the dugout, Stallings wanted it shooed away, believing it was a bad omen. The same for cigar butts and any other trash in his immediate vicinity. Chicago third-baseman Henry "Heinie" Zimmerman liked to stroll by the Boston dugout and scatter bits of torn-up paper; when the Braves played in Philadelphia, manager Pat Moran had people in the box seats behind the visitors' dugout do the same thing. Stallings was even superstitious about Opening Day, believing if his team won, it probably wouldn't do well from then on. Such was the man Gaffney entrusted to lead his Boston Braves out of the doldrums.

Early in December, at the annual meeting of the club's directors, Stallings was elected to the board and became a minor stockholder, while Herman Nickerson moved from the sports desk of the *Boston Journal* to become club secretary. Gaffney told the local press Stallings would have a free hand to do what he wanted with the team. At his new manager's behest, Gaffney hired Fred Mitchell as a player-coach. Mitchell, a Cambridge, Massachusetts, native whose unlikely given name was Frederick Francis Yapp, had pitched in the American League for Boston and in the National League for Philadelphia and Brooklyn before dropping back to the minors. In 1910 he came back up as a catcher, appearing in sixty-eight games for Stallings's New York team. Mitchell would be the Braves' third-base coach, work with the pitchers, and generally serve as what Stallings termed "my right eye."

In his annual late-winter run-down for the monthly *Baseball Magazine* on prospects of the different major-league teams, William A. "Wild Bill" Phelon of the *Cincinnati Times* wrote that with Johnny Kling's departure, Stallings had no catching talent, and Phelon didn't think much of the rest of his players. Phelon couldn't see how the Braves "can possibly rise about seventh, or how [they] can even get out of the eighth hole unless complete demoralization overtakes the clubs ahead."[8]

If Phelon (and nearly everybody else) thought the Braves' prospects for 1913 were pretty bleak, those of the Chicago Cubs looked a lot better, especially under their renowned new manager. As Stallings was signing his three-year contract with Gaffney, Johnny Evers was signing for five years at $10,000 per year with Charles W. Murphy, president of the Cubs. The son of a saloonkeeper, Evers was a native of Troy, New York, and thus nicknamed the "Trojan" by baseball writers. He had been the middleman in the celebrated Tinker-to-Evers-to-Chance infield on the 1906–1908 and 1910 champions. Bothered by headaches from numerous "beanings," manager Frank Chance quit playing after the Cubs' six-game loss to the Philadelphia Athletics in the 1910 World Series. Following also-ran seasons in 1911 and 1912, he resigned as Cubs manager and ill-advisedly signed to manage the American League's forlorn New York team. Tinker, alongside whom Evers had played since 1902 but to whom he hadn't spoken for years, went to Cincinnati to replace Roger Bresnahan as Reds manager. Eighteen months into the future, the baseball lives of George Stallings and Johnny Evers would fortuitously entwine.

Evers was thirty-one years old, a left-hand batter, and a lantern-jawed, scrawny 5'9" and 140 pounds. He was excitable, temperamental, and as fiercely focused on winning as was Stallings. Whereas Stallings specialized in matchless profanity, Evers was acid-tongued and hard on nearly everybody—umpires, teammates, even himself—so much so that he had earned another nickname, the "Crab." Editor F. C. Lane of *Baseball Magazine* acclaimed him "the greatest of all second basemen."[9]

Lane's accolade would have been hotly disputed by American League partisans of Cleveland's Napoleon Lajoie and the Athletics' Eddie Collins. In fact, later generations might have difficulty understanding the high regard in which so many of his contemporaries—sportswriters, managers, many fellow players (if few umpires)—held a player whose skills weren't extraordinary for a major-league ballplayer. Mostly it had to do with Evers's leadership qualities and the fierce competitiveness he brought to his work. He could be a truly inspirational leader on the field, and he possessed an abundance of what would later be called "baseball smarts." According to Rabbit Maranville, Evers kept scrapbooks of critical comments sportswriters wrote about other players, the idea being that he might be able to exploit some shortcoming a particular player exhibited. "Every player in the National League had a place in that scrapbook."[10]

Yet Evers had experienced a variety of personal misfortunes. Ostensibly he had a good marriage, having wed Helen Fitzgibbons in New York City in January 1909 and fathered a son and daughter. But during the 1910 season, he wrecked his new automobile in Chicago, killing passenger John McDonald, his close friend. For five weeks Evers was out of the lineup with what was reported as "nervous prostration"; then, with the season nearly over, he broke his ankle sliding in a meaningless game in Cincinnati and had to sit out the World Series. His partner in his shoe store in Troy swindled him out of $9,600 and fled the state, forcing Evers to sell the stock in his Chicago shoe business at a loss. All told, his financial reverses amounted to $25,000. After all that, he suffered a complete emotional breakdown and played in only twenty-two games in 1911. Yet he came back in 1912 to bat .341, in the second season in which the major leagues used a new cork-centered baseball. That livelier ball produced a big spike (temporary, as it turned out) in Evers's and many other players' offensive numbers.

Evers got off to a bad start as manager. Rumors surfaced during the Cubs' seven-weeks of spring training in Tampa that he frequently lost his temper and squabbled with various players. When the train carrying the team arrived in Chicago, Evers asked trainer Bert Semmons if he had awakened the players and informed them they were to report at West Side Park for practice at 1:30. Not getting the respectful answer he wanted, Evers cursed Semmons, who hit him in the jaw and knocked him into a seat. Semmons then handed the keys to the clubhouse to Evers and quit on the spot. Later Semmons, who had been with the Cubs for six years, complained that Evers had nagged him all spring.

Murphy signed the recently deposed Roger Bresnahan—former star catcher for the Giants and also former manager of the St. Louis Cardinals—to a three-year contract as a player and as Evers's "assistant," at a salary of $6,334 per year, plus a $10,000 bonus. Murphy thereby created a season-long difficult relationship between Evers and Bresnahan, whose total pay exceeded the new manager's.

Meanwhile the Boston Braves did spring training in Athens, Georgia, a town of about fifteen thousand. They held their practices on the field of the local University of Georgia baseball team. Three weeks of almost daily rain—part of a weather system causing the Ohio and other rivers to overflow and to inundate the Cincinnati ballpark—hampered Stallings's effort to get a good sense what kind of team he had. Francis Eaton, the *Sporting News's* Boston correspondent, looked over the contingent in Athens and judged them no better than last year's. Lefty Tyler and Hub Perdue were still on hand, along with Bill Sweeney, Art Devlin, and John Titus, a thirty-seven-year-old outfielder obtained from Philadelphia during the previous season. Stallings also had outfielder J. Bentley "Cy" Seymour, who had played in the minors the past two years after fifteen major-league seasons. Seymour's presence prompted A. H. C. Mitchell of the *Boston Journal*, correspondent for *Sporting Life*, to comment sourly, "we, in Boston, have seen so many veterans unloaded on the National League team that we look with suspicion on any more of them."[11]

Among other newcomers were Ralph "Hap" Myers, a tall first-baseman up from the Eastern League, who had earlier played three years in the American League; pitcher Bill James, a big, blond, twenty-one-year-old right-hander purchased along with catcher Bert Whaling for a hefty $8,000 from Seattle (Northwestern League), where James had won twenty-nine games; and outfielder Les Mann, who had played for Stallings at Buffalo. Another rookie was Joe Connolly, a left-hand-batting outfielder drafted by Washington and sold to the Braves just before the start of the season. Starting out as a pitcher, the twenty-seven-year-old Connolly had bounced around the minor leagues for seven seasons before landing at Montreal, where he batted .313 in 1912.

Infielder Bill McKechnie was drafted from St. Paul of the American Association. McKechnie had played in the majors with Washington and Pittsburgh, but he was never much of a hitter; after appearing in one game with the Braves, he was claimed by the New York Giants for the $5,000 waiver price. (McKechnie would have a forty-eight-year career in professional baseball and make his place in its history as the manager of four National League pennant-winners with three different teams.)

Then there was Judson Fabian "Jay" Kirke, who had joined the Boston team from the Southern Association the previous season. A husky six-footer, Kirke had batted .320 in 103 games for the 1912 Braves, but he was a defensive liability wherever he was stationed. Kirke was a player, observed Eaton, "who can certainly hit, but who as a fielder can only retrieve."[12] After appearing in thirteen games for the Braves, Kirke was sold to Toledo (American Association). Except for past-time stints with Cleveland in 1914 and 1915 and the Giants in 1918, he would spend the rest of his thirty-year baseball career in the minors, as one of the outstanding hitters in minor league history.

For 1913, Rabbit Maranville would be paid $2,400, good money for a rookie. But Stallings seemed bent on having as his regular shortstop Art Bues, who had played for him at Buffalo and incidentally (or not so incidentally) was his wife's nephew. Stallings overheard Maranville complaining about that and gave the young man a stern lecture on who was running the ball club. But when the Braves reached Atlanta, playing their way north toward the season-opener (as teams did in those days), Bues fell ill. When the team left, Bues stayed behind, suffering from what was probably strep throat. Stallings had no choice but to pencil in Maranville for the remaining exhibition stops in Charlotte, Richmond, Baltimore, and Washington.

On Thursday, April 10, 1913, the Braves opened the season in the Polo Grounds in New York, wearing their new blue road uniforms with red trim. With Art Bues still unavailable, Maranville was at shortstop. As he usually did when the Giants opened at home, John McGraw held back the great Christy Mathewson for Saturday's game, which was usually the biggest attendance day of the week. Hub Perdue held the Giants scoreless, while the Braves scored eight runs on Jeff Tesreau. Catcher Bill Rariden homered; Maranville made two hits, did some nice fielding, and clinched his job. When Bues rejoined the Braves, he got into two games before being sent back to the minors.

The rain that had plagued the Braves all spring continued along the east coast, keeping them idle until April 14, when they opened at home in white uniforms trimmed in red and blue. Boston Mayor John F. "Honey Fitz" Fitzgerald (grandfather of a future U.S. President) threw out the first ball, but Gaffney, recuperating from abdominal surgery, missed the opener. His recovery would take until mid-summer. Mathewson was in good form, defeating Perdue and two other pitchers, 4–3. Bill Sweeney was ejected after arguing with umpire Charles "Cy" Rigler, the Braves' first run-in with an umpire in 1913, although there would be plenty of others that season and in seasons to come. Stallings used seventeen players; throughout the coming season, he would use more of his roster than contemporary managers usually did.

The Braves also lost their next six games, all with the Giants and Brooklyn. They finally won again on April 24, when Bill James, in his first start, pitched a twelve-inning shutout, beating Brooklyn's Frank Allen 1–0. By mid–May, however, the Braves had won only five times in twenty-two tries. "Boston broke from the post with much fire and fury," Bill Phelon wrote, "but the Braves soon calmed down, and, after a few distressing interviews with superior people, meekly began retreating toward the coal hole."[13] By May 5, when they finished losing three times in four tries in Ebbets Field, Brooklyn's new steel-and-concrete ballpark, they had won only four of sixteen games.

Two months later, however, they had become a respectable ball club. In large part that had to do with the emergence of Dick Rudolph as one of Stallings's top three pitchers. A native of the Bronx, New York, and a Fordham University dropout, Rudolph was undersized as pitchers went, at 5'9½" inches tall and 160 pounds. He carried the nickname

"Baldy" because at the age of twenty-five, he had already lost most of his hair. Rudolph had pitched professionally since 1906, including brief trials with the Giants in 1910 and 1911. John McGraw hadn't seen much to like in Rudolph, but in 1912 he had an outstanding year in the International League, compiling a 25–10 record for pennant-winner Toronto.[14]

Rudolph was again with Toronto the following spring, but after losing his first start to Newark, he quit the team in discouragement, convinced that he would never make it to the major leagues to stay. At that point Fred Mitchell, who had played at Toronto, contacted owner Jim McCaffery and asked about buying Rudolph. Reluctant at first, McCaffery agreed to sell Rudolph to the Braves when Gaffney offered him $4,000 and agreed to include Charles "Buster" Brown, a run-of-mill left-hander. The deal done, Rudolph joined the Braves and signed a contract for $2,900.

Stallings used young Bill James sparingly, starting him only ten times. But Rudolph pitched in thirty-three games, finishing with a 14–13 record and a respectable 2.92 earned-run average. "He wasn't fast," Fred Mitchell recalled of Rudolph, "but had a good curveball, which he mixed with a spitball, and he almost read the batter's mind. I've often sat on the bench with him and heard him tell whether a batter would take or hit. He made a real study of his profession."[15] (Until it was outlawed before the 1920 season, the spitball was perfectly legal. By the century's second decade, numerous pitchers at all levels of baseball were throwing spitballs and various other "trick pitches.")

After winning ten of fifteen games on their first trip to the four western cities, the Braves found themselves in the rarified air of fifth place, with a 24–28 record. When asked how well he thought his team might do, Stallings replied, "I don't have the faintest idea where I'm going to wind up with this ball club, but I'll tell you one thing—I'm going to beat someone.... I'm not going to finish last in this man's league." Tim Murnane and A.H. C. Mitchell marveled at Stallings's drive and determination. Murnane called him the hardest-working man in baseball; Mitchell observed that when the Braves were at home, he had them out for morning practice every day (presumably with the exception of Sundays). "No manager that Boston has ever had pays more attention to his charges than does Stallings."[16]

Now Bill Phelon praised Stallings as having "got the Braves to performing intelligent team work such as they never developed in recent summers." A month later, although they had slipped to sixth at 32–41, John E. Wray, sports editor of the *St. Louis Post-Dispatch*, wrote that the Braves' rise was "the most interesting achievement in the baseball world.... By filling in the holes with veteran timber and injecting a little of his own pep and ginger into the club, [Stallings] has his men going now."[17]

Late in July, after splitting sixteen games on their home stand, the Braves went west in sixth place with a 38–55 record. Stallings didn't accompany his team, instead putting Bill Sweeney in charge and traveling to Buffalo to be with his wife, who had undergone an appendectomy. He rejoined the Braves in Pittsburgh, but when they returned home, he shuttled back and forth between Boston and Buffalo, as his wife's post-operative condition steadily worsened. Eunice Davis Stallings died on Thursday, August 29, in all probability from infection and ultimately peritonitis—in a time when infection-fighting antibiotics were far into the future. Her funeral was held the following Monday.

In Stallings's absence, the Braves endured a seven-game losing streak in St. Louis, Cincinnati, and Pittsburgh, but they continued to jockey with Brooklyn for fifth and sixth places. Sweeney was absent part of the time, too. On August 26, in a 3–0 loss in Pittsburgh, Sweeney vociferously protested when Cy Rigler wouldn't make a catcher's inter-ference call; Rigler ordered him out of the game. When the umpire filed his report to the National League office in New York City, league pres-ident Tom Lynch suspended Sweeney three games for abusive language. Whereupon Jim Gaffney sent Lynch a telegram (which he made public) criticizing Lynch's umpires and sarcastically suggesting he travel around the league to see for himself how bad they were. Meanwhile Sweeney took the train to New York to tell Lynch his side of the altercation, to no avail.

Stallings rejoined the Braves in New York on September 2, a day after they lost a Labor Day doubleheader to McGraw's Giants, who were way ahead of Philadelphia and cruising to a third-straight pennant. But because the Phillies swept two from Brooklyn, the Braves remained tied for fifth place with the team variously known as the Superbas, Bride-grooms, or Trolley Dodgers. By then only six players who had been with the Braves on Opening Day remained on the roster; Cy Seymour and Art Devlin, who had seen some grand days with the Giants, were among those released. Among the new players were two from the International League: Jack Quinn, a twenty-nine-year-old right-hander, who had won eighteen games for Stallings in 1910 at New York and nineteen this season for Rochester, and Charles "Butch" Schmidt, a husky first-baseman who had batted .321 with Rochester. Displacing Hap Myers, Schmidt hit a solid .308 in twenty-two games for the Braves.

Stallings wanted at least a fifth-place finish and continued to drive his players in the remaining month of the season. On September 11, during a wild 12–11 loss in Cincinnati, the Braves and Reds engaged in a notable brawl that began when Maranville, trying to break up a double play, barreled into Joe Tinker. The Reds' shortstop and manager exchanged punches with Maranville, whom he outweighed by thirty pounds. Quickly players from both teams converged, with Hap Myers taking over the fight with Tinker from his little teammate. Order was restored after umpires Hank O'Day and Bob Emslie ejected several combatants. After reading O'Day's account of the fray, Tom Lynch levied fines of $50 on Tinker and Maranville and a stiff $100 on Myers for running on the field and attacking Tinker, and also suspended the Reds' manager for cursing O'Day.

The Braves lost three of four games at Redland Field, split a pair of games in Pittsburgh, and lost two of three in Chicago before ending their last western trip in St. Louis, by sweeping a three-game series from the hapless Cardinals. Miller Huggins's team would end the season with only fifty-one wins, six fewer than the Browns, their American League counterparts. It was a bad baseball year for St. Louis fans.

In Philadelphia the Braves played three doubleheaders in five days and won only three games out of seven, although their 9–7 victory on September 27 mathematically eliminated the Phillies from the pennant race. Returning to South End Grounds, they dropped one game to the champion Giants, then swept a doubleheader, with Lefty Tyler pitching an 8–0 shutout in the nightcap. Brooklyn split a doubleheader with Philadelphia, which left Boston a game and a half ahead of the Superbas in the competition for fifth place.

After a rainout, the Braves and Brooklyn played out the season at South End Grounds. On October 3, the Braves won a single game; the next day they took a doubleheader, followed by another rainout on Saturday. So they concluded the season with a record of 69–82 (plus three ties) to Brooklyn's 65–84. After losing that Labor Day doubleheader to the Giants, the Braves won seventeen of their last thirty-one games. Although they ended 31.5 games from first place and ten games from fourth-place Pittsburgh, they had done better than any Boston National League team since 1902. It wasn't a miracle, but what Stallings accomplished, using forty-six players at one time or other, was at least as impressive as what he had done in 1909 and 1910 with the New York Yankees.

Long accustomed to sorry endings to Boston National League seasons, the baseball press in New England and in much of the rest of the country hailed Stallings's achievement. "Stallings," bubbled the St. Louis writer W. J. O'Connor, "inherited the greatest aggregation of jokers that any manager ever took hold of this spring" and "imbued them with the fighting spirit which wins." He was "the dynamic force which has lifted the team out of the rut." The *Chicago Tribune's* Irving Ellis "Sy" Sanborn credited Stallings with reviving National League interest in Boston, developing enough young players "to make people sit up and notice his team for next year," and, not least, making a profit for the ownership.[18]

Sanborn was probably correct that Gaffney and associates, with the league's smallest payroll, had made a profit. Attendance at South End Grounds increased by nearly 90,000 over 1912, whereas the defending World Series champion Red Sox, barely beating out Chicago for fourth place, lost nearly 160,000 customers.

Only five Boston players had at least four-hundred official times at bat, as Stallings juggled his lineups and players came and went. Offensive output moderated somewhat from the previous season; the National League's collective batting average dropped ten points, American League teams by six points. Rookie Joe Connolly led the Braves with a .281 average and fifty-seven runs driven in. Hub Perdue had the best pitching record at 16–13, followed by Dick Rudolph's 14–13. Lefty Tyler, often getting little run support, won sixteen games but lost seventeen. Stallings's pitchers led both major leagues with 105 complete games.

In his first full season in the majors, Rabbit Maranville batted only .247 and committed forty-three errors in 143 games. But the Braves' pocket-size shortstop became a big hit at South End Grounds and around the league with his all-out hustle and especially his belt-buckle catches, which, the *Boston Globe's* Melville E. Webb wrote, "always get a laugh." Late in July, some two-hundred people from Springfield honored him

George "Lefty" Tyler. Under George Stallings, he came into his own as a big-league pitcher (George Bantham Bain Collection, Library of Congress).

and Les Mann, another Springfield native, with a "day," a common gesture by hometown people in a period before ballplayers made enough money to buy everything themselves. Besides the inevitable floral horseshoes, Maranville and Mann received a variety of gifts, even including a live rabbit for Rabbit. Webb extolled Maranville "as the shiftiest, nerviest little player that wears spikes and as a player whose very enthusiasm for the game he plays makes watching his work one of the greatest pleasures of a baseball matinee."[19]

Lavish praise for a youngster only a year away from Class B who had registered a mediocre batting average in his first full season in the major leagues. But Boston sportswriters and local National League fans, long starved for some excitement, had enjoyed the antics of the colorful little Rabbit and the unexpectedly competitive team Stallings put on the field. The best was yet to be.

2

1913–1914: "The fact that Evers will play second"

Rabbit Maranville spent the offseason of 1913–1914 having the time of his young life. Jim Gaffney had raised his salary to $3,500, pretty big money for a bachelor. He earned a couple of thousand more performing on the Keith vaudeville circuit with Tommy Griffith, an outfielder the Braves had purchased from New Bedford. Beginning at the National Theatre in Boston early in November, they toured theaters around New England with a baseball comedy routine featuring songs written by Griffith, anecdotes by Maranville, and finales in which Rabbit either slid across the stage or made a belt-buckle catch of a ball tossed down from a box seat. His sliding stunt in a Lewiston, Maine, theater ended with a dive into a bass drum in the orchestra pit, when his foot hit an uneven board. (Or so he told the story many years later.) The two ballplayers closed their act in Springfield, where Rabbit even found time to play basketball in a Springfield league (under rules that would make the game hardly recognizable to later generations).

Now Maranville could also afford his first automobile, or "motor car." Those early autos—ungainly contraptions, nearly all of which had open seating and were hard to start, to maneuver, or to stop quickly— had become popular among ballplayers and other young men with substantial money to spare. But "automobiling" players—inexperienced operators who were inclined to drive recklessly—worried baseball owners and managers, given the frequency with which their valuable employees were involved in accidents. Sure enough, Maranville had a wreck that winter, although he wasn't injured. But out in California, Bill James, given a $600 raise to $3,000, suffered a mild concussion and scalp wounds when he was thrown from his auto and into a pile of stones near his home at Oroville. Johnny Evers told F. C. Lane of *Baseball Mag-*

azine he still hadn't gotten over the wreck in Chicago that killed his close friend John McDonald. He had given up driving automobiles; even riding in taxis gave him a "nervous tremor," as did being driven around Troy by his brother Joe.[1]

Meanwhile Stallings relaxed on his plantation at Haddock and hosted hunting parties that included fellow–Georgian Ty Cobb; Harry "Bud" Fisher, who drew the popular syndicated "Mutt and Jeff" comic strip; and George Stinson, manager of the Macon South Atlantic League team.

If the 1913 season had been a generally satisfying one for Stallings and his players (at least for those players who managed to remain with the team), it had been a frustrating, strife-ridden year for Evers. Hugh Fullerton, the syndicated Chicago baseball writer, had predicted in the spring Evers wouldn't get the loyalty from his players Frank Chance had received, which is what happened. The Cubs' manager and second baseman played well afield, batted a solid .284, and directed the Cubs to a third-place finish, only a half-game behind runner-up Philadelphia. After August 1, the Cubs had the best record in the National League. Yet Evers's players complained to the press about his chronic nagging and frequent temper outbursts. Outfielder Mike Mitchell, sold to Pittsburgh late in July for the waiver price, said he was glad to leave Evers and "his awful temper, which he cannot control."[2]

Evers's particular antagonist among his players was Heinie Zimmerman. "Zim," as his teammates called him, or "the Great Zim," as he liked to refer to himself, was a muscular six-footer and one of the best in the National League with a bat in his hands. In 1912 the native New Yorker had achieved what would later be termed the Triple Crown, leading the league in batting average (.372), home runs (14), and runs batted-in (103), as well as doubles (41). As with many other players, Zimmerman's batting average tailed off in 1913 (to .313), but he still drove in ninety-five runs. Yet Zimmerman, an indifferent fielder, had also led the league's third-basemen in errors the past two seasons.

He was also frequently surly and resentful of authority, both his managers' and the umpires'. In May 1913, his strained relationship with Evers came to a head in Philadelphia. Before the game, Zimmerman told Evers he didn't feel well, to which Evers replied he would either play or not get paid. The game was in the early innings when umpire Bill Byron ejected Zimmerman "for making a kick on a play which did not even call for a protest," as one writer described it.[3] As Zimmerman dawdled getting off the field, Evers berated him for getting needlessly thrown out. After he dressed, Zimmerman sat in the center-field bleachers and yelled insults at his manager. Cubs president Murphy backed Evers on that occasion, as he did in July, when Evers intervened in an argument Zimmerman was having with Roger Bresnahan. Whatever Zimmerman did on that occasion—whether he physically threatened Evers or just cursed him—cost him a $200 fine and brief suspension.

But a month later Murphy sided against his manager when Evers and Bresnahan had a falling out. With first-string catcher Jimmy Archer injured, Bresnahan took his place, but Evers didn't like his work and benched him in favor of third-stringer Tom Needham. Murphy took a hand in the situation, ordering Evers to put Bresnahan back behind the plate. Evers had to comply, but his and Murphy's relations steadily deteriorated.

Then, Murphy found fault with Evers's managing in the post-season city series, played since 1903 between the Cubs and the American League White Sox when neither Chicago team was in the World Series. As usual, the series was well attended, with the White Sox winning it, four games to two. Murphy claimed that cost him the $10,000 he could have made on a seventh game, which would have been played in the Cubs' West Side Park.

That winter the shared monopoly Murphy and his peers in the two major leagues enjoyed came under a direct threat from a group of ambitious and well-heeled men seeking to cash in on professional baseball's soaring popularity. Led by James Gilmore, a wealthy Chicagoan, they announced that in 1914 their Federal League would operate as a third major league in eight cities, half of which were big-league cities, half members of the International League and American Association. The Federals would be in direct competition with both the National and American league in St. Louis and Chicago and with the National League in Brooklyn and Pittsburgh. In 1913, when the Federal League operated with semipro players and former professionals outside Organized Baseball (the two major leagues and the minor leagues the majors officially recognized), the major-league bigwigs had dismissed or ignored altogether the new organization. Now they realized they faced a real menace to the baseball status quo.

The Federal League financiers also announced their intention to sign the best players they could from anywhere within Organized Baseball, at higher salaries than their present owners were paying them (which probably accounts for the nice pay raises Gaffney gave Maranville and James, as well as Dick Rudolph, who would be paid $3,500 in 1914). Moreover, the contracts the Federals offered would omit the reserve clause, under which, since 1879, clubs had possessed the exclusive option to re-sign players year after year, as long as a club wanted to.[4]

The Federals meant business. They were successful in each city in obtaining playing sites—renting and fixing up former major-league parks in Brooklyn, Baltimore, and Pittsburgh and renovating and expanding local semipro parks (St. Louis, Indianapolis, Buffalo, Kansas City). For his Chicago Federal League entry, Charles Weeghman, who had become wealthy from his chain of "quick lunch" restaurants, was having built a modern steel-and-concrete ballpark on the city's north side that would seat about 15,000 and outclass the Cubs' wooden, nineteenth-century–style West Side Park. John Ward had so much faith in the Federal League venture that he temporarily put aside his law practice to become business manager of the Brooklyn Tip Tops—so nicknamed for brothers Robert and George Ward (no relation to John Ward), who operated the local Tip Top Bakery and financed the Brooklyn entry.

So Johnny Evers spent nearly two weeks of his offseason on trains, traveling around the country to get Cubs players' signatures on contracts before the Federals could get to them. Later he claimed he saved Murphy $25,000 in players' salaries. He also visited the Cubs' Tampa spring-training site and generally made plans for 1914. After all, Evers was working under a five-year contract—or so he thought.

On February 10, 1914, Evers and Murphy were both in New York City at the Waldorf Hotel, attending the National League's annual winter meeting. In a session of the league's owners, Murphy announced that Evers had resigned as Cubs manager and would be replaced by Hank O'Day. A former pitcher, O'Day had managed Cincinnati in 1912 after umpiring in the National League for sixteen years. He resigned the Cincinnati job amid well-founded rumors the Reds were obtaining Joe Tinker to become their player-manager. O'Day then returned to the league's umpiring staff for 1913.

Upon hearing Murphy's announcement, Jim Gaffney left the room and hurried downstairs to the lobby to talk to Evers, presumably about whether he would be willing to join the Boston Braves. Later John Tener, who had succeeded Tom Lynch as National League president, also took Evers aside for a talk. Meanwhile Cubs secretary Charles Thomas gave out Murphy's written statement to the assembled press corps. Sam Weller of the *Chicago Tribune* acidly characterized the document as "one of Murphy's well known interviews with himself." Philadelphia manager Charles "Red" Dooin commented, "This [Evers' firing] is playing into the hands of the Federal League with a vengeance."[5]

Evers' firing—which it what it was—created a sensation and came as a shock to nearly everybody, including Evers. "What particularly galled me," he told F. C. Lane later, "was the fact that certain people knew all about the move before I had any light on the matter myself." But Evers also said that while he had heard nothing from Murphy or anybody else, "I had an inkling that O'Day was being considered.... " He also vehemently denied he had resigned. Evers mistakenly assumed Murphy would have to pay him for the remaining four years of his manager's contract. But when he signed the contract in the fall of 1912, William E. Locke, president of the Philadelphia Phillies, had witnessed the signing and told him he had signed "over a trap door." Locke noticed Murphy had inserted a provision that he could still terminate the manager's contract at his discretion. Said Evers, "I confess I have never been very keen in analyzing a contract."[6] (Unfortunately for Evers, Locke wasn't available to confirm his "trap door" judgment, having died the previous year.)

Evers had actually signed two contracts, as manager but also as a player. He had been paid $6,000 per year to manage, $4,000 to play. Presumably Murphy expected him to be at second base for the Cubs in 1914, but Evers declared, "I will never play for Murphy again under any circumstances." He acknowledged talking to Federal League representatives, "but I would rather be with the 'old boy'" (meaning the National League).[7] In fact, at the Knickerbocker Hotel in New York, Evers had met with Charles Williams, business manager of Weeghman's Chicago club, and Joe Tinker, who had jumped from the National League to play shortstop and manage the "Chifeds." They offered Evers a $15,000 contract for 1914 plus a $30,000 signing bonus. For all their past animosity, Joe Tinker was anxious to have Evers. (Whether Evers would have been willing to be managed by Tinker is another question.)

Charles Webb Murphy was the prototype of the self-important, meddlesome, often overbearing club owners who have populated professional baseball until fairly recently. A native of Wilmington, Ohio, Murphy had been a reporter for Cincinnati newspapers and a press agent for the New York Giants. In 1905, at age thirty-seven, he borrowed enough money from Charles P. Taft, publisher of the *Cincinnati Enquirer*, to buy a half-interest in the Cubs from Jim Hart. Taft, plus Frank Chance and a few other minor investors, bought the other half. Over the years Murphy had increased his holdings in the franchise to fifty-three percent.

Murphy's entry into baseball ownership turned out to be perfect timing; the Cubs under Chance's leadership were about to start their run of four pennants and two World Series victories in five years; and booming attendance at the Cubs' West Side Park made Murphy a rich man. But over the years his high-handed manner had alienated his fellow owners in both leagues, as well as Ban Johnson, the American League's imperious president, who wasn't reluctant to meddle in National League affairs. "The American League has become tired of the blunders of this man," Johnson pontificated, "and for the good of baseball I think a change in the ownership of the Cubs is necessary." Johnson went on say league president Tener should be "clothed" with the kind of power he had in the American League, and to call for a "purge" of "enemies of the sport."[8] Avowing to remain as Cubs owner, Murphy threatened to sue Johnson for slander.

Evers wired Troy, New York, to urge his legal adviser to hurry to New York City with the two contracts he had signed. (Of course Evers should have sought some legal advice a year and a half earlier, before signing the manager's contract Murphy drew up.) He was to meet with Gaffney the morning of February 14. Meanwhile the National League's board of directors examined the contracts, ruled them valid, and also ruled that contrary to Murphy's claim, Evers hadn't resigned. At last Murphy's peers had run out of patience. His abrogation of the contract of one of the league's reigning stars was simply too much to abide.

Murphy had suggested a trade whereby Evers would go to the Braves in exchange for Bill Sweeney and Hub Perdue, but Evers would have none of it. "I am going to make Murphy pay for the way he has treated me," he told everybody who cared to listen. "I want him to lose money by not being able to get anything in return for my services."[9]

On February 21, Tener, Taft, Harry Ackerland (who had bought Chance's stock), and John Conway Toole, the National League's legal adviser, met for four hours in Cincinnati and finally voted to ban Murphy from ownership in the league. Taft bought out Murphy, paying $503,800 for his fifty-three percent of the Cubs. Murphy gave up his idea of suing Ban Johnson. In his $60,000 Chicago home, Murphy sat on pillows to comfort an aching back and bragged to reporters how he had started on a shoestring and now was worth a million dollars. "I am a very happy man," said Murphy, "because I haven't a thing to worry about; nobody is calling me names and criticizing me, and it seems as if a large weight has been lifted from my shoulders."[10]

Besides the buyout money (about $8 million–$10 million in today's dollars) Murphy would also receive income from the rental of the Philadelphia National League ballpark, which he and Taft had bought from William E. Locke in 1912. (In 1916, Murphy paid to have an opulent theater built in his native Wilmington, Ohio, at a reported cost of $250,000. Naturally, he named it for himself.[11])

So ended the Murphy-Evers saga, which a contributor to *Baseball Magazine* thought "will go down in baseball history as one of the shining examples of loyalty vs. ingratitude in America's national game." With the approval of the league's board of directors, Evers signed a four-year contract with the Braves for $10,000 per year, plus a $25,000 signing bonus. His contract also provided that he would receive a $2,000 bonus if the Braves won the pennant, $1,500 if they finished second, and $1,000 if they finished third. As Lane concluded, "Never was a player more fortunate in his misfortunes than John Evers...."[12] With Murphy out of the picture, Evers had no problem with the Cubs being compensated. Gaffney and George Stallings kept Hub Perdue (for the time being), but they sent Bill Sweeney to the Cubs along with an undisclosed amount of cash.

"Remembering the work done by Manager Stallings last year," commented the *Christian Science Monitor*, "as well as the fact that Evers will play second, it is hard to place Boston other than in the first division." Stallings later said that when he got Evers, he knew he had a pennant-winner. That was hindsight of massive proportions, but in fact the Braves' prospects for 1914 looked better than they had in many years. In mid–February, Evers came down to Boston from Troy, talked over things with Stallings and Gaffney at Hurlburt's Hotel, met the press at the Braves' offices in the Paddock Building, and then was the guest of honor at a banquet at Hurlburt's. Stallings announced Evers would be the Braves' captain.

John E. Wray, sports editor of the *St. Louis Post-Dispatch*, thought little of the Braves' chances in 1914. "Stallings," he wrote, "appears to have butted into a situation beyond him when it comes to making a pennant fight with the material at hand." Yet while Bill Phelon picked the Giants to take the pennant again, he predicted either the Braves or the Cubs would finish in second place. Frederick G. Lieb thought "George Stallings is due to horn his way into the first division…. though fourth is perhaps the limit with his present band." Hugh Fullerton, touring the southern training camps, considered the Braves "almost certainly a first-division ball club—and if Stallings has luck in developing pitchers and catchers, it may be a serious pennant contender." Even John McGraw, in his syndicated newspaper column, termed the Braves "a trouble-maker" and "liable to finish in the first division." McGraw praised Stallings for having "done wonders with this club."[13]

Stallings had his pitchers and catchers assemble early at his plantation at Haddock, where Fred Mitchell worked with them. Subsequently the team as a whole gathered in Macon. Unlike Athens, Macon was a good-sized city of something more than forty-thousand, billing itself as "the heart of Georgia." The Boston players lodged at the Hotel Dempsey, in considerably better quarters than had been available the previous spring in Athens, and practiced in Central City Park. Stallings had everybody down for breakfast by 8:30. The players were at the ballpark by 9:30 for an hour and a half's practice. After a lunch break and rest, they were back on the field by 3:00.

Federal League agents haunted all the major-league and higher-minors training sites. The Braves' manager knew they had approached Maranville and George Tyler, and he was determined to keep them away from his players at Macon. When Harry "Doc" Gessler, manager of the Pittsburgh Federals, showed up at the Hotel Dempsey, Stallings had him served with an injunction, obtained under Georgia's contract labor laws, to prevent Gessler from having any contact with his men. (Georgia's laws—similar to those in other Southern states—forbade attempts to hire anyone who was under a labor contract. Such laws were intended to keep laborers, mostly black laborers, from leaving farms where they worked.[14])

Stallings's personnel bore little resemblance to what he had started with in the spring of 1913. Besides Evers, the newcomers included outfielders Tommy Griffith from New Bedford (New England League) and Larry Gilbert from Milwaukee (American Association); infielders Charlie Deal from Providence (International League) and Oscar Dugey from Waco (Texas League); and little Dick Crutcher and tall Gene Cocreham, who had both pitched the previous season in the Western League, for St. Joseph and Topeka, respectively. Tall, goose-necked Harry Morgan "Hank" Gowdy had played sporadically at catcher and first base for the New York Giants. In 1911, Gowdy was a throw-in with infielder Al Bridwell when the Giants acquired infielder Charles "Buck" Herzog from the Braves. Stallings saw Gowdy's potential as a full-time catcher and optioned him to Buffalo, where he played the position regularly in 1913.

Paul Strand, a left-handed pitcher who had joined the Boston team the previous September from Walla Walla of the Northwest League, was still only twenty years old but already in his third year in professional ball. Infielder Jack Martin had played in the American League for New York in 1912 until a Walter Johnson fastball shattered his jaw. After a year back in the minors, he was drafted by Boston. George Davis, who had pitched for Rochester in 1913, was a graduate of Williams College. Now pursuing a law degree at Harvard, Davis wouldn't join the Braves until June. First base belonged to Butch Schmidt, who had taken over the position the last few weeks in 1913.

Federal League operators, offering big increases in salaries and often multi-year contracts, had cut pretty heavily into the ranks of the major leagues and the top-level minors. By the spring, only the Chicago White Sox and reigning World Series champion Philadelphia Athletics hadn't lost anybody to the upstart circuit. The Braves had drafted outfielder Edward "Dutch" Zwilling from Denver of the Western League, but Zwilling signed with the Chicago Federals. Walter Dickson, whose 1913 record for the Braves was a pallid 6–7, jumped to the Pittsburgh Federals (where he would lose twenty-one games); Bill Rariden, who had split catching duties with Bert Whaling, went to Indianapolis; and infielder Fred Smith joined Pittsburgh. Charles "Tex" McDonald, another infielder, had batted .357 in sixty-two games in 1913 after coming to the Braves from Cincinnati. He signed with Buffalo.

Jack Quinn also deserted the Braves for the new league, Quinn after signing his contract for the coming season. Stallings had counted on Quinn to pitch as effectively for him as he had in 1910 when both were with New York. Gaffney filed a $30,000 damage suit in a Maryland court to force the Baltimore owners to compensate him for the loss of Quinn— only one of a flock of suits and countersuits ensuing from the machinations of the Federal Leaguers, branded in most of the baseball press as "outlaws" and "invaders." Except for Quinn and perhaps Rariden and McDonald, none of the players the Braves lost figured prominently in Stallings's plans for the coming season.

That included Hap Myers. Myers had been sent down to Rochester in the deal for Jack Quinn and Butch Schmidt, with the stipulation that if Myers failed to report, the Braves would pay Rochester $3,500. That Gaffney ended up having to do, because Myers signed with the Brooklyn Federals. Myers was one of eighty-one current or former major-leaguers and 115 minor-leaguers who had opted for the new league by the spring of 1914.

Although the tall first baseman had been popular with the fans at South End Grounds, according to Stallings, "Myers would let ground balls go over the base for two baggers that were baseball crimes."[15] Myers, though, was convinced Stallings wanted to send him back to the minors because he had been active in the Baseball Players' Fraternity. The Fraternity was another troublesome matter club owners were having to contend with.

The president of the Players' Fraternity was David Fultz, a former National League player who had graduated from Brown University and was now a New York attorney. Organized in 1912, the Fraternity sought to gain members not only among major-league players but minor-leaguers as well. Initially Fultz set forth modest goals for his organization, such as getting club owners to honor everything in players' contracts and to make efforts to curb spectators' abuse such as had prompted Ty Cobb to go into the grandstand in New York and beat up a heckler in May 1912.

The emergence of the Federal League moved Fultz to broaden his program, although, to the relief of operators of teams throughout Organized Baseball, he didn't yet attack the inviolable reserve clause. Now Fultz proposed that the owners pay players' expenses in traveling to spring-training sites as well as eliminate the hated ten-day clause, whereby, even though a player was under contract, he could be released with only ten-days' notice. Within a year or so, the Fraternity had enlisted a large number of players in both the majors and minors, including such luminaries as Cobb, Tris Speaker, and Christy Mathewson, with Brooklyn first-baseman Jake Daubert serving as its president. Early in 1914, in a meeting in Cincinnati, the major-league owners agreed to a few concessions to the Fraternity, such as observing all contract provisions and picking up travel expenses to spring training, but the ten-day clause remained.

Fultz wanted to change the essentially feudalistic relationship between owners and players, but he proved not to be the kind of leader he needed to be. When the club owners declared their determination to blacklist any and all players signing with the Federals, Fultz went along with the blacklist, thus in effect affirming the reserve clause and vitiating whatever ambitions he had for eliminating or at least modifying it.

If the Braves lost relatively little to the Federals, other teams weren't so fortunate, especially in the National League. Most of the top stars of the period—such as Cobb, Tris Speaker, Eddie Collins, and Joe Jackson—were American Leaguers. Though tempted by the money the Federals flashed, nearly all of the game's foremost performers (including such National League standouts as Christy Mathewson and Grover Cleveland Alexander) stayed with their clubs for big salary increases, often under multi-year contracts. Cobb held out during the first part of the season but eventually signed for $15,000; beginning in 1915 he would work under a three-year contract at $20,000 per year. When Speaker disembarked in New York harbor at the end of a celebrated around-the-world baseball tour organized by John McGraw and Chicago White Sox owner Charles Comiskey, Federal representatives met him with a lavish offer. Speaker decided to stay with the Boston Red Sox, signing a two-year contract for $18,000 per year, which, at least temporarily, made him the highest-paid player in baseball history.

As the three leagues—two established major leagues and one pretender—prepared for the 1914 season, the Federal League's ultimate failure was by no means a foregone conclusion, despite the bravado of the

National and American league owners and the three members of the ruling National Commission. Some teams had been especially hard hit by Federal League raids, none more so than the Philadelphia Phillies, second place finishers in 1913. Although they kept the brilliant Alexander, the Phillies lost their other two front-line pitchers: twenty-seven-game winner Tom Seaton (Brooklyn) and fourteen-game-winner Ad Brennan (Chicago). Those three had accounted for 72 percent of the Phillies' wins in 1913. The Philadelphia team also lost the left side of its infield: shortstop Mickey Doolan and third-baseman Otto Knabe, both topnotch players, who signed with Baltimore. Knabe became the "Terrapins" player-manager.[16]

It was the common opinion among baseball observers that the defection of sizable numbers of big-league players to the Federal League would diminish the quality of play in 1914, especially in the National League. A little more than a month into the season, Hugh Fullerton described the National League as "suffering from general debility."[17] However that may be, what George Stallings and his mostly rebuilt Boston Braves did that year would become part of American sports legend and lore.

3

1914: "I feel the pennant fever buzzing"

The Braves' exhibition trip north toward the 1914 season-opener climaxed in Washington, where they lost twice to the team then usually called the "Nationals." In the first game, Walter Johnson struck out seven and gave up four hits in seven innings in a contest that ended 7–4. On Tuesday, April 14, they began the season in Ebbets Field, Brooklyn, with about 12.000 people in the stands and about 10,000 seats unoccupied. It was the managerial debut of fifty-year-old Wilbert Robinson, who had been the catcher and John McGraw's teammate on the famous Baltimore Orioles three-time pennant winners (1894–1896) in the old twelve-team National League. For three years Robinson had served as McGraw's coach, until they had a falling-out in the aftermath of the Giants' third-straight World Series defeat the previous October, losing in five games to Connie Mack's Athletics.

For the season opener—and only for that game—the Braves took the field dressed in their blue road uniforms with swastikas sewn on the front of their caps. Of course later generations would be horrified by the exhibiting of a swastika under any circumstances, but in the decade before the German Nazis appropriated it as their movement's symbol, the swastika was widely regarded as a symbol of good luck—as it had been so regarded in many different cultures for thousands of years.

After the usual pregame ceremonies, league president John Tener, a former big-league pitcher himself, threw out the first ball. Robinson's starter was right-hander Ed Reulbach, who had been part of Frank Chance's stellar pitching staff on the 1906–1910 Cubs. Stallings countered with George Tyler and a lineup that included four players who were effectively rookies: Charlie Deal at third base, Butch Schmidt at first base, Larry Gilbert in center field, and Tommy Griffith in right. Hank

National League President John Tener throwing out the first ball on opening day, April 14, 1914, in Ebbets Field, Brooklyn. The Braves lost, 8–2 (George Bantham Bain Collection, Library of Congress).

Gowdy was behind the plate. Joe Connolly in left field plus Johnny Evers and Rabbit Maranville, already being hailed as the majors' foremost "keystone" duo, filled out the lineup.

That all three of Stallings's outfield starters were left-hand batters was an indication of how he intended to use his outfielders during the season: Lefty batters versus right-handed pitchers, righty batters versus left-handed pitchers. McGraw had done some of that with his Giants teams, but Stallings would use "platooning" (as it came to be called much later) to a greater extent than any manager had been willing to do up to that time.

Reulbach gave up two runs in seven innings before giving way to Edward "Jeff" Pfeffer, a big right-hander who was beginning an excellent big-league career. Pfeffer held the Braves scoreless the rest of the way, while Brooklyn hit Tyler hard for eight runs. The Braves committed four errors, two by Griffith in right field. It wasn't an auspicious beginning to a season in which the team Stallings had put together was supposed to be at least a first-division club (although given Stallings's peculiar superstition about not winning the season-opener, he may have thought it a good omen). After an off day on Wednesday, rookie right-hander Raleigh Aitchison shut out the Braves, 5–0, Dick Rudolph taking the loss.

Stallings then took his team to Philadelphia, where they were beaten in two of three games. On Saturday the 18th, Hub Perdue lost to Roy "Rube" Marshall, one of only six games Marshall would win all season. Grover Cleveland Alexander outpitched Rudolph on the 22nd, but in between the Braves won for the first time, Dick Crutcher working a tidy 4–3 game to defeat Joe Oeschger.

At least the Braves had a successful home opener. On April 23, in typically chilly temperature, James Michael Curley, Boston's new mayor, threw out the first ball. Evers and Deal hit doubles and Connolly tripled in a 9–1 thumping of Brooklyn's Pat Ragan and two other pitchers. Tyler pitched all the way despite issuing eleven walks. But Brooklyn won the last two games in the series; two home losses to the Giants followed, then another defeat by Philadelphia before the Braves found their bats again and handed Alexander one of the worst beatings of his illustrious career, scoring thirteen runs on fifteen base hits, including Connolly's home run. Rudolph managed to hold the Phillies to seven runs for his first victory of the season.

On May 11, after McGraw's Giants swept a three-game series in New York, the Braves were dead last with a 3–12 record. One of the games was a tough 2–0 loss, Christy Mathewson over Tyler, who gave up eleven hits to Mathewson's nine. The decisive play was probably a diving catch by center fielder Fred Snodgrass, who then threw to second base to double up the runner. The Braves were convinced Snodgrass had trapped the ball, but base umpire Cy Rigler—with whom Stallings and his carryover players from 1913 bore a grudge—ruled it a catch. Captain Evers, who had his own history with Rigler from his years with the Cubs, stormed onto the field to argue the call; while Stallings, confined to the bench in street clothes, exercised his vocabulary of expletives. Gaffney, sitting in his Polo Grounds box, took Rigler to task at the end of the game; the next day Gaffney and Stallings met with Tener in his Manhattan office to protest Rigler's umpiring. Then and in subsequent similar episodes, Tener calmly affirmed his satisfaction with his umpiring staff.

The Braves began their first tour of the western cities with a one-

Umpire Charles "Cy" Rigler, 1914. Though burly and tough, Rigler didn't cow the famously disputatious Braves (George Bantham Bain Collection, Library of Congress).

game stopover in Pittsburgh, which ended in a 1–1 tie. In Cincinnati they caught a hot ball club. Although James allowed only three hits, former New York Giants stalwart Leon "Red" Ames blanked them 1–0. Towering Dave Davenport shut them out again the next day, 6–0, Tyler taking the loss; and on May 15 left-hander Earl Yingling bested Crutcher, 4–2. While the Braves moved back to Pittsburgh, Ames defeated his old team 9–1; thereby Cincinnati, under shortstop and first-year manager Buck Herzog, rose to third place, only the second time in three seasons the Reds had reached that high in the standings.

At Pittsburgh's Forbes Field (which, when it opened in 1909, had been the National League's first steel-and-concrete ballpark) Boston took the first of a three-game series, 4–1, James winning for the first time, but lost the other two to the Pirates, the league's early front-runners. The Braves did better in Chicago, winning the first two games before losing the third, 2–1, on Bill Sweeney's ninth-inning single off Rudolph, in a game in which Maranville committed three errors. They won the series finale, 8–2, James getting the win, although Tyler finished the game. The three victories must have been especially pleasing for Evers. While his team was trailing the rest of the league, the Cubs under Hank O'Day were only a notch higher in the standings.

Yet that last game in Chicago was also the origin of bad feeling between Evers and James. Evers took his role as captain with utmost seriousness and felt free not only to coach but criticize his teammates on the field. The Braves were mostly a collection of young players; by comparison Evers, who would turn thirty-three that summer, was a grizzled veteran. Fifty years later James revealed that at one point in the Chicago game, he motioned for Evers to move over before he made his next pitch. Evers changed positions, then moved back. The batter hit the ball through the infield where Evers would have been if he had stayed where James wanted him. Stallings, seeing the two were angry with each other, motioned for Tyler to relieve James. Afterward, in the visitors' dressing room, the twenty-two-year-old pitcher told Evers he had to admit he had been right in trying to get Evers to re-position himself. "Evers blew a fuse," James recalled, "and I never was able to make him like me."[1]

It could be that, at least at that point in his young life, James wasn't particularly likeable. Late in June, during a series in Boston with

Philadelphia, the big pitcher took offense at something a local reporter (whose identity wasn't publicly revealed) had written about him, invited the man into the Braves clubhouse, and proceeded to beat him up—presumably as teammates looked on. That hardly endeared James to the Boston baseball press.

The Braves continued to play pretty well in Robison Field in St. Louis. Maranville's four hits helped give Tyler a 3–2 win. The Cardinals won the next day, but on May 27 Boston concluded its first western tour by winning a raucous 7–4 finale, Rudolph outlasting left-hander Harry "Slim" Sallee. Maranville hit a bases loaded home run in the second inning. At various points in the game, Cy Rigler ejected Evers and St. Louis third-baseman Alvin "Cozy" Dolan and center fielder Lee Magee; afterward Schuyler Britton, whose wife Helene Robison Britton had inherited the St. Louis franchise from her uncle, wired John Tener that "for the good of organized baseball in St. Louis," Rigler shouldn't be assigned to work future games at Robison Field.[2] Stallings's men entrained for Philadelphia, still having won less than a third of the time.

Besides his team's poor play, Stallings wasn't happy with baseball affairs in general. As usual, he was complaining about the league's umpires, who were, he submitted, even worse than in 1913. After thinking about that for a minute, he acknowledged it would be impossible. As for the Federal League, he predicted its ruin, because it was "too much flavored of the bush to attract attention at major league prices." But he also didn't think American and National league owners could afford to pay players the salaries being forced upon them by competition from the Federals. "A major league franchise today isn't worth a chew of tobacco," he grumbled. "It will not be for three years to come."[3]

Stallings's mood didn't improve in Philadelphia and Brooklyn. Boston lost a single game and split a Decoration Day doubleheader with the Phillies before moving on to Brooklyn, where they played two doubleheaders in a row (to make up for April rainouts), losing three of the four games, then dropping a single game to reduce their record to 10–24. In the five games, the Braves scored only thirteen runs.

Finally back in South End Grounds, at the start of a thirty-one-game home stand crowded with more makeup doubleheaders, they split four games with Cincinnati, which had taken over second place from Pittsburgh. Hub Perdue won the opener, 7–2, which ended Red Ames's seven-game winning streak. The next day Tyler was the losing pitcher, 6–4, and after the mandatory Sunday hiatus, Bert Niehoff's home run over the short right-field fence and Tom Clarke's single in the ninth inning beat James, 3–2. Otto Hess, a Swiss-born left-hander, pitched the best of his eleven starts that season, edging fellow-left-hander John "Rube" Benton, 3–2, in the fourth game. That put Boston's record, as of June 9, at 13–28.

Herzog's Reds left Boston in second place with a 28–18 record; Cincinnati fans, whose teams had never won anything in the National League, were talking pennant. Such hopes wouldn't be sustainable. That month the defection to the St. Louis Federals of Dave Davenport and Armando Marsans, a Cuban infielder-outfielder, significantly weakened the Reds.

At that point the Braves had the worst team batting average in the league, a puny .225, and had scored only 105 runs, an average of 2.5 per game. "George Stallings," read an entry in *Sporting Life's* weekly "National League Notes," "is desperately trying to land some sort of hitter to grace his Boston outfield. Outside of the fact that any trio he starts are bad judges of fly balls, poor throwers and mediocre stickers, his Boston garden looks fine."[4]

Stallings and Gaffney needed to get some help. But while they were putting out trade feelers, the Braves erupted for an 11–2 battering of Pittsburgh and went on to sweep the Pirates in four-games. The high point of its season so far, the Boston club's sweep was a major setback for the Pirates and the great Honus Wagner, who despite his forty years, was still at shortstop or occasionally third base every day. Wagner wasn't the fearsome hitter and far-ranging fielder he had once been, but many people, not just in Pittsburgh but other places, would have liked for the universally admired "Dutchman" to play on one more pennant-winner. Yet the Pirates' early showing proved illusory; manager Fred Clarke's team was on its way to a seventh-place finish.

The Braves' revival continued when Hank O'Day's Chicago Cubs came in for four games, beginning on Tuesday, June 16. In pre-game doings, Bill Sweeney, still popular at South End Grounds, received gifts from local admirers who had arranged a "day" for him with the Boston management. The Cubs won the series opener, 7–5, Larry Cheney outlasting Otto Hess. On Wednesday the Braves won by the same score,

Crutcher and big Jim Vaughn both pitching all the way. On the 18th, Bunker Hill Day, Boston swept the holiday doubleheader, 6–3 and 7–3, behind Tyler and James. That put their record at 20–29. Although the Braves were still in last place, three games behind Chicago, they had won seven of their last nine. It seemed they were about to start playing the kind of baseball expected of them.

Gaffney was finally were able to arrange a deal for players Stallings thought would give his lineup more punch. Tommy Griffith, batting .106, was gone, demoted to the American Association. On June 26, Boston sent Hub Perdue, with a 2–5 record, to St. Louis for outfielders George "Possum" Whitted and Ted Cather. Those two, together with Les Mann, became Stallings's outfield against left-handers. A few days later the Braves also traded Jack Martin, who had subbed occasionally for Charlie Deal, to Philadelphia for 5'6" Josh Devore, who was supposed to provide needed outfield and basepath speed. (Devore's main claim to notoriety was his desperate running catch in deep right-center field at Fenway Park to save game three of the 1912 World Series for the Giants.)

Devore joined Joe Connolly and Larry Gilbert as Boston's lefty-batting outfielders, although a few weeks later Boston sent Cincinnati cash for Herbie Moran, still another outfielder. The veteran Moran, thirty years old, was an inch shorter than Devore and also hit from the left side. Including Oscar Dugey, who was in the outfield occasionally, Stallings had eight outfielders to shuffle. He had also settled on Hank Gowdy as his first-string catcher, with Bert Whaling as his backup.

Boston's new players didn't help much—at least not right away. After a four-game split with St. Louis, on June 24 the Braves began a six-game series at South End Grounds with the first-place Giants. They managed to hold their own with John McGraw's league-leaders, dividing a doubleheader to start the series, with Rudolph winning the opener. Perdue, in his last outing as a Brave, lost the nightcap. The next day Paul Strand relieved James in the third inning and hit a game-winning double in the ninth off Jeff Tesreau. On the 26th the teams played another twin bill, which the Giants swept, 10–6 and 8–4. Boston won the single game finale, 4–2, Rudolph besting Richard "Rube" Marquard. The Braves' June 25 victory over New York actually got them out of last place by four percentage points, although their doubleheader loss the next day dropped them back into the cellar.

After the Sunday layoff, the next day's single game with Philadelphia was rained out. People reading their newspapers that Monday, June 29, might have taken note of what then seemed an obscure happening the previous day in Sarajevo, in the Austro-Hungarian province of Bosnia. A Serbian nationalist had assassinated Austrian Archduke Francis Ferdinand and his duchess. That event would eventually lead to significant changes in the lives of all Americans, including those who played professional baseball; but in the summer of 1914, those changes were still a long way off.

On Tuesday and Wednesday, the Phillies defeated Boston in back-to-back doubleheaders, with Alexander the victor in two of the four games. James, Crutcher, George Davis, and Rudolph took the losses. Brooklyn, now in seventh place, moved into South End Grounds, won a single game, and swept the traditional Independence Day double-header, 4–3 (Reulbach/Tyler) and 7–5 in eleven innings (Pat Ragan/James). After the Sunday off day, the Braves closed their home stand with still another doubleheader, beating Wilbert Robinson's team in both games. Rudolph out-dueled Pfeffer 3–1; in the nightcap, Crutcher pitched the best game of his big-league career, shutting out the opposition while the Braves scratched a single run off Frank Allen.

After losing nine times in fourteen games with the other three eastern clubs, the Braves' record was a lackluster 28–40. Midway through the season, they were still looking up at the other seven members of the National League. Yet it was a tightly bunched league; Boston was only fourteen games behind the league-leading Giants. By then Chicago had moved up to second place; in his weekly syndicated column, John McGraw named the Cubs as the team the Giants would have to beat for the pennant.

If the Boston team's showing so far had been disappointing, Stallings and Gaffney nonetheless moved to tie up players they considered their most valuable, to keep them out of the hands of the Federal Leaguers. Evers, making $10,000 per year, was already under contract through 1917; now Maranville, Gowdy, Rudolph, James, Tyler, and Schmidt signed new contracts running through 1916. All of the new contracts carried sizable pay increases beginning in 1915, including $7,500 per year for Rudolph, $4,000 for James, and $5,400 for Tyler. Moreover, the contracts all omitted the despised ten-day release clause. Gaffney,

46

no doubt mindful of Maranville's auto wreck the previous winter, also took out a $25,000 insurance policy on his little shortstop.

The Braves left South Station on the evening of July 6, 1914, for Chicago, where they were to start their next tour of the western cities. On the way they stopped over in Buffalo for an exhibition game with the local International Leaguers. Although most players disliked such occasions, the visiting club's share of the gate receipts from in-season exhibitions in minor-league cities helped pay travel expenses, especially for the less-prosperous outfits.

The stopover in Buffalo could have been something of a homecoming for Stallings; instead it turned out to be a total embarrassment for the Braves' manager. The Buffalo team pounded his second-string pitchers for fifteen runs, while Boston was held to three. When the players returned to the train station, they found Stallings in a volcanic mood. As Maranville later described the scene, he greeted them with "Big league ballplayers, you call yourselves, eh! You're not even Grade A sand lotters. I'm ashamed of you all." Stung and hurt, Maranville and his mates "were still ripping mad when we arrived in Chicago."[5]

They proceeded to take three games out of four from the Cubs, Rudolph winning the last game 5–2. The three defeats dropped Chicago to third place, behind player-manager Miller Huggins's surprisingly competitive St. Louis team. Next the Braves split a four-game set with the Cardinals. The first game, on Sunday, July 12, was an easy 12–5 victory; Boston got to ace spitballer Bill Doak and Hub Perdue for fifteen hits. The suffocating heat and humidity that made ballplayers hate playing in St. Louis in mid-summer forced both Tyler and Doak to leave the game; Crutcher pitched a scoreless six innings, although under the scoring rules then in effect, Tyler was credited with the win. Another Boston win the next day, 8–7, had the *St. Louis Post-Dispatch's* W. J. O'Connor touting the Braves' pennant chances and especially Maranville's quickness and Evers's infield generalship. "Evers," O'Connor wrote, "so maneuvers the Braves' infield that it is impossible to get a single on a ground ball."[6] (One wonders about Bill James's reaction upon reading that.) But with Stallings resting Evers, St. Louis won the remaining two games, Perdue bettering Tyler and his old team, 3–2, and Slim Sallee outpitching Otto Hess, 5–3.

The following three-game series in Cincinnati was a Boston sweep;

Stallings's pitchers allowed the Reds only five runs. In the last game, on July 19, the Braves scored three times in the top of the ninth inning to win the game for James, 3–2. With that the Braves improved their record to 36–43 and vacated last place, displacing Pittsburgh in the standings. This time they were out of the cellar for good, because they shoved the Pirates deeper into eighth place by winning three single games at Forbes Field and dividing a doubleheader. Tyler pitched shutouts in the first and fifth games, Rudolph and James in the second and third. Boston's only loss was an 8–4 thumping suffered by Crutcher and Davis in the nightcap of the July 23 doubleheader.

The Braves, having won fourteen of their last eighteen games, including an 11–4 mark on the western trip, came home in fourth place. The league standings were changing almost daily, so that the Braves had risen from eighth to fourth in only four days. It was the first time in twelve years a Boston National League team had been in the first division that late in the season. When the team arrived at South Station on the evening of July 24, Stallings told them to be at the ballpark an hour ear-

Johnny Evers. His inspirational leadership and fiery competitiveness made up for his unexceptional playing skills (George Bantham Bain Collection, Library of Congress).

lier than usual. In the clubhouse the next morning, Tyler remembered, Stallings delivered one of "his fiery speeches," which "put blood in our eyes for the game that day." He said from then on he was depending on his "Big Three" of Rudolph, James, and Tyler to carry the team; and if anybody let down his pitchers, he would be back in the minor leagues in 1915.[7]

Fiery speeches or not, that afternoon Stallings's team disappointed an overflow Saturday crowd at South End Grounds by losing to Chicago, 5–4. Jim Vaughn and Otto Hess combined to give up five ground-rule doubles hit into the spectators standing around the outfield. It was a particularly tough day for umpire Bill Byron; not only was he harassed by the Boston players throughout the game, but as he left the field at game's end, somebody tossed a pop bottle and hit him in the head.

That defeat still left Boston only nine games behind the Giants, with Chicago (2½ behind) now back in second place and St. Louis (5½ behind) in third. But with the exception of W. J. O'Connor in St. Louis, as yet nobody seemed to take seriously the Braves as pennant-contenders.

That changed after Stallings's players reeled off a nine-game winning streak. They beat the Cubs in the remaining two games of their Boston stay and swept four from St. Louis. The Braves' Saturday, August 1 win over the Cardinals, 4–3, drew a huge overflow estimated at 22,000, thought be the biggest National League turnout in Boston history. They won three games from Pittsburgh—the first two of which were shutouts, by Rudolph and James. The Thursday, August 6, game was a thriller, which the Braves won, 5–4, when Maranville hit a home run in the tenth inning off Charles "Babe" Adams. Although he also had two singles and stole two bases in that game, Maranville later revealed he was murderously hung over from long-term partying the night before at the home of Harry Levine, a well-to-do wine importer who lived in the Boston suburb of Hyde Park. Besides Maranville, the other Braves on hand were Gowdy (who organized the party), Schmidt, Devore, Cocreham, James, and Whaling. Rabbit drank champagne—lots of it—for the first time in his life. Pittsburgh won the series finale, 5–1, to break Boston's winning streak, Crutcher and Davis again failing against Fred Clarke's team.

The fact that seven Braves were out partying most of the night before a game that might figure critically in the pennant race was indicative of

Stallings's way of dealing with his players. During games he might fume and rage at them, but once they left the ballpark, he didn't concern himself with their comings and goings. Unlike John McGraw and some other managers, he didn't enforce a curfew on road trips or have them spied upon both on the road and at home. As long as his players showed up ready to play, Stallings let them alone.

Johnny Evers missed the last two games with Pittsburgh and a three-game series with Cincinnati that followed, as a consequence of still another personal misfortune. Word came from Troy that his five-year-old daughter Helen (named after her mother) had died of scarlet fever. When Evers reached his home, he found that his little son was also near death with the same highly contagious disease. John Jr. would recover, although he was still desperately ill when Helen was buried on Sunday, August 9, following a Roman Catholic funeral mass. Then Evers's departure for Boston was delayed another day by local health authorities, who insisted he have all of his clothes as well as his luggage fumigated to purge whatever scarlet fever "germs" they might have on them.

As is often the case when a couple loses a child, the death of the Evers's daughter aggravated already worsening circumstances in their marriage. Even though Evers had brought his wife and children with him to spring training in Macon, she complained about his long absences from home and family (such as have often strained the marriages of professional athletes). Within a few years Helen Evers would take John Jr. and move away from Troy. Given the couple's Catholic faith, divorce was out of the question, so she would obtain a legal separation, the terms of which gave her custody of their son and lifetime alimony.

On August 8, while Evers was away from the team, Gaffney and Stallings made still another player deal, obtaining third-baseman James Carlisle "Red" Smith from Brooklyn for the waiver price. Charlie Deal was a capable fielder, but he couldn't get his batting average out of the low .200's and was nursing a sore leg. The twenty-four-year-old Smith, a South Carolinian and a graduate in engineering from Alabama Polytechnic Institute (later Auburn University), was one of the league's better players. He had batted .286 and .297 in the past two seasons; in 1913 his forty doubles led the majors. But he didn't get along with Wilbert Robinson, having been part of a faction that wanted Jake Daubert named manager when Bill Dahlen was fired.

Smith's discontent affected his play; batting only .245 after ninety games, he had come in for quite a lot of razzing from the spectators at Ebbets Field. Mordecai "Three Finger" Brown, former ace Cubs pitcher and current manager of the St. Louis Federals, was wooing Smith. When Brooklyn president Charles Ebbets, fearing Smith was about to jump, put him on waivers, the Braves quickly grabbed him.

Upon Smith's arrival in Boston, the first thing Stallings told him was that he was raising his salary. As if that weren't enough to buoy Smith's confidence, Stallings assured him, "Red, you're the man we've been looking for. You're the man we've needed on this club. You're the man who's going to win the pennant for us." "After that," Smith recalled a half-century later, "I felt like a million dollars."[8]

Also after that, the newcomer presumably didn't mind Stallings's insistence on morning practices and his daily lectures on yesterday's game and pep talks for today's. That wasn't the way things had been under the easy-going Robinson. Evers described Stallings's morning sessions: "He can stand up there for half an hour and talk of the game of the day before, never using a note or a score card, and call attention to a dozen plays the players did not see or have forgotten."[9]

Tim Murnane could barely contain his excitement about the Braves' surge in the standings. "I admit," declared the

James "Red" Smith. His acquisition in August 1914 was a major factor in the Braves' pennant drive (George Bantham Bain Collection, Library of Congress).

Boston Globe's white-maned sports editor, "that I feel the pennant fever buzzing."[10] Joseph Lannin, a New York hotel owner and developer who had bought a majority interest in the Boston Red Sox the previous winter, offered the Braves the use of bigger Fenway Park for their remaining home games. Although Lannin charged a modest rental fee, Gaffney and Stallings were only too happy to accept the offer.

The three games with Cincinnati that closed the home stand resulted in two wins and a thirteen-inning tie. Having pushed their record to 51–46, the Braves began their next road trip with a scheduled four-game series versus the Giants. At that point they were still in fourth place, six and a half games behind John McGraw's team, which, unlike 1913, was finding itself in a tough race.

What happened in the three games played in the Polo Grounds should have convinced any remaining doubters about the Braves' ability to contend for the pennant. And as various Boston players said later on, they left New York confident they could actually win it. Rain prevented the game scheduled for Wednesday the 12th. Before the Thursday game, Rudolph was honored by the Bronx Elks Club; among the various gifts he received was an unusual one: a diamond-studded elk's tooth. The balding right-hander rewarded his admirers by pitching well enough to gain a 5–3 decision over Rube Marquard. The next day the Braves slapped Jeff Tesreau and Al Demaree for eleven hits and seven runs, while James held the Giants to three. They won the Saturday finale in ten innings, 2–0, Tyler pitching a masterful three-hitter to beat Christy Mathewson. That evening the Boston players happily boarded their train for Cincinnati, now pursuing the Giants by only three and a half games.

Meanwhile the National League's board of directors met secretly to hear McGraw's criticism of the league's umpires (Bill Klem excepted). Bill Byron, McGraw complained, was "absolutely incompetent." But however McGraw felt about John Tener's umpires, in his weekly ghosted column for the Wheeler syndicate he stuck to his prediction that his Giants would come out on top. He believed that on the Braves' upcoming road trip, "one or two defeats will be liable to break the club.... Once stopped, I figure the Braves will be stopped for good." With his fourth-straight pennant increasingly endangered, McGraw went on in a vein that read a lot like sour grapes: "I don't contend that any club has played good ball. If any had, the Braves would never have climbed from last place to their present place in six weeks' time." Mike Donlin—a onetime Giants star McGraw had brought back mainly out of sentiment—was even less impressed by the Braves. "I want to say," he told a St. Louis reporter with added emphasis, "that BOSTON HASN'T THE CLASS TO WIN."[11]

Opinion was rather different in Boston. "The wonderful spurt of the Braves has turned Boston daffy," reported the *Boston Journal's* A. H. C. Mitchell in the weekly *Sporting Life*. Mitchell noted that when the result of the Saturday game in New York was posted on the Fenway Park scoreboard, the crowd cheered for five minutes, ignoring the Red Sox–Yankees game on the field. The Braves had won twenty-six of their last thirty-four games, for which Mitchell gave Stallings the credit. The Braves' success "only goes to show what intelligent management can do. Stallings is a great organizer of a ball club. There is probably none better in the business."[12]

The series in Cincinnati opened on Monday, August 17, with a doubleheader. The Braves won both, the first an 11–1 walkover for James, the second a hard-earned 5–3 win for Rudolph. Red Smith's wild throw lost the next day's game, Crutcher taking a tough 3–1 loss. Phil Douglas, a hard-drinking, often dominating spitballer, was the winning pitcher. The series' last encounter was another close one, Tyler topping Red Ames, 3–2. The Giants' second loss in Pittsburgh cut New York's lead to two games.

In Pittsburgh, the Braves won two of three, then lost two of three in Chicago. Rudolph had a bad outing at West Side Park on August 26, being knocked around in a 9–6 loss that broke his eleven-game winning streak. But the Giants were stumbling as well, losing all three games in Cincinnati, so that on August 26 they were tied with the Braves at 59–48, with St. Louis (62–53) and Chicago (58–53) close behind. Tyler, for whom the Braves' seemed to have extraordinary trouble scoring, lost 1–0 in the last game in Chicago; Larry Cheney pitched a gem, allowing only one hit. The single Cubs score came on first-baseman Vic Saier's seventh-inning home run (one of eighteen he hit that season).

Heinie Zimmerman followed Saier's homer with a drive to left-center field, which he tried to stretch into a double. When he slid into second base head first, Evers (whose feelings for the "Great Zim" hadn't improved since 1913) slammed the ball onto his neck. Zimmerman (whose feelings for Evers hadn't changed, either) jumped up and began grappling with Evers. Maranville (as he described it in his posthumously published memoirs) "tried every angle to get at Heinie," finally landing a blow that split Zimmerman's upper lip. "For an instant, then," according to a Chicago reporter's eye-witness account, "Zimmerman, Evers and Maranville were in a tangle back of second base. They were then hidden from view by a flock of athletes and two umpires, who rushed to the scene." Other players from both teams joined the fray, which went on for a couple of minutes before umpires Ernie Quigley and Mal Eason managed to get everybody separated. The three who had initiated the disturbance were ordered out of the game, as well as Butch Schmidt, who denied hitting anybody. The Chicago reporter thought the fight "probably was the worst perpetrated on a big league diamond in recent years." After reading the umpires' report, president Tener fined Evers and Zimmerman $100 apiece and Maranville $50.[13]

The Giants, having lost nine of their last eleven games, followed the Braves into Chicago, while the Boston team played a four-game series in St. Louis that was relatively peaceful. Home runs by Walton Cruise and Lee Magee and Alvin "Cozy" Dolan's tenth-inning double off Rudolph accounted for all the Cardinals runs in a 3–2 victory, which put the Cardinals in second place, half a game ahead of Boston. Now W. J. O'Connor, stirred by the local team's showing, was predicting the Braves' pitchers would "crack soon."[14] But Boston won the remaining three games, while the Giants got back on their feet, also winning three of four from the Cubs.

On their way home, the Braves played a doubleheader and three single games in Philadelphia. Red Dooin's Phillies, relying almost entirely on the pitching of Alexander and Erskine Mayer, were struggling in the second division. Their struggles continued, because the Braves won four of the five encounters. With Evers on the bench with a stomach complaint, Boston swept the September 2 doubleheader with some lusty batting: 7–5 (Rudolph) and 12–5 (James). In a matchup of big pitchers in Brooklyn, Jeff Pfeffer held New York to two runs, while Rube Marquard was cuffed for six.

That put the Braves in first place and dropped the Giants to second for the first time since May 30. On the 3rd, though, the Giants regained the lead by taking a doubleheader, while Alexander shut out the Braves for eight innings, then gave up four runs in the ninth before escaping with 7–4 decision. Back in the lineup, Evers didn't last beyond the second inning, when Bill Klem tossed him for arguing balls and strikes.

Evers must have used some pretty strong language in his exchange with Klem, because Tener slapped a three-day suspension on him. On Friday, with Whitted at second base, James gave up thirteen hits but held on for a 6–5 win in twelve innings, with the winning run tallied on a squeeze play executed by Gowdy and Schmidt. Alexander was the losing pitcher in relief. Klem was still taking no backtalk, ejecting Herbie Moran and Phillies outfielder George "Dode" Paskert for taking exception to his work behind the plate. And on Saturday, Boston closed the series with a fine performance by Gene Cocreham, in one of his three starting assignments during the season and his only complete game. The tall Texan yielded a single run, while the Braves scored seven on Mayer and executed four double plays.

Meanwhile in Brooklyn, Marty O'Toole, picked up from Pittsburgh on waivers, pitched the Giants to a 4–3 win.[15] McGraw's team ended the series at Ebbets Field with a doubleheader split: A free-hitting 9–5 decision for Al Demaree, followed by a 4–1 loss, veteran left-hander Nap Rucker throttling the Giants with his slow curveballs. That left the Braves and Giants in a flat tie at 67–52. Out west, St. Louis lost four of five games (with a tie) to Pittsburgh and slipped to fourth place, with a 64–61 record. Third-place Chicago had won four of its last six and stood at 64–59. So it was still a four-way race.

That was the situation on Sunday, September 6, when the Braves arrived home and were greeted at the station by a large contingent of their long-unrequited supporters. A Labor Day doubleheader versus the Giants was in the offing, with a single game scheduled for Tuesday. Since that ignominious July day in Buffalo, the Braves had won thirty-nine of fifty-one games, with one tie. Tim Murnane announced to his readers that for the rest of the season, he wouldn't travel with the Red Sox (who were in second place in the other league, though well behind the Athletics), but would stick with the Braves. Stallings and his players possessed a big advantage over the other contenders, in that they were about to begin a home stand that would run for twenty-six games.

Encomiums for Stallings continued, even from American League scribes. A. E. Batchelor, the *Sporting News'* Detroit correspondent, doubted that apart from his three pitching mainstays, plus Evers,

Maranville, and a handful of others, Stallings had any big-league caliber players. Batchelor thought Stallings's success could be summed up in an epigram from poker-playing: "Life isn't so much in holding a good hand as in playing a poor hand well."[16]

In that period, doubleheaders were always scheduled on holidays; the home team nearly always scheduled the games for mornings and afternoons and charged separate admissions. In the eastern cities, most people could attend their favorites' games only on Saturday afternoons (unless they worked six-day weeks, as most wage-earners still did) and holidays. Separate admissions on holidays were a particular imposition on workers' pocketbooks, but that had been the practice for decades, and there wasn't much point grumbling about it.

The two games on Monday, September 7, in Fenway Park attracted a combined paid attendance—as reported by club secretary Herman Nickerson—of 74,163, surely the biggest one-day turnout up to then in the history of either major league. Expansion of Fenway Park's open-seating areas before the 1912 World Series had increased its capacity to about 32,000, close to that of the Polo Grounds. Both games were played before overflows of spectators, who stood behind ropes in front of the right- and center-field bleachers and on the ten-foot incline—dubbed "Duffy's Cliff" for the Red Sox's star left fielder—at the base of the left-field fence.

In the morning, Rudolph was matched against Mathewson, who was in the midst of the last good season of his storied career. The Braves showed no more respect for the universally admired "Matty" than for any other opposing player, calling him, among other things, "milk legs," in reference to his knock-kneed walk. McGraw made an early exit, banished from both games for berating umpire Bob Emslie, "whose eyesight for base decisions was none too good all day," according to the *New York Times* reporter on the scene.[17] Rudolph held the Giants to four runs, but Mathewson allowed only three until the bottom of the ninth inning, when Evers, his suspension served, lifted a single into left field to drive in Josh Devore and Herbie Moran and win it, 5–4. Much of the crowd poured onto the field to hoist Evers and carry him to the home team's third-base dugout. With the field and then the ballpark cleared, everybody waited about three hours for the first pitch of the afternoon game.

Those hours were the duration of the Braves' sole occupancy of first place. The afternoon game was something of a debacle for the home team, which committed four errors. Tyler and Jeff Tesreau pitched scorelessly for three innings before New York scored a run in the fourth. Then the Giants pounded Tyler for four more runs in the sixth, another four in the eighth, and added a final run, off Crutcher, in the ninth. Tyler gave up twelve hits before leaving with nobody out in the eighth inning. Tesreau struck out ten Braves, permitted a single run (in the seventh inning), and coasted most of the way. Once again the two teams were in a first-place tie.

The most memorable part of a game that Boston fans would wish to forget came in the seventh and the start of the eighth inning. Tyler, already down 5–1, threw close to center fielder Fred Snodgrass's head four times, finally hitting the button of his cap. Bill Klem motioned him to first base, but on his way Snodgrass veered close to Tyler and, as he told it fifty years later, "I stood in front of that guy and called him everything I could think of. He never said a word. Finally, when I ran out of adjectives, I went over to first base."[18] Snodgrass then thumbed his nose at Tyler (which could be taken either as a mild insult or as an obscene gesture); in response, Tyler tossed the ball in the air and dropped it, pantomiming Snodgrass's muff in the twelfth inning of the deciding game of the 1912 World Series—an infamous miscue that opened the door for the Red Sox's winning rally. Tyler got out of that inning unscathed, before being driven out in the eighth.

When Snodgrass trotted out to center field for the bottom of the eighth inning, the standees behind the ropes unleashed a torrent not only of verbal abuse but of pop bottles, food, paper wads, and whatever else they could find to throw in Snodgrass's direction. Snodgrass answered with more nose-thumbing. With people pushing against the ropes, it appeared the situation was about to get out of hand. At that point His Honor Mayor James M. Curley left his third-base box and attired, in Snodgrass's recollection, in swallowtail coat, top hat, and spats and accompanied by two policemen, stormed onto the field to demand umpires Klem and Emslie remove Snodgrass from the game. Klem ordered Curley off the field, while the policemen shooed the spectators back from the ropes. Tesreau retired the Braves without incident, after which second-baseman and acting manager Larry Doyle judiciously replaced Snodgrass with Bob Bescher for the ninth inning. (Subsequently Curley wrote John Tener insisting the league president fine or suspend Snodgrass for thumbing his nose at the mayor's constituents; Tener simply let the matter drop.)

So on Monday, September 8, the Boston and New York teams were again tied, at 69–53. With some 17,000 customers amply accommodated in the Fenway Park grandstand, pavilion, and bleachers, Bill James restored Boston's lead with a three-hit, 8–3 victory, despite issuing seven walks. The Braves touched up Marquard, Art Fromme, and George Wiltse for fifteen hits; Marquard, famed for winning nineteen consecutive games two years earlier, lost for the ninth time in a row. Meanwhile the Cubs were hanging in the race with a 69–59 record.

Although he didn't intend to stop relying on his Big Three to carry his team to the pennant, Stallings did add some late-season pitching strength. Gaffney purchased Tom Hughes, a thirty-year-old right-hander who had pitched for Stallings at New York and then spent the past four seasons in the Eastern/International League. This season Hughes had won twenty games for Rochester.[19]

On the 9th Philadelphia came into Fenway Park for back-to-back doubleheaders and a single game. The Phillies took the opener, 10–3, but in the nightcap George Davis, relying on a spitball and curve, pitched a 7–0 no-hit game, one of six decisions he would have that season after joining the Braves in June. Two Phillies reached base on Red Smith's errors; Davis walked three others. All three passes came in the fifth inning, but the Harvard law student struck out one batter and got another to hit into a double play. Rudolph and James were in fine form for the next day's doubleheader, Rudolph shutting out the Phillies, 3–0, James easing to a 7–2 win in the second game—the big Californian's sixth victory in the past fourteen days.

The Braves had to battle to win the single game, 6–5, beating Eppa Rixey, a 6'6" left-hander. Stallings used Crutcher, Strand, Davis, and Cocreham, who got credit for the win. Maranville lofted a sacrifice fly to score Whitted in the ninth inning. Whitted made three errors subbing for Evers, the Braves' captain having drawn another three-day suspension for a row with umpire Eason the day before. According to Tim Murnane, Gaffney had ordered Evers to stop getting thrown out of games, and Stallings wasn't on the umpires as much as usual. At the close of the games with Philadelphia, Boston's record was 73–54.

The Giants continued to flounder, dropping two of three games at home to Brooklyn and three of five in Philadelphia, while the Braves won two of three from Brooklyn. Tyler lost his third-straight game in the opener, to Raleigh Aitchison, 4–3. Rudolph, given four runs in the fifth inning, won the next day, 4–3; and on Tuesday the 15th, James survived to get the 7–5 decision despite giving up fifteen hits. At 75–55, Boston had built its lead over an increasingly frustrated John McGraw to a full three games. New York catcher John Meyers (who like nearly every player with even partial American Indian ancestry, had to put up with being called "Chief") later said, "We got discouraged, because everybody in the country seemed to be pulling for the Braves and rooting against McGraw."[20] That wasn't far from the truth.

St. Louis, by sweeping four games in Cincinnati from the Reds, had again displaced Chicago in third place. At 71–63, Miller Huggins's Cardinals had developed pennant aspirations of their own by the time they arrived in Boston for three single games. And by then W. J. O'Connor, admittedly a Cardinals partisan, seemed about tired of Evers's behavior. Yet he wrote about him with grudging admiration, terming him "an expert goat-getter." O'Connor asserted that the last time the Braves were in St. Louis, Evers "fought the Cardinals, the fans, the umpire and the Braves. He antagonized his own men as much as the enemy.... Once the game begins he hasn't a friend on the field. What's more, he doesn't want one." Yet *Baseball Magazine* editor F. C. Lane hailed "Evers the invincible" for overcoming his personal troubles and "playing his position with a steadiness, a brilliance, and a dash ... cheering his men on to victory, unwilling to let his own troubles interfere with their pennant hopes."[21]

In short order, the Braves dispatched whatever pennant hopes the Cardinals had. On Wednesday, September 16, before the first game of the St. Louis series, Evers's admirers honored with the gift of a silver service. (Yet the cloud that seemed to hang over Evers was still around; that same day, the new home in Troy he had paid for with his Boston signing bonus was burglarized.) With the score 3–3 in the eighth inning, Evers led off with a walk to start a three-run rally that broke Tyler's three-game losing streak. Rudolph pitched superbly the next day, holding St. Louis to one run while the Braves scored five on Slim Sallee. On Thursday, James and Bill Doak, the Cardinals' ace spitballer, battled for twelve innings, until the umpires decided it was too dark to continue with the score 1–1. The Cardinals left Boston eight games behind and effectively out of the race. Chicago was also out of it, having lost four of six games in Pittsburgh and two of three in Brooklyn. In New York, the Giants swept three games from Cincinnati and gained a half game on the leaders.

The Braves extended their winning streak to eight games by sweeping a three-game set with Pittsburgh and the opening game of three-consecutive doubleheaders with dead-last Cincinnati. James bested Red Ames in the first game of the September 23rd doubleheader, but in the nightcap Cincinnati finally won after nineteen-straight losses, Charles "King" Lear throwing a shutout while the Reds scored three times in the ninth inning on George Davis. Tyler pitched a shutout of his own the next day, 5–0; the second game ended in a 2–2 tie; and on Friday, Rudolph won the third shutout of the series, 2–0, followed by James's 4–2 decision.

In New York, the Giants blew whatever lingering pennant chances they had by losing five straight to Chicago and St. Louis. At nightfall on the 25th, the respective records of the Braves and Giants were 84–56 and 77–64. The Giants players could start making plans for the offseason; for the first October since 1910, there would be no World Series games in the Polo Grounds.

What the Braves had accomplished since July left most people simply dazzled. Grantland Rice, at thirty-three already a widely syndicated sports columnist, liked to enliven his columns with verses that were less-than-classic but sometimes memorable. His paean to the Braves, with references to Kaiser Wilhelm II and the war going on in Europe, exemplified the former:

> Wild Bill of Germany, they say,
>   Can beat the Frenchmen to a mush;
> J. Bull in any sort of play
>   Can batter back the Kaiser's rush;
> And Russia with a savage blow
>   Can drive the Austrians like slaves;
> But tell me this—before I go
>   What clan can check those pop-eyed Braves?[22]

The Braves just kept on winning. With Frank Baker and Eddie Collins of the American League champion Athletics in the Fenway Park grandstand to scout them, they beat Chicago's two best pitchers in another doubleheader. Tyler topped Jim Vaughn, 6–2, in a game featuring Maranville's three-run home run; Otto Hess coasted to a 12–2 battering of Larry Cheney. The next afternoon James gave up twelve hits and six runs and loaded the bases in the top of the ninth inning, but still managed to come out with a 7–6 victory. The Giants won a doubleheader from Pittsburgh, Marquard ending his twelve-game losing streak in the nightcap, but it was too late for heroics by Marquard or anybody else on the New York team.

On Friday, September 29, the Braves won the pennant, thereby breaking the Pittsburgh–Chicago–New York axis that had dominated the National League since 1901. In his first outing as a Brave, Tom Hughes (who joined the team too late to be eligible for the World Series) pitched a three-run, five-hit victory. Cheney allowed only three hits, but in the fifth inning he walked four batters in a row to give Boston its first run, and Moran scored another on an infield out. The Braves won it in the bottom of the ninth inning when Evers walked, went to second on a sacrifice bunt, and scored the pennant-clinching run on Whitted's single. In various ways, the game was typical of the way the Braves had won much of the time. At that point their record was 89–56; the Giants', 80–65.

The Braves' triumph moved Joseph Kelly, Pittsburgh's *Sporting Life* contributor, to offer a tongue-in-cheek recipe for a pennant-winning team:

> *Take a club that bats in the aggregate somewhere around the .247 mark, that fields about second or third, that ranks sixth in the long range hitting, that has one lad in the herd who can land among the leading sluggers of his league, and but one player who can swipe bases among the upper ten, have practically every man on the club a cast off, and in general have the aggregation described—during the first months of the season, of course—as a bunch of misfits, mix with George Stallings, and serve piping hot.*[23]

Boston's remaining ten games were all away from home, in New York and Brooklyn. Six games were scheduled in the Polo Grounds, including two doubleheaders. About three hundred Royal Rooters, in five day coaches and three parlor cars, rode the train down from Boston, dancing in the aisles during stops in Providence, New London, and New Haven.

On September 30 the Royal Rooters watched the Braves drive out Tesreau with four runs in an eventual 7–1 win for Rudolph. The second game was a 7–7 tie. Joe Connolly had seven hits in nine at bats in the two games: four singles, a double, and two triples. On Thursday, October 1, Boston scored twice in the top of the ninth inning to win it, 7–6, Davis going all the way. Tyler had a bad outing on the 2nd, losing 11–5. In the next day's doubleheader, Stallings rested Gowdy in favor of Fred Tyler, Lefty's younger brother, who was being given a late-season trial. Hess won the opener, 4–1; in the nightcap Crutcher gave up a lone hit (by Marquard) but walked four batters in the fourth inning for the only New York run. Marquard pitched a five-hit shutout. The teams split their season series, eleven games apiece. Except for Marquard's shutout, the Braves had done some pretty strong hitting in the six games in the Polo Grounds.

The regular season closed in Brooklyn on October 5 and 6 with a pair of doubleheaders, the fourteenth and fifteenth the Braves played over the last six weeks of the season. Fred Tyler worked both twin bills in Ebbets Field, so the youngster was behind the plate for three-consecutive doubleheaders.[24] In the first doubleheader, Stallings's men continued to pound the ball: a fifteen-hit, fifteen-run barrage in support of Crutcher, who held the opposition to two. The only remarkable thing about the game was that in the eighth inning, Brooklyn right-hander Don Carlos Patrick "Pat" Ragan, pitching in relief, struck out three Braves on nine pitches—a feat performed only twice before in the American League and once in the National League. Ragan also worked the nightcap, a 9–5 win decided on Les Mann's bases-loaded home run. Hughes was the winning pitcher.

Even though he had the pennant clinched, Stallings continued to drive his team, whereas Connie Mack was resting his regular players. Stallings didn't work any of the Big Three after Tyler's trouncing in New York, but he kept his infield regulars in the lineup and continued to use his outfield combinations as he had all season. For that he drew some criticism, which seemed justified when, in the ninth inning of the first game of the season-closing doubleheader in Ebbets Field, Red Smith broke his right ankle and tore the ligaments above the ankle sliding into second base. Boston lost, 3–2, to Jeff Pfeffer, Davis taking the defeat. In a game that meant nothing to Boston, Stallings lost the services of his crack third-baseman, who had compiled a .314 average and driven in thirty-seven runs in 207 times at bat since coming to the Braves. It was all too reminiscent of what had happened to Johnny Evers four years earlier. The news of Smith's injury prompted gamblers to up the World Series odds in Philadelphia's favor from 2–1 to 3–1.

In the visiting players' clubhouse between games, the Boston players were downcast. Then, Stallings related a few months later, he tried a little psychology. For the last game of the season, he put a patchwork lineup on the field. Besides keeping Fred Tyler at catcher, Stallings had Strand pitch and Whitted play first base. Charlie Deal was at third base, Mann at shortstop, and Oscar Dugey at second. Stallings said he wanted "to prove to my ball players that one man's loss could not wreck a ball team. The way the substitute club beat Brooklyn restored the confidence that the injury to Smith had destroyed."[25] Whether or not it worked out that way, or whether it was even necessary, Boston won 7–3, in a game called after seven innings.

The Braves finished with a 94–59 record, with five ties. Their margin over the runner-up Giants was a stunning ten and a half games. While that should have been enough to make a believer of John McGraw, he was still in his sour grapes mood, grumbling that the Braves couldn't have beaten either his Giants or the Cubs in 1908. St. Louis's Cardinals, for whom "Spittin' Bill" Doak won twenty games with a 1.72 earned-run average (the majors' best), ended in third place at 81–72, a thirty-game improvement over 1913.[26] Chicago was fourth. That wasn't good enough for the Cubs' owners, who replaced Hank O'Day with Roger Bresnahan. Brooklyn narrowly beat out Philadelphia for fifth place, with Pittsburgh and Cincinnati bringing up the rear.

From July 8, when they began the road trip that lifted them out of last place and into the National League pennant race, the Braves' record was 66–19, a .776 winning percentage. They had a winning record against every team in the league except New York, with which they split their season's series, and Brooklyn, which beat them thirteen times in twenty-two games. They dominated the western clubs: Pittsburgh (17–5), Chicago (16–6), St. Louis (15–6), and Cincinnati (14–8). Only St. Louis and, oddly, seventh-place Pittsburgh committed fewer errors. Sparked by the middle-infield play of Evers and Maranville, Boston led both major leagues with 143 double plays.

W. J. O'Connor was wrong; the Braves' pitchers didn't crack, despite the pile-up of doubleheaders. Rudolph's final record was 26–10 with a 2.35 earned-run average; James's was 26–7 with a 1.90 ERA; Tyler's was 16–13 with a 2.69 ERA. Rudolph completed thirty-one games; James, thirty; Tyler, twenty-one. Rudolph had an eleven-game winning streak; James got credit for nineteen of his last twenty decisions. Between them, the Big Three worked 939.3 innings and pitched in 126 of the Braves' 158 games (including the five ties). Heroic work, indeed, even in a period when front-line pitchers were expected to take the mound every third or fourth day and finish what they started.

The Braves' team batting average was only .251, but one way or another they managed to score 657 runs, bettered only by the Giants. Of the full-season players, Joe Connolly led the team in batting average

George Stallings with (left) Bill James and (right) Lefty Tyler and Dick Rudolph, sitting in the visitors' dugout in the Polo Grounds, New York, probably right after they had clinched the pennant back in Boston. The three pitchers combined for sixty-eight wins in 1914 (George Bantham Bain Collection, Library of Congress).

(.306), as well as home runs (9). Despite batting only .246, Maranville drove in the most runs (78).

Pennant celebrations in Boston would have to wait. The World Series was scheduled to begin on Friday, October 9, so Stallings took the Braves directly to Philadelphia from Brooklyn and booked them into the Majestic Hotel, not far from both the National League and American League ballparks. They would begin practice the next day on the National League grounds. Stallings intended for his players to be rested and prepared to take on Connie Mack's champions, winners of three of the last four American League pennants and three of the last four World Series.

4

1914 World Series: "What chance do predictors stand against miracles?"

George Stallings brushed aside worries about the absence of Red Smith and having to play weak-hitting Charlie Deal in his place, and boldly predicted a sweep in the World Series. That must have sounded like the sheerest bravado to sportswriters in the various major-league cities, most of whom thought otherwise. Of twenty scribes writing for daily newspapers queried by the *Sporting News*, twelve picked the Athletics; only four at least liked the Braves' chances; the remaining four didn't know or wouldn't say. The *Philadelphia North American's* George M. Graham predicted an Athletics sweep; E. A. Schneider of the *Detroit Free Press* thought Philadelphia would win in five games. The two Boston writers in the survey differed, the *American's* Fred Hoey favoring the Braves, the *Journal's* Francis Eaton picking the Athletics. The *Cincinnati Post* asked three unidentified managers and five players what they thought; they all gave the nod to Philadelphia.

Bill Phelon, though, believed Boston could win it. "If any club now in the business is equipped and out fitted to defeat the Mackmen," he wrote in *Baseball Magazine*, "it's the Boston Braves.... The reputed invincibility of the Athletics won't buffalo the Braves."[1]

It had been a curious season for Connie Mack's Athletics. Although they finished a comfortable eight and a half games in front of Boston (99–53 to 91–62), for much of the season they seemed to play sluggishly. In md–July, following three losses to Detroit and the St. Louis Browns, their record was 44–32, and Washington and Detroit weren't far behind them. Then they won thirty-eight of their next forty-four games and moved out to a big lead, which they held despite losing five in a row in

September to the red-hot Red Sox and ten of their last twenty-six games.

Yet the situation in Philadelphia wasn't a happy one. All season long Federal League agents had buzzed around Mack's players, and he had heard plenty of talk about the big salaries and bonuses the Federals were paying. Among the buzzing agents was Danny Murphy, who had played for Mack for twelve years, and whom Mack had found a managing job in the upper minors. Instead Murphy signed with the Brooklyn Federals and sought to lure various old teammates to the new league. Moreover, whereas the Philadelphia ball club had been praised for the players' closeness and unselfishness, by 1914 various personal resentments and cliques had developed. Some of it had to do with Mack's choice of third-string catcher Ira Thomas to be team captain after Danny Murphy ostensibly retired. Some of it also had to do with the presumption by Eddie Collins, the Athletics' splendid second baseman, to criticize teammates for their on-field mistakes, as Johnny Evers presumed to do with his fellow Braves. Collins, though, had published some of his critical comments in his syndicated newspaper columns, which he actually wrote himself.

Ban Johnson had long inveighed against such syndicated columns, published under the names of players and managers but nearly always ghosted by sportswriters. Yet while Johnson usually dominated baseball's ruling National Commission and ran American League affairs pretty much as he wanted, he hadn't been able to put a stop to the practice.[2]

Although at that time Mack held only a minority interest in the Philadelphia franchise, which was still mostly owned by Benjamin Shibe, he was in complete charge of everything having to do with players. He was five years older than George Stallings, but as a player, manager, and investor, he had been in professional baseball exactly the same amount of time. Like Stallings, Mack managed from the dugout in street clothes, in Mack's case usually in dark suit, high starched collar, and derby. His method of positioning the outfielders by waving his scorecard was already famous. In contrast to Stallings's volatility, Mack dealt with his players in an avuncular manner, rarely scolding them for an on-field mistake, instead taking them aside afterward to explain why it happened. Most of Mack's players were genuinely fond of him.

The "Tall Tactician," as the baseball writers had dubbed Mack, had a reputation for recruiting educated young men, something his admirers

Connie Mack, Ira Thomas, and Jimmy Isaminger of the *Philadelphia North American*, in the home dugout, Shibe Park Philadelphia. Thomas, a rarely used catcher, was the Athletics' captain and Mack's right-hand man (George Bantham Bain Collection, Library of Congress).

tended to exaggerate.[3] In fact, "college men"—meaning virtually anybody who had at least attended a college or university—were scattered around both major leagues. The best-educated of the Athletics was Eddie Collins, a bona fide graduate of Columbia University.

Stallings was a relatively wealthy man, something Mack, who came from a working-class New England background, had never been. Such people can be either lavish spenders when they have a little money or tight-fisted to the point of parsimony. Mack was pretty tight-fisted, which meant the Athletics' payroll was considerably smaller than might have been expected for such a consistently successful team. Mack could tell his players the same thing New York officialdom would be telling Yankees players from the 1930s into the 1960s: Besides whatever they were being paid, they could usually look forward to a World Series share.

Moreover, Mack and Shibe hadn't tied up their best players with multi-year contracts to keep them out of the clutches of the Federals, as Jim Gaffney and Stallings had done. That didn't bode well if the Federal

League—which, contrary to widespread predictions, had completed its full schedule with most of its franchises ostensibly in good shape—continued to raid the two older leagues.

The Athletics would be less equipped financially to resist those raids than in past years. They played in a first-class ballpark, five-year-old Shibe Park, in the nation's third-largest city, and had no Federal League competition. Yet home attendance had plunged from 571,896 in 1913 to 346,641. The two major leagues had lost nearly three million customers as a consequence of Federal League competition, the perception that defections to the new league had diminished the level of play, and then a downturn in the economy in the season's second half, in the midst of uncertainty over the effects of the European war. It could also have been that much of Philadelphia's fandom had simply become bored by the Athletics' success.

So the Philadelphia players went into the World Series in some cases discontented, in others distracted, and generally overconfident. Tall and lean Charles Bender was Mack's ace right-hander. (Being part Ojibway and having grown up on a Minnesota reservation, Bender of course was called "Chief," although he always signed his name "Charles," which is what Mack called him.) Bender was so convinced the Braves were "a bunch of bush league hitters" that he wouldn't go to New York to scout the last Braves-Giants series, choosing to remain in Philadelphia in direct disregard of Mack's orders.[4] By contrast, Christy Mathewson and even John McGraw himself, as well as Pat Moran (the new manager of the Phillies and a member of the Cubs in 1910), Danny Murphy, and Harry "Rube" Vickers, who had once pitched for Mack, advised Stallings on the strengths and weaknesses of the Philadelphia players.

Whatever internal tensions the Athletics experienced, they remained an outstanding ball club, as well as a veteran one. The infield of John "Stuffy" McInnis at first base, Eddie Collins at second, Jack Barry at shortstop, and Frank Baker at third—on which somebody placed a collective $100,000 price tag—had remained intact since 1911. Outfielders Eddie Murphy, Amos Strunk, and Reuben "Rube" Oldring had been with Mack over the same years. In his second season, Wally Schang had become a first-rate catcher as well as a timely hitter. The Athletics scored the most runs and made the fewest errors in either major league.

As had been the case for the past ten years, Mack's pitching staff was anchored by Bender and by left-hander Eddie Plank. The 1914 Athletics didn't have a twenty-game winner, but seven pitchers won at least ten games. Bender led the staff with seventeen, including a streak of fourteen consecutive victories. Plank, at thirty-nine, was beginning to fade, but he still posted a 15–7 record. Mack had also used five young pitchers, all of whom performed well: right-handers Bob Shawkey and Leslie "Joe" Bush won sixteen games apiece; Weldon Wycoff, another right-hander, won eleven, as did left-hander Herb Pennock; and left-hander Raymond "Rube" Bressler won ten.

Buoyed by their manager's assurances and by their blazing pennant-winning pace, the mostly young Braves players were plenty confident they could handle the favored Athletics. But to make sure they were as mentally prepared for combat as possible, Stallings tried some more psychology, which he may or may not have cooked up with captain Evers's connivance. What happened has been given in various accounts—by, among others, Evers in his ghosted syndicated column and by Rabbit Maranville in his posthumously published memoirs. Probably the most reliable version appeared shortly after the event in the *Hartford Courant*, based on what Mack said took place.

Already irked upon finding out Bender hadn't scouted the Braves, Mack then had a nasty telephone encounter with their manager. After practicing on the Phillies' grounds on Wednesday, October 7, Stallings wanted to accustom his players to Shibe Park by holding practice there the next day. Mack claimed he and Stallings had agreed the Braves could work out in Shibe anytime on the afternoon of the 8th except from 2 to 3, when the Athletics had scheduled their practice. Then, Mack said, he heard early on the morning of the 8th that Stallings had accused him of unsportsmanlike behavior. He phoned the Braves' manager at the Majestic; they argued over who had agreed to what; Stallings charged both Mack and the Philadelphia club with double-dealing, to which Mack pointed out that the Athletics hadn't practiced at either West Side Park in Chicago in 1910 or the Polo Grounds in 1911.

Presumably the phone conversation ended after Stallings threatened to punch Mack in the nose. Whether or not Stallings had planned it all just that way, the dispute had the desired effect, according to Maranville. "It made us all very angry at Connie Mack, and we all said then and there, 'Practice or no practice, we will beat them anyway.'"[5]

On the morning of the Series opener, Stallings, not a bit mollified, was leaving the hotel with his players when a man accosted him, offering to bet him the Athletics would win it. Stallings grabbed the man by the collar, shook him, and hit him in the jaw. Several Braves players quickly pulled him away and got him into the elevator. Mack allowed himself to be quoted as saying, "The trouble with Stallings is that the novelty of winning a pennant has disturbed his balance."[6]

So while the weather on the afternoon of October 9 was agreeable, relations between the two managers were decidedly frosty. Stallings wouldn't even have his team use the Shibe Park visitors' clubhouse; instead the players donned their uniforms at the Phillies ballpark and rode in taxis to Shibe Park. Before the game, Stallings and Mack refused to pose together for photographers.

Meanwhile the Royal Rooters—who had followed the Braves from New York—paraded onto the field singing "Tessie," their theme song

Hank Gowdy, "Honey Fitz" Fitzgerald, and Boston friends before the first game of the 1914 World Series, Shibe Park, Philadelphia. Fitzgerald, former Boston mayor, was the unofficial leader of the Royal Rooters (George Bantham Bain Collection, Library of Congress).

since they rooted the Boston Americans to victory in the first "modern" World Series in 1903. Then former Mayor Fitzgerald led the contingent of Bostonians to the upper-deck seats reserved for them, where they continued with "Tessie," to the growing annoyance of Philadelphia partisans.

The reserved upper-deck seats they occupied cost $3 each, as did those in the lower grandstand above the sixth row. Box seats and the first six lower-grandstand rows went for $5; seats in the pavilions down the left- and right-field foul lines cost $2; and a place on the bleacher benches in left field could be had for a dollar.

In pregame ceremonies, Fitzgerald awarded Stallings a diamond stickpin; current Mayor Curley gave him a solid gold bat and Evers a solid gold baseball; and Hank Gowdy's friends gave him a gold watch and chain. Then the *pièce de résistance*: Eddie Collins took possession of a new Chalmers "30" automobile, his prize for being named the most valuable player in the American League. Collins had enjoyed another brilliant season, batting .344, stealing 58 bases, and leading both major leagues with 122 runs scored.

As expected, Mack chose Bender to start his tenth World Series game. Known as a "money pitcher," Bender had won six games and lost three in Series play, going back to the Athletics' five-game defeat by New York in 1905, when he hurled Philadelphia's only victory. Stallings, of course, would stay with his well-rested Big Three, starting Rudolph in the opener, then using James and Tyler in games two and three. Departing from the all-lefty-batting outfield he had used against right-handed pitchers, Stallings put George Whitted in center field in place of Larry Gilbert, and listed him fourth in the batting order. Apparently Stallings didn't consider either Gilbert or Josh Devore up to the competition.

As Bender took the mound, a crowd of 20,562 paying customers, as well as numerous baseball officials and other dignitaries with passes, didn't quite fill Shibe Park. In St. Mary's Hospital in Brooklyn, Red Smith followed the progress of the Series via a telephone hookup. Fred Mitchell took his accustomed place in the third-base coach's box; Bill James coached first. (Throughout the Series, James and Rudolph would alternate coaching at first.) Harry Davis, a handyman who had been with Mack since the inception of the American League, would be the Athletics' third-base coach; Jack Coombs, who had won eighty games for

Mack from 1910 to 1912 before illness and arm trouble sidelined him, would coach at first.

In the top of the first inning, Bender retired Herbie Moran, Johnny Evers, and Joe Connolly without incident. Eddie Murphy singled to lead off the home half of the inning but, with one out, unwisely tried to go from first base to third on Frank Baker's foul ball far back of first. Butch Schmidt caught the ball running away from the foul line, then fired across the diamond to Charlie Deal for an easy tag-out.

At the start of the second inning, Bender walked Whitted. After Schmidt fouled out, Hank Gowdy bounced a double off the left-field fence to score Whitted. Maranville drove in Gowdy with a single over second base, but Deal ended the inning by hitting into a double play, Barry to Collins to McInnis. 2–0, Braves.

Bender kept the Braves from scoring in the second and third innings; Rudolph held Philadelphia scoreless until the third inning, when McInnis walked and came around to score on Amos Strunk's hit to right field that got by Moran and rolled to the fence. That was the extent of the damage, because Rudolph struck out Jack Barry; Evers fielded Wally Schang's grounder and threw to Deal, who tagged out Strunk; and Bender's grounder forced Schang. 2–1, Braves.

The fourth inning was scoreless. In the fifth, with two out, Gowdy drove the ball over Strunk's head to the center-field fence for a triple. Maranville singled again to bring him home, but was doubled off first base when Deal popped up a bunt attempt, after which Rudolph struck out. Again the Athletics failed to score on Rudolph, who mixed his spit-ball, curve, and occasional fastball with increasing effectiveness.

The Braves broke the game open in the sixth inning. After Moran fouled out to Barry behind third base, Evers singled, Connolly drew a walk, and both scored on Whitted's triple to deep right-center field. Schmidt singled in Whitted, at which point Mack waved Bender out and signaled in Weldon Wycoff. It was a historic moment in Athletics history—the first time in five World Series that Mack had taken out a starting pitcher. Wycoff walked Gowdy but retired Maranville to get out of the inning. 6–1, Braves.

The Athletics could do nothing against Rudolph in the sixth or seventh innings. The Braves tacked on a seventh run in the eighth when Schmidt singled and took third base on Gowdy's third hit. Then Stallings

Charles "Chief" Bender. A great pitcher but a big disappointment in the 1914 World Series (George Bantham Bain Collection, Library of Congress).

rubbed it in, signaling for a double steal. Gowdy took off for second, and Schmidt stole home as Jack Lapp, who had replaced Schang, threw too late to get Gowdy. 7–1, Braves.

That's the way it ended. By the top of the ninth inning, much of the crowd was already heading for the exits. After Wycoff retired Boston in order, Rudolph gave up a double to Baker, who went to third as Maranville threw out McInnis. There Baker remained, because Strunk popped out to Evers and Maranville also threw out Barry.

It was a stunning defeat for the Athletics, who had never lost a World Series game that badly since a 9–0 pasting by the Giants in the third game in 1905—and in fact had lost only three games in Series play since 1905. Gowdy, who had averaged an unimposing .243 in 336 times at bat during the season, finished with a single, double, triple, walk, and even a stolen base. Rudolph pitched a five-hitter; as he savored his achievement, he received a telegram from New York: While the game was in progress, his wife in the Bronx had given birth to a ten-pound baby girl.

That night Whitted, a clean-living young man, celebrated the victory by eating too much of a chocolate cake his mother had mailed from his home town of Durham, North Carolina. Unable to sleep with a bad case of indigestion, he went to Stallings's room at 4 a. m., expecting him to be in bed, only to find the manager at a desk diagramming plays. Whether or not Stallings had ever studied medicine, he served as the team's physician. He got out a chest full of bottles, gave Whitted something for his indigestion, and sent him back to his room.

The next afternoon, with Bill James and side-arming left-hander Eddie Plank warming up in front of their respective dugouts (as pitchers did then and would continue to do for the next forty years or so), Stallings went to a right-hand batting outfield. Whitted remained in center; Ted Cather replaced Connolly in left; Les Mann replaced Moran in right. The paid attendance was exactly the same as on Friday.

Both pitchers were on their games. James threw mostly fastballs, a few curves, and an occasional spitter; Plank, the proverbial "crafty left-

Johnny Evers and Eddie Plank, before the second game of the 1914 World Series, Shibe Park, Philadelphia. Plank was about to pitch his last game for Connie Mack (George Bantham Bain Collection, Library of Congress).

hander," kept the Boston batters off balance with a variety of pitches thrown at different speeds, although he lacked his customary fine control. Neither team scored for five innings, although the Braves threatened in the sixth when, with two outs, Plank walked Gowdy for the second time and hit Maranville. But Deal forced Gowdy, Baker unassisted. In the bottom of the seventh, Collins beat out an infield hit; then one of the most-accomplished base-runners in the major leagues was picked off on James's quick throw to Schmidt for the third out.

The game was still scoreless when the Braves came to bat in the ninth inning. After Maranville grounded out to Barry, Deal hit a fly ball to center field that Strunk misjudged. It went over his head for a double; Deal then made it to third base when Schang's throw to Barry picked him off second and Baker was late covering his base. For the fourth time, Plank struck out James, but Mann sliced a short fly ball that fell just out of Collins's reach in short right field, scoring Deal with the game's first (and only) run. Mann took second when Plank's pitch got away from Schang. Evers drew a walk, but Barry fielded Cather's grounder and tossed to Collins for the force out, ending the inning.

The bottom of the ninth started ominously for James, who had handled the Athletics easily up to then. Barry drew a walk and stole second base as Schang struck out. Mack sent up Jimmy Walsh, a left-hand-batting substitute outfielder, to bat for Plank, and Walsh worked James for another base-on-balls. With the tying and winning runs on base, Eddie Murphy hit a sharp grounder just to the left of second base; Maranville, shading toward the bag for the left-hand batter, fielded the ball, stepped on second, and threw to first for the game-ending double play.

James had outdone Rudolph's performance on Friday. He permitted the Philadelphia batters only a single and double and struck out eight. Although he walked three, because of the Braves' three double plays, he faced only twenty-eight batters. Plank gave up seven hits, struck out six Braves, walked four batters, and hit one. He was undone in the ninth inning by Strunk's misplay of Deal's fly and Baker's unaccountable failure to be in position to tag Deal. Yet for many, the key play occurred in the sixth inning, when Schang doubled past Deal and took off for third base as Gowdy scrambled after a short passed ball. Bill Byron—whom John Tener had named to work the Series despite numerous complaints about his umpiring—called Schang out. An on-field press photographer's photo, published the next day, appeared to show Byron had missed the call.[7]

As they had done yesterday, the Royal Rooters, led by "Honey Fitz" Fitzgerald, paraded around the field in triumph singing "Tessie." Meanwhile the players packed for the trip to Boston to resume the Series on Monday, October 11, the 10th being a Sunday. When the Braves arrived at Back Bay Station on Sunday morning, they had intended to go directly to their residences, but they were met by a delegation of fans who told them a big crowd was waiting to greet them at South Station. So Stallings and his players rechecked their bags and got back on the train. At South Station they found a welcoming throng estimated at 10,000 that included a brass band, whose renditions violated state and city laws against Sunday amusements. But inasmuch as Mayor Curley was part of the throng, nobody would have cared except for Boston's strict Protestant Sabbatarians (whose influence was steadily diminishing in the Irish-Catholic-controlled city).

To accommodate as many people as possible, Fenway Park had been outfitted the same way it had been for the 1912 Red Sox-Giants World Series, and the same strange ground rules would be in force. Box seats were added along the front of the grandstand from first to third base, bleachers were built behind a low fence in front of "Duffy's Cliff" below the left-field fence; a solid three-foot fence was placed in front of the center-field bleachers; and the same odd barrier as in 1912 was erected in front of the distant right-field bleachers: a three-foot-high enclosure that had a plank baseboard and railing but also an eighteen-inch gap between the board and railing. Any ball hit against the left-field wall or into the temporary bleachers in front of the cliff would be a ground-rule double; so, incomprehensibly, would a ball hit *over* the left-field fence. A hit clearing or bouncing over the center-field barrier would be a home run, as would anything hit or bouncing over or *through* the open barrier in right field.

Every bit of seating—regular-season as well as temporary—was occupied by game time; the bleachers had been full for hours. Prices were a bit cheaper than in Philadelphia: Box seats cost $5; reserved seats, $3; and those in the pavilion, $1. One could sit in the bleachers or stand somewhere for only 50 cents. The paid attendance was 35,520, which didn't include some 350 sportswriters from across the United States as well as nine from Havana. Of course the mass of people also included the Royal Rooters, who filed into their reserved grandstand seats down the left-field line.

In his syndicated column (one of several ghosted for various players and managers during and shortly after the Series), Johnny Evers claimed that when the teams came on the field, the Athletics "were inclined to be friendly and chatty, and this is always a sign of nervousness and loss of heart. But they did not receive any encouragement from us along those lines, because we were out there to play ball and not to chat."[8]

In pre-game ceremonies, Evers received his own Chalmers "30," his prize for being named the National League's most valuable player. (One wonders what he might have done with the automobile, inasmuch as he had sworn off driving several years earlier.) In any fair comparison, Evers wouldn't have seemed in a class with Eddie Collins. Evers had put in a solid year, batting .276 and leading his league in fielding at his position. But not only had Collins outhit him by 68 points, but the Athletics' second baseman had driven in 81 runs to Evers's 33, scored a third more runs, and stolen almost five times as many bases. Because of suspensions and his daughter's death, Evers had missed nineteen games, whereas Collins had played in all but six.

Stallings sent Lefty Tyler to the mound for the third game. Mack might have come back with Bender on two days' rest; instead he chose one of his youngsters—twenty-one-year-old Joe Bush. Not much bigger than Dick Rudolph at 5'9" and 175 pounds, Bush had won thirteen games as a rookie in 1913 and then confirmed his status as a front-line major leaguer in the present season. Although he would later be credited with inventing the fork-ball pitch, early in his career he relied on a fastball that was good enough to earn him the nickname "Bullet Joe." With the Braves now facing a right-hander, Stallings kept Whitted in center field and returned Connolly to left field and Moran to right. Mack, evidently displeased by Strunk's critical misplay in Saturday's game, put Jimmy Walsh in center field.

Tyler got off to a shaky start. Eddie Murphy sliced a single down the left-field line; Rube Oldring sacrifice-bunted him to second base, and he scored when Connolly in left field dropped Collins's fly ball. As Baker struck out, Collins stole second. That proved unnecessary, because

Tyler issued a walk to McInnis. With one run in and two men on base, Collins proceeded to kill the rally by getting caught off base for the second time in two games, Tyler to Evers. In the bottom half of the inning, with two out, Evers singled and stole second but died there when Whitted struck out. 1–0, Athletics.

While Tyler kept Philadelphia from scoring in the second and third innings, the Braves tied the game in the second. With two out, Maranville walked, stole second base, and came home on Gowdy's ground-rule double into the temporary bleachers in left field. But the Athletics took the lead again in the fourth inning. Collins led off by popping out to Evers; Baker went down swinging for the second time. But McInnis doubled into the left-field bleachers, as Connolly dived head first into the spectators in a vain try for the ball. McInnis scored on Walsh's single to left. Barry ended the inning by grounding out to Maranville. 2–1, Athletics.

Whitted began the bottom of the fourth by grounding out to Collins. Schmidt singled to center field and went to second as Collins threw out Deal. Maranville hit a blooper down the right-field line that barely fell foul, as it was called by umpire George Hildebrand.[9] Maranville hit another blooper to the same immediate vicinity that neither Collins nor Murphy could reach. It wasn't much of a hit, but it was enough to bring home Schmidt with the tying run. Maranville then stole second base and continued to third on Schang's errant throw. After Gowdy walked, Stallings tried to bring off another double steal. This time, though, Collins's return throw to Schang beat Rabbit to the plate. 2–2.

For the next five innings, Tyler and Bush each settled down and held the opposition scoreless; Collins's single in the sixth and Baker's double in the ninth—neither of which eventuated in anything—were the only base hits either pitcher allowed over that span. Both still looked in command as the game went into extra innings.

That changed in the tenth inning. Schang led off the Philadelphia half with a single. Bush struck out, but Schang was safe at second base when Tyler was slow fielding Murphy's dribbler; Murphy reached first on the fielder's choice. The runners advanced on Oldring's ground out, Evers to Schmidt; then Tyler walked Collins to load the bases. Baker got his second hit of the game on a hot grounder that got away from Evers;

when Evers held the ball instead of making a quick throw home, Murphy scored behind Schang. McInnis made the third out on a fly ball to Whitted in center field. 4–2, Athletics.

It seemed the Athletics might actually turn the Series around, until Gowdy, the first batter to face Bush in the bottom of the inning, drove a home run into the temporary bleachers in deep center field. Josh Devore batted for Tyler and struck out, but Bush gave a critical base on balls to Moran, who raced to third base on Evers's single and scored the tying run on Connolly's fly ball to Walsh in center field. Whitted killed the rally by popping out to Baker. 4–4.

Only two days after pitching an arduous complete game, Bill James came on to work the eleventh inning. After retiring Walsh and Barry, he walked Schang. Mack was staying with Bush, who struck out again. But Bullet Joe was still strong, easily retiring Schmidt, Deal, and Maranville to send the game to the twelfth inning. In a period before daylight-savings time, the mid–October northern darkness was closing in; street lights and lights in buildings near Fenway Park had come on. The umpires had agreed the twelfth would be the last inning played.

Eddie Murphy led off by drawing James's second walk and went to second base on Oldring's tap in front of the plate, which Gowdy pounced on and fired to Schmidt. Collins could have put the Athletics ahead, but all he could manage was a pop fly to Deal at third, after which James walked Baker. That set up a force play, which is what happened when McInnis hit a hopper to Evers, who flipped to Maranville for the third out.

Bush still had no answer for Gowdy, who bounced another double into the left-field bleachers. Stallings had Les Mann run for him and sent up Larry Gilbert to pinch hit for James. Mack ordered Gilbert walked intentionally, and Stallings signaled Herbie Moran to lay down a sacrifice bunt. Bush got to the bunted ball quickly, but in trying to cut down Mann at third base, he threw it by Baker into left field. Mann scored before Oldring could retrieve the ball and make a throw.

If it was probably the best day of Hank Gowdy's seventeen-years in the big leagues as a player, it was also probably the toughest loss of Joe Bush's big-league career, which would also last seventeen years, include four additional World Series, and conclude with 193 regular-season victories. Bush held the Braves to nine hits and struck out four, but because of his wild throw, the game was the first in World Series play to end on

80

an error. As had been the case in the 1912 Series, the additional seating areas around the Fenway Park outfield decidedly affected the course of the game, more so for Bush than for the two Boston pitchers.

A few months later, in an article in *Baseball Magazine* appearing under his and Stallings's names, Evers sought to explain his apparent bonehead play in the tenth inning, when he held the ball as Schang and then Murphy crossed the plate. In Evers's account, Baker's hard-hit ground ball took a bad hop, hit him in the chest, and bounced away. When he picked up the ball, believing the game was already lost, he kept his head down as the two runners scored. Stallings praised Evers's teammates for lifting his spirits when he got to the dugout, which was all well and good, except that the magazine's baseball-savvy readers must have scratched their heads and wondered why in the world, with Boston coming to bat in the bottom of the inning, the never-say-die Trojan would have assumed the game lost.

But inasmuch as the Braves ended up winning, few among the 34,365 people jammed into Fenway Park for game four would have dwelled on Evers's mistake. Whereas the weather in Philadelphia and for Monday's game in Boston had been fairly pleasant, today was overcast with a cold wind blowing from the northwest. The chilled spectators consumed many gallons of hot coffee.

As everybody had expected from Stallings, he called on Dick Rudolph to try to bring the Series to an end. The bearing of the Philadelphia players as they came on the field was akin to that of children about to take castor oil. While the Royal Rooters filed in to the strands of "Tessie," twenty-three-year-old right-hander Bob Shawkey warmed up in front of the visitors' dugout. Bender was nowhere to be seen. For various reasons, Mack had lost faith in his "money pitcher," who hadn't worked since Friday and only five-and-a-third innings then. Mack also kept Amos Strunk on the bench, again starting Jimmy Walsh in center field.

Rudolph held the Athletics scoreless innings through four innings, although the Athletics almost scored in the top of the fourth. With one out, Baker singled off Schmidt's mitt and made it around to third base on McInnis's hit to left field. But Deal made a fine play, grabbing Connolly's throw in short left and firing the ball to Evers to thwart McInnis's effort to stretch his hit into a double. Baker was held at third, and Walsh went down swinging for the third out.

The Braves couldn't do anything against Shawkey until the bottom of the fourth. It began with a walk to Evers. Connolly hit a sharp ground ball to Collins, who fumbled the potential double-play ball and had to settle for throwing out Connolly. Whitted got a base hit on another grounder that ticked off Collins's glove. As Collins scrambled for the ball, Evers kept running and made it to third base, from where he scored on Schmidt's slow grounder to Barry at shortstop. Gowdy could only contribute a weak roller to Shawkey. 1–0, Braves.

Philadelphia got the run back in the top of the fifth inning. Barry's bounder went over Deal's head for what would be his only base hit of the Series. After Schang grounded out, Evers to Schmidt, with Barry taking second base, Shawkey drove a double between Connolly and Whitted to score Barry. Shawkey went to third as Evers threw out Murphy, but Rudolph struck out Oldring. 1–1.

Maranville started the bottom of the fifth inning by grounding out, Barry to McInnis; Deal followed by grounding out to Baker. But Rudolph kept the inning alive with a single to center field; Moran followed with a double to left-center, and Rudolph heeded Fred Mitchell's hold-up sign at third base. On the vaudeville circuit that winter, Maranville related that the morning before every Series game, he and seven Catholic teammates took communion, and that they prayed in a critical situation Evers would get a base hit. That may have been the kind of yarn for which the puckish Rabbit had already become known, but whatever the truth, Evers did come through. On a 3–2 pitch, he shot a single past Shawkey into center field to score both Rudolph and Moran, as Walsh had trouble picking up the ball. Then the Trojan rather marred his heroics by getting caught off base by Shawkey. 3–1, Braves.

In the top of the sixth, Maranville saved Rudolph a base hit by fielding Collins's hot shot back of second base and throwing him out, after which Baker and McInnis went quietly. Left-hander Herb Pennock, only twenty, took the mound for Philadelphia in the bottom of the inning, which prompted Stallings to send up Les Mann to hit for Connolly. Mann lined out to left field, but Whitted and Schmidt followed with singles. Gowdy again showed he was mortal by striking out; on a double-steal attempt, the husky Schmidt, less than fleet-footed, was caught between first and second and run down by McInnis.

Seventh inning: Walsh started the top of the inning with a single and ran to second base on a wild pitch to Barry. Then Walsh strayed too far off the base, and, as Barry struck out, Gowdy picked him off on a peg to Evers. That probably wasn't the key play some later made it out to be, because Rudolph also struck out Schang. In the bottom half of the inning, Pennock walked Rudolph with two out but got Moran to foul out.

Rudolph had no trouble retiring Pennock, Murphy, and Oldring in the eighth. Pennock again issued a two-out walk, to Whitted, who stole second base and went to third on Schang's passed ball. He remained there as Schmidt struck out.

Down to their last three outs, the Athletics could do nothing with Rudolph. Collins led off the top of the ninth inning by striking out. Evers threw out Baker on a routine grounder, and McInnis ended the Series with another ground out, Deal to Schmidt.

Joyous fans rushed onto the field from all directions and hoisted Evers, Maranville, and Gowdy onto their shoulders. Collins and team captain Ira Thomas quickly made their way to the Braves' dugout to congratulate the victors. Mack himself lingered in a corner of the visitors' dugout until, following speeches to the crowd by Stallings, Gaffney, and Mayor Curley, the Boston manager had left the field. Mack then disappeared into the exit from the dugout to the clubhouse.

The festivities in Fenway Park went on for some time. As one sportswriter described the scene, "it was almost dusk before the last celebrator ceased to whoop and snake-dance around the bases."[10] Then the Royal Rooters, with Maranville at their head and with thousands of other Bostonians joining them, paraded from Fenway Park to the Copley Hotel, where they serenaded the Athletics with "Tessie" and assorted other ditties.

It was the first World Series to end in a four-game sweep, as well as the first Series victory for the National League since 1909. Ever since the inauguration of the four-out-of-seven format in 1905, rumors had cropped up—spread mostly by grumbling gamblers who had lost money—that this or that game had been thrown to give the club owners at least one more big attendance day. Some were prepared to believe that when the Athletics lost the second game of the 1913 Series, they did so to insure a big gate for game five in Philadelphia. After the Athletics had disposed of the Giants in five games, Mack remarked at a banquet in his honor that he would like to see a four-game sweep to prove baseball's integrity. On that cold October afternoon in Boston, he got his wish.[11]

With the exception of Bender, one could hardly fault the work of Mack's pitchers, but at bat the Philadelphians had been little short of pathetic. As a team, the Athletics averaged .172 on nine hits in twenty-two times at bat, which produced six runs. It was a particularly dismal Series for Eddie Collins, who batted .214, was sometimes shaky afield, and got caught off base twice.

Rudolph was masterful in his two starting assignments, James even more so in game two. Although the young right-hander struggled a bit in relief of Tyler in the third game, he did well enough to come out the winner. Red Smith's bat might have come in in handy at times, but even though Charlie Deal only had one safe hit and grounded into three double plays, he handled third base flawlessly and made a key play in the last game.

Collins's counterpart generally outplayed him. Evers registered five singles and two doubles in sixteen times at bat for a .438 average.

Eddie Collins. The 1914 World Series was perhaps the low point in his brilliant career (George Bantham Bain Collection, Library of Congress).

Although Gowdy went hitless in the fourth game (with his parents, who had traveled from Columbus, Ohio, for the game, in the grandstand), he was sensational otherwise. The lanky Ohioan batted .545 on six hits in eleven official times at bat, including three doubles, a triple, and the Series' only home run.

Throughout the four games, the Braves kept up the same kind of verbal harassment they had used on opponents all season. Some even targeted the dignified Mack, whom they called a "scab" because, they had heard, he discouraged his players from joining the Players' Fraternity. Editor Francis Richter of the weekly *Sporting Life*, published in Philadelphia since 1882, sniffed at the Braves' "noisy coaching from the bench. In this matter the Boston players were particularly active, and quite offensive, and in Boston their howls in chorus from the dugout could be heard in the press box on the roof of the grandstand."[12] Having covered baseball in the rough and rowdy eighties and nineties, Richter could hardly have heard anything from the Braves he hadn't heard on ball fields twenty years earlier.

Yet Richter also noted the Athletics' "lack of ginger," which "amazed the home crowds." "The dope went wrong," commented *Baseball Magazine* editor F. C. Lane. "The strongest [sic] club played with a listless apathy unworthy of a second division contender." Seventeen years later, in a syndicated chapter from his autobiography, Mack summed up what he thought had gone wrong with his ball club: "… knowing the mental turmoil of the players and their utter lack of purpose, spirit and industry in the games, it was anything but a surprise to me." And in a 1938 article in the weekly *Saturday Evening Post*, he explained the Athletics' defeat in similar terms: "Our players were simply more bitter against one another than interested in the series."[13]

The period in which the 1914 Series took place was one in which much was made of "breaks" that decided games. Lane wrote that if the Athletics had gotten a few breaks, the outcome might have been different. "But this year, the breaks fell all the other way." Breaks or not, for Lane the Braves' sweep was "a defeat more utter and crushing than has before been witnessed in a World Series."[14]

Yes, the "dope" had been wrong. Evers took a swipe at Hank O'Day, who had managed the Cubs to a distant fourth place that season. O'Day predicted it would be the Athletics who swept the Series. "Hank," Evers told a reporter, "doesn't predict any better than he does some other things." Or as Ring Lardner put it, in the vernacular of a semi-literate fan, "Us wise old owls was teached a lesson. I'm one bird that won't never go strong again on the predictin' stuff."[15]

The Braves had finally made a believer of John McGraw. American League umpire Billy Evans, in his syndicated column on the Series, quoted McGraw's latest assessment of the Boston team: "When you watch the club practice, you can't see much class to it, but before the game is over, their aggressive tactics make you think they are trying to drive you off your own ball field."[16]

The following winter, Jim Gaffney said that at the beginning of June, after watching the Braves lose four times in five games in Ebbets Field, he thought Stallings ought "to take that ball club and dump them in the ocean…. No man other than a miracle worker could have whipped that team I saw in June into a world beater by October." In fact, "Miracle Man" and "Miracle Braves" were what Stallings and his players were already being called in the baseball press. As F. C. Lane put it, "What chance do predictors stand against miracles?"[17] Right after the Series, Gaffney tore up Stallings's old contract and signed him to a new one, for five years at the same $12,000 per year.

The total attendance for the four games was 111,009, which returned receipts of $225,739. Each Boston player's share came out to $2,812. 28; each Philadelphia player got $2,031.65. For most members of both teams, that money more than doubled their regular-season salaries. For Johnny Evers, 1914 had been an exceedingly lucrative year, starting with the $25,000 signing bonus Jim Gaffney paid him. He was under a $10,000 yearly contract, which also specified a $3,000 bonus if the Braves won the pennant. So his earnings for the year (not including whatever he received for his ghosted Series column) totaled at least $41,000, an immense sum for that time. Gaffney also gave Rudolph, James, Tyler, Maranville, and Gowdy bonuses of $1,000 each.

The Braves' Series shares and whatever other income they garnered in 1914 meant that for the first time in their lives, they, as well as the Athletics, would have to pay personal income taxes. The new federal tax law—enacted the previous December to offset revenue losses from import taxes under the 1913 tariff act—exempted people with annual incomes of less than $3,000, which of course included the vast majority of Americans. But incomes from $3,000 to $20,000 were taxed at 1 percent, those above $20,000 to $50,000 at 2 percent. Evers would have to pay twice as much as Stallings or any of the other players—a whopping $800–$850 or so.

When the Athletics players got back to Philadelphia, they dropped by Shibe Park, picked up their Series checks, and quietly left for their homes in the city and various parts of the country. Mack and Ben Shibe told the city's mayor they wanted no banquets or other occasions to honor the team. Although their fans could have had no inkling of what lay ahead, in fact the Athletics' debacle in the 1914 World Series marked the end of an era in the team's history. If the future looked bright for Stallings and his players, the next decade would be a bleak time for American League baseball in Philadelphia.

5

1914–1915: "I don't see how they can beat us"

Some owners might not approve of the practice, but once their contracts expired, players were free to make extra money playing ball in various venues—what had come to be called "barnstorming." So only five days after the World Series, two teams—one consisting of American League players led by Ira Thomas, the other of National Leaguers led by the longtime manager, executive, and promoter Frank Bancroft—began an odyssey that would eventually take them to Hawaii. The tour wasn't nearly as ambitious or as publicized as the around-the-world trip led by John McGraw and Charles Comiskey a year earlier, but it was ambitious enough.

The makeup of the teams justified their billing as "all-stars." Among the American Leaguers were Joe Bush, Jimmy Walsh, and Eddie Murphy of Philadelphia; Boston outfielder Duffy Lewis and first-baseman Dick Hoblitzell; Detroit infielder George Moriarty; Cleveland shortstop Ray Chapman and pitcher Willie Mitchell; New York pitcher Leonard "King" Cole; and another Bill James, a 6'4" right-hander who had won fifteen games the past season for the St. Louis Browns. With the Braves' Bill James, plus Grover Cleveland Alexander, Jeff Tesreau, and Hippo Vaughn, the National Leaguers clearly had the advantage in pitching. Among other National Leaguers on the trip were New York shortstop Art Fletcher and outfielders Fred Snodgrass and George Burns, Pittsburgh outfielder Max Carey, and Philadelphia infielder Bobby Byrne and catcher Bill Killefer.

The teams played their first game on Sunday, October 18, in Minneapolis, with Bush besting James. Then they rode the Great Northern Railroad on to Mandan, North Dakota, and Forsythe, Hamilton, and Missoula, Montana, before reaching Spokane, exhibiting their skills to crowds made up mostly of people who had never seen big-leaguers in action. Playing each other almost daily, they moved on to Potlatch, Walla Walla, Bellingham, and Seattle, Washington; Lewiston, Idaho; Portland, Oregon; and San Francisco, Oakland, Sacramento, Porterville, Modesto, and Petaluma in California. Then they sailed to Hawaii, playing as a mixed team versus the Oahu All-Stars, before cruising to Molokai, where they were met by swimmers diving for coins they tossed overboard and enjoyed festive outdoor dinners. After six games in the Islands, the teams returned to California for matchups in Fresno, Bakersfield, and San Diego. At the end of their ten-week travels, the All-Nationals had won twenty-nine games, the All-Americans twenty one, with two ties. Bancroft reported that each player made $1,331.55 after expenses.

While Bill James was making a tidy addition to his year's income, Dick Rudolph was getting to know his baby daughter. Interviewed at home in the Bronx by Bozeman Bulger of the *New York Evening World*, he said she was born at 3:00 p. m. on October 10, "just as Deal was making that winning run" in the Series' second game. Although he couldn't join his family until after the Series, "I was thinking about home and that baby all the time." Then he asked Bulger, "Have you at last decided that we have a good ball club and aren't simply lucky?" He went on to talk about pitching to the Athletics, "the worst suckers on a curveball I ever pitched against in my life. I was so surprised when I saw them missing ordinary curves that I could hardly believe my eyes." Rudolph claimed he actually didn't throw many spitballs, mainly going to his mouth as a bluff.[1]

Hank Gowdy got a hero's welcome upon his arrival in Columbus, where he had once served as bat boy for the local American Association Senators. He rode in a nighttime parade down High Street to the state capitol, where Governor James M. Cox and Mayor George F. Karb praised him to the cheers of a crowd local newspapers estimated at 40,000. Evers received similar tributes when he got back to Troy, although the occasion was dampened by the death of his mother-in-law late in October. In Augusta, Georgia, a couple of hundred prominent citizens held a banquet to honor Stallings as well as local resident Ty Cobb (who had won his eighth consecutive batting title).[2] Joe Connolly got a big reception when he returned to his home in Putnam, Connecticut, as did Les Mann in Lincoln, Nebraska, and Lefty Tyler in East Derry,

New Hampshire. After he got home, Tyler bought four-hundred acres near Nashua, which he said he intended to turn into a dairy farm.

Rabbit Maranville later claimed that following the World Series, Joe Fleming, an agent for Charles Weeghman's Chicago Federal League club, made an appointment with him and Johnny Evers. In Maranville's account, Fleming "laid down $100,000 in front of Evers and $50,000 in front of me as a bonus with a three-year contract to play for the Chicago Feds." Neither would take the offers because, Maranville quoted Evers as saying, "when I sign a contract I live up to it." Jim Gaffney, Evers went on, "is honest and square and has always been on the level with me and I shall do the same to him." Maranville added, "Those are my sentiments too."[3] That the encounter with Fleming took place is undoubtedly true, as well as the response of the two ballplayers. But the figures Maranville mentions would have to be wild exaggerations. Not even Weeghman was throwing around that kind of money.

The vaudeville stage again beckoned to Rabbit Maranville. In

Joe Connolly. The little outfielder led the 1914 Braves in batting average and home runs (George Bantham Bain Collection, Library of Congress).

Boston he began another tour of New England theaters on the Keith circuit, performing twice per day with a professional vaudevillian named Ed McHugh and still usually ending his act with a belt-buckle catch. He also got married to a young New Bedford woman named Elizabeth Shea, and survived another automobile wreck while taking a Springfield newspaper cartoonist on a hair-raising ride in the Berkshire Hills. Neither was injured. After Maranville finished his vaudeville tour, he was the guest of honor at several banquets in New England and played some more basketball, for the Holyoke team. In a talk to Boston College students, he claimed sign-stealing had been a big reason for the Braves' success in 1914. Asked about that, Stallings commented, "Maranville either has been misquoted or is dreaming."[4]

After being feted in Columbus, Hank Gowdy returned to New York to team with Dick Rudolph for an appearance at Hammerstein's Theatre. The catcher enlightened the audience on signals he used; the pitcher talked about his repertoire of deliveries. As they left the stage, Gowdy was overheard to say, "It's a crime to take the money." "Some of those in the audience," commented an anonymous contributor to *Sporting Life*, "are said to have entertained ideas upon the matter very similar to those held by the honorable Hank."[5]

A quarter-century earlier, Tim Murnane had been writing for the *Boston Globe* when Mike "King" Kelly, the greatest baseball celebrity of his time, was appearing in offseason theatrical productions, but Murnane had never approved of ballplayers performing in vaudeville. Where Stallings was concerned, Murnane made an exception. Stallings signed a contract with the Keith circuit to appear six nights a week, with matinees on Saturdays, for $2,000 per week. The venerable *Boston Globe* sports editor knew the Braves' manager had six-hundred bales of unsold cotton worth $30,000. "I needed the money, and I had to get it," Stallings told *Baseball Magazine's* F. C. Lane.[6]

Although the British and French governments would subsequently be placing orders in the United States for huge amounts of everything from cotton and foodstuffs to iron and steel, and would borrow billions from American creditors to finance their war with Germany and Austria-Hungary, the closing off of the central European market initially precipitated a sharp downturn in overseas commerce, including the market for American cotton.

"It is bread and butter," Stallings explained about his vaudeville engagement as he sat in the lobby of his New York hotel. "It is facing the mob in front of the foot lights with knees knocking together in order to get hominy and bacon for a lot of blacks down in Georgia," who, he said, numbered sixty at the Meadows. "Believe me, when I am through with this I am going to stick to legitimate stuff on the ball field."[7]

Stallings debuted on October 26 at the Keith Palace in New York. Jim Gaffney, National League secretary John Heydler, and International League president Ed Barrow attended his opening performance, which consisted mainly of an analysis of the past season and his Braves players. One observer described him as "a nervous, mild-mannered, courtly gentleman who has nothing except words of praise for his 'kid' team." "This 'kid' team of mine," he assured his audience, "is not a bloomer or mushroom team. It is a fine ball team and will be a fine ball team for some time to come." The *New York Tribune's* Heywood Broun thought that while the Braves' manager did all right, "Stallings can hardly do justice to himself on the stage. All his best stuff would be deleted by the censor."[8]

A century later, many Americans would have wanted to censor a playlet being staged in Boston's west end at the same time as Stallings's vaudeville turn. A group called the St. Joseph's Total Abstinence Society presented a two-act, three-scene farce entitled "The Frolic of the Braves," to celebrate the team's World Series victory. Performed at St. Mary's Theatre, the playlet featured performers in blackface banjo-strumming, dancing, and supposedly depicting the carefree life of the people who worked on Stallings's Haddock plantation. A segment representing a banquet for the champions had waiters in blackface doing a "buck dance" as they served the banqueters.

(That display of racial insensitivity took place in the city considered the cradle of the abolitionist movement, but then and for long afterward blackface "humor" was a staple of popular entertainment. Many comedians—often Jewish—appeared in blackface; professional minstrel companies toured the country; and white school children, adolescents, and college students corked their faces, rouged their lips, and performed in minstrels for local audiences.[9])

If George Stallings found himself in need of quick money, presumably Johnny Evers's finances were in excellent shape. Yet his personal woes continued. So far in 1914, Evers had lost his little daughter and mother-in-law and almost lost his infant son. Now he almost lost his own life. Early in December he traveled from Troy to Chicago to participate in an indoor baseball game, the proceeds from which were to go to the widow of Jimmy Doyle, a former Cubs teammate, and also to Cardinals shortstop Arnold Hauser, whose parents, wife, and two children had all died within a few months in 1913, causing him to have a mental collapse and to miss the entire 1914 season.

When Evers left Chicago for New York for the National League's winter meetings, he had a bad cold, which he later said he caught playing in the drafty arena where the benefit game was held. After arriving on December 8, he dropped in on the meetings at the Waldorf Hotel, then went to dinner with Jim Gaffney, but he was feeling so rotten he had to return to his room at the Hotel Somerset and go to bed. Gaffney's personal physician determined Evers had developed pneumonia, a major killer in that time. Gaffney wired Helen Evers to come to New York as quickly as possible; she arrived on the 10th to find her husband critically ill and being tended by two nurses. Evers was confined to his room until two days before Christmas, when he returned to Troy, pale and skinnier than ever. Sometime in January he left his family in and moved to a site in the Adirondacks, where he undertook to live outdoors in bitter cold, convinced that such a regimen would strengthen his lungs and generally reinvigorate him.[10]

The Braves' 1914 home attendance of 382,913 led the National League. That exceeded the previous franchise record, set in 1897, by nearly 50,000 and even topped what the Giants drew in the Polo Grounds, by 16,000 or so. And there were the two big World Series crowds in Fenway Park. Gaffney paid off the $225,000 mortgage on South End Grounds inherited from the Russell estate and borrowed $600,000 to finance a much larger ballpark in a different location. He also extended his agreement with Joseph Lannin for the continued use of Fenway Park during 1915 while the new ballpark was being constructed. That was good news not only to Braves fans but to the rest of the league's club owners, most of whom had lost money in 1914. They could look forward to the continuation of bigger revenues from their shares of the gates in Boston.

At the National League's December meeting, the owners voted to cut costs by reducing the May 1–September 1 roster limit from twenty-five to twenty-one. That left George Stallings in a decidedly unhappy frame of mind. Although his most-valued players were under multi-year contracts, in directing his team to the pennant, he had used his full roster and planned to do the same in 1915. He was especially put out that he had to drop Fred Mitchell, on whom he had relied to work with the pitchers, and reclassify him as a scout. Josh Devore received his release; others would have to be evaluated in spring training and the early weeks of the season. The American League owners, presumably at Ban Johnson's behest, voted to keep the twenty-five-man limit. It didn't seem to occur to the National Leaguers that not only had they made more players available to the Federal League; they may also have put their pennant-winner at a disadvantage in World Series play.

That winter Stallings authored (or had ghosted) a series of syndicated newspaper columns. He acknowledged that Federal League raids had weakened several other National League teams and worked in favor of the Braves. Despite having to do with fewer players in 1915, he exuded confidence. His Big Three pitchers ought to be as good as ever, and the addition of Tom Hughes, who had pitched well after joining the Braves the previous September, would make his staff even stronger. So Stallings was ready with his prediction: "Let me say baldly and without any apologies for the statement, that I expect my club to win the National League championship again next season, and later the World's Series. I don't see how they can beat us."[11]

Stallings maintained he was always with his team, from his morning clubhouse "'skull' rehearsal" throughout the day. On the road, with Gaffney's approval he always put up his players at the best hotels, and "I do not flee from the hotel with friends as soon as I arrive in town, but I am around just with my team." He liked to spend most of the time with his young players. Besides teaching them baseball, "I can get a good line on their characters and figure the best way to handle them to get out all the baseball there is in them."[12]

However confident Stallings might be about his team's prospects, he still saw room for improvement, particularly in its run production. He would have liked to acquire the troublesome Heinie Zimmerman, whom he believed he could make an even better ballplayer, although nothing came of whatever overtures he may have made to the Cubs, if he made any at all. Instead he approached William F. Baker—who had succeeded the late William E. Locke as majority owner of the Philadelphia Phillies—about a deal for outfielder Sherwood Magee.

Though mostly forgotten in subsequent generations, "Sherry" Magee, as he was familiarly known, was one of the finest players of his time. An eleven-year major-leaguer, he had joined the Phillies directly from a semi-pro team in Carlisle, Pennsylvania. Right-handed all the way, a well-put-together 5'11" and 180 pounds, Magee was a potent offensive force, having batted above .300 five times and topped the National League in 1910 with a .331 mark. In the past season he hit .314 and led the league in base hits, doubles, runs driven in (for the third time), total bases, and slugging average. His seventy-three home runs since 1904 were the most anybody in either league had accumulated in that span. Magee was also one of the league's foremost base-stealers and an outstanding fielder. In short, he was exactly the ballplayer Stallings thought he had to have.

But like Zimmerman and Johnny Evers, Magee was an often-difficult teammate. He "crabbed" at their mistakes, bragged about his own abilities, and was quick to anger. A local sportswriter called him "one of the most hot-headed players in either big league."[13] On July 10, 1911, in a game in Philadelphia with St. Louis, first-year umpire Bill Finneran called him out on strikes. When Magee threw his bat in the air in disgust, Finneran whipped off his mask and ordered him out of the game. Magee grabbed the umpire and hit him in the face with his left fist, knocking him to the ground and apparently rendering him unconscious. Reviving quickly, the bloody-faced Finneran went after Magee, but base umpire Cy Rigler and a Phillies player restrained him and sent him off to a nearby hospital to get patched up. League president Thomas Lynch hit Magee with a $200 fine (a big one for that day) and announced his suspension for the rest of the season, although he lifted it after thirty-six days.[14]

For 1914, Phillies manager Red Dooin named Magee team captain, and he reportedly put aside his self-centeredness and became "the greatest team worker we had," according to a teammate.[15] Though still only twenty-nine years old, he expected to be named manager when Dooin was fired after the season and Pat Moran succeeded him. Disgruntled, Magee started talking to Baltimore Federal League officials. That alarmed Philadelphia president Baker, whose team had already been badly damaged by defections to the Federals, and who now faced the likelihood of losing his best player and getting nothing in return. So Baker was willing to negotiate with the Braves. The day after Christmas, Magee was dealt to Boston in return for an undisclosed amount of cash and two players, to be named later. He signed a two-year contract for about $6,000 per year.

When he read of the deal, George Whitted hurried from his home in Durham, North Carolina, to see Stallings, who was back in Georgia, being feted at a banquet in Macon and hosting Gaffney and his wife and several Boston and New York writers at the Meadows. Whitted declared he didn't want to be included in any deal for Magee, and if he were, he wanted $3,000, which he figured would be about what another World Series share would be. Initially Stallings backed out of sending Whitted to the Phillies and signed him to a Boston contract for 1915. But on February 10, the Braves' manager concluded the transaction, sending Whitted and Oscar Dugey to Philadelphia. Fans in Boston were left to wonder how Stallings, who already had one "crab" in Evers, would get along with a second one.

In one of the newspaper columns syndicated under his name, Stallings asserted, "I don't believe that a single man on the payroll would leave the Boston club now under any condition."[16] He may have been referring to players on the payroll as of December 1914; Charlie Deal and Les Mann must have delayed signing their contracts. Deal no doubt assumed that with Red Smith back at third base, he wouldn't play much, whereas the acquisition of Magee made Mann expendable. Besides, Mann had informed Stallings he wanted a three-year contract at $3,500 per year, which he wasn't going to get. So Deal and Mann signed Federal League contracts, Deal with St. Louis, Mann with Chicago. (In 1915, Deal would bat .323, though appearing in only sixty-five games; Mann, as the pennant-winning Whales' regular center fielder, would bat .308.)

Stallings also mentioned that Jack Quinn, who the previous winter had jumped to the Baltimore Federals after signing a Boston contract, admitted to him he made a mistake, despite leading the league with twenty-six wins. Gaffney announced he was withdrawing his suit for $30,000 against the Baltimore owners. "Inasmuch as my club won the world's championship," joked Gaffney," I'd get a lot of sympathy about Quinn, wouldn't I?"[17]

If Stallings and Gaffney seemed little concerned about the Federal League, Pittsburgh owner Barney Dreyfuss was still angry over the effect of the "outlaw" circuit on his own Pirates. As Dreyfuss told a reporter for the *New York Press*, he blamed the team's 1914 collapse after its strong start on the fact that "The Feds never left us alone a minute[;] our players talked, played, and ate 'Feds.'" Connie Mack knew exactly how Dreyfuss felt. "The Federal League" he told one of the Philadelphia papers in the summer of 1915, "wrecked my club by completely changing the spirit of the players."[18]

In the aftermath of the Athletics' ignominious World Series showing, Mack undertook a drastic overhaul of his once-proud champions. Late in October he asked waivers on Chief Bender, Eddie Plank, and the long-ailing Jack Coombs. For the time being, Mack wanted that to remain confidential among the American League club owners, and he was angry when he learned Detroit manager Hugh Jennings had revealed the news during an Atlantic City vaudeville appearance. Mack and Jennings weren't on good terms anyway; the Athletics' manager had been told that in the 1911 and 1913 World Series, Jennings rooted for the Giants and John McGraw, his close friend and former teammate on the old National League Baltimore Orioles.

However all that may be, when no American League club claimed any of the three pitchers, Mack released them all outright. Coombs signed as a free agent with Brooklyn, where he would eventually make a successful comeback, but at that point he was of little value. Not so Bender and Plank. Mack could have tried to sell or trade his two pitching mainstays, but his attitude seemed to have been that if they were so bent on going to the Federal League, he would speed their departure. Plank signed with the St. Louis Terriers and, at the age of forty, would win twenty-one games for a team that would lose the 1915 pennant to Chicago by only a few percentage points. Bender joined a poor Baltimore team and would have a miserable year, finishing with a 4–16 record. At thirty-one, he seemed all but washed up.

On December 8, twenty-seven-year-old Eddie Collins went to the Chicago White Sox for a record $50,000; Charles Comiskey signed him to a five-year contract at $12,000 per year. Although Mack sold Collins because he needed the money, the deal was also a byproduct of Walter Johnson's jump to the Chicago Federals. Ban Johnson—fearing that the

97

loss of the game's top pitcher to Comiskey's local Federal League competition would weaken one of his league's strongest franchises—convinced Collins to consent to the sale. Of course as things turned out, Collins's transfer from Philadelphia to Chicago wasn't really necessary, because Johnson ended up back with Washington.

Hard-hitting Frank Baker refused the contract Mack sent him, flirted with the Federals, and decided to stay home in Maryland for the entire 1915 season. Early the next year, Mack sold him to the New York Yankees for a hefty $37,500. By mid-season 1915, Mack had dealt away Jack Barry, Herb Pennock, and Bob Shawkey; Stuffy McInnis, Wally Schang, Rube Oldring, and Amos Strunk would follow them in a year or two. From a 99–55 record in 1914, the Athletics plummeted to 43–105, finished seventeen games behind seventh-place Cleveland, and sold 146,223 tickets, fewest in the majors. It would be 1922 before one of Mack's teams escaped the American League cellar.

At the beginning of 1915, the Federal League still appeared to be a going concern. Yet while reliable attendance statistics aren't available, the reality was that several of its teams had lost heavily in the league's inaugural season. High salaries paid to lure established major-leaguers, the costs of building new ballparks or renting old ones (such as Washington Park in Brooklyn or Exposition Park in Pittsburgh), and the legal expenses involved in the various suits by big-league teams and counter-suits by the Federals—all of that added up to mounting indebtedness. The Indianapolis entry was a financial failure despite having edged Chicago for the pennant by one game and having the league's batting and base-stealing champion in Benny Kauff. Multi-millionaire oilman Harry Sinclair bought the Indianapolis team and moved it to Newark, New Jersey, where it would have to compete with the local International Leaguers, not to mention the Giants and Yankees across the river. In the absence of a reserve clause in their contracts, Federal League players could move from team to team in the offseason, unless they had signed multi-year contracts. Kauff signed with the Brooklyn Tip Tops.

Despite their money problems, Federal League teams continued their raids on National and American leaguer rosters. Rube Marquard, tempted by an offer of $10,000 per year from Robert B. Ward of Brooklyn, swore out an affidavit that he wasn't under contract to the Giants and accepted a $1,500 signing bonus, when he was actually still under a two-year contract with the New York club. Marquard's status remained in dispute all winter. After the Giants reimbursed Ward for his signing bonus, the wayward left-hander gave up and reported to McGraw for spring training at Marlin, Texas. (In his first start in 1915, on April 15, Marquard would pitch a no-hit game versus Brooklyn.)

Yet besides Bender and Plank, a number of prominent players left the National and American leagues to play in the new league in its second season, including infielders Hal Chase (White Sox to Buffeds), Lee Magee (Cardinals to Brookfeds), Mike Mowrey (Cardinals to Pittsfeds) and Ed Konetchy (Pirates to Pittsfeds), and pitchers (Ed Reulbach (Brooklyn to Newfeds) and Hugh Bedient (Red Sox to Buffeds). The caliber of play in the 1915 Federal League would probably be higher than in the previous season, while that in the two older leagues—especially the National League—probably would be a bit lower.

Like other club officials and managers in the National and American leagues, Stallings remained bitterly hostile to the interlopers. At still another banquet in Augusta in his honor, he said he wanted to help the local South Atlantic League team and pledged $100 for four season tickets. Then Stallings learned the ballpark had been rented to the Pittsburgh Federals for spring training, whereupon he phoned the Augusta president that he could keep the tickets.

Les Mann had been one of Stallings's favorite players; his loss wasn't insignificant. But with his pitching staff intact, and anticipating that having Sherry Magee in the lineup would make for more potent offense, Stallings assembled his players in Macon and again put them up at the Hotel Dempsey. Odds-makers had made the Braves 8–5 favorites to repeat as National League winners.

Yet as has often been the case on pennant and World Series winners, some players were unhappy with what they were being paid. Jim Gaffney, carrying a much bigger payroll than the one he inherited in the fall of 1912, wasn't at all receptive to players' complaints. "All winter long," reported an anonymous New York Times sportswriter, "President Gaffney has handled his players in the way of contracts with an iron hand." He refused pay increases to players he had signed to long-term contracts the previous summer, even when they talked about jumping to the Federals. Bill James had become a particular malcontent, writing from California to a Boston friend that he wouldn't report for spring training until he got a new contract at $7,000 per year. James was under contract for the next two seasons for $4,000 per year, and Gaffney said he had promised the big pitcher another $1,000 bonus if the Braves won the pennant. "If the boy changes his mind," Gaffney said, "well and good. But he will not get a penny more than the $4,000 and that $1,000 bonus. I told him he was foolish to sign for two years. He told me he knew his business. And there you are."[19]

After talking with Federal agents on the way to Macon, James showed up about two weeks late, in a frame of mind that hadn't improved. Now he was claiming his work in 1915 had been worth $50,000 to Gaffney. The Boston president wired Federal League head James M. Gilmore in Chicago to make sure Gilmore knew James was under contract for the next two years. He disapproved of "chasing after" players who were threatening to go over to the Federals, he told reporters, and he wouldn't take back anybody who had jumped his club. Tim Murnane wrote that because of James's assault on a local sportswriter the previous summer, the feeling toward him in Boston wasn't good. The *Globe's* James C. O'Leary and Walter Hapgood, sports editor of the *Herald*, were especially hostile to James. The *Sporting News* joined in, editorially taking Gaffney's side in his dealings with the pitcher.[20]

Just before the Braves began spring training, Stallings negotiated the purchase of infielder Eddie Fitzpatrick from Toronto. Fitzpatrick could play second base, shortstop, third base, or the outfield. When Evers arrived in Macon, he said he weighed fifteen or twenty pounds more than at the end of the World Series, and felt fine. Others, including Stallings, weren't so sure. Fitzpatrick would turn out to be a valuable handyman.

Sherry Magee reported on schedule and with high hopes of playing on a pennant-winner for the first time in his career. On March 2 he donned his uniform and went out to Central City Park. Trying for a low running catch, he stepped into a hole in the rough outfield and fell heavily on his right shoulder. Stallings examined the shoulder and pronounced it not broken.

Although Magee had to nurse the shoulder through the rest of spring training and the exhibition games, at Macon he was fit enough to join Maranville in one of his adolescent hijinks: breaking up an Evangelical Protestant church service and, when local police were called,

Sherwood Magee as a member of the Philadelphia Phillies in 1914. Magee joined
the Braves the next season but was never the player he had been with the Phillies
(George Bantham Bain Collection, Library of Congress).

joining a Salvation Army Band, borrowing a tambourine and drum, and collecting coins from passersby. Yet the star outfielder on whom Stallings was counting to energize his offense would play the 1915 season in pain, hit with little power, and throw with difficulty.

The previous winter Stallings had declared, "I don't see how they can beat us." At Macon he said he saw McGraw's Giants as the only club Boston would have to contend with. But on the eve of the 1915 season, Bill Phelon looked at the Braves' current situation and thought otherwise. If Magee and Evers couldn't play up to form and with Whitted gone, Phelon believed "the Braves have as much chance to cop the flag as I have of kissing the Empress Dowager of England."[21] In fact, the Braves' troubles had just begun.

6

1915: "We're not going to wait until July this year"

While the United States remained at peace in the spring of 1915, the war convulsing nearly all of Europe since the previous August had already taken hundreds of thousands of lives. The western front had settled into indecisive trench warfare, characterized by costly French and British attacks and German counterattacks. On the eastern front, Imperial Russia's armies struggled over great expanses of territory against German and Austro-Hungarian forces, with neither side able to gain much advantage. The baseball season would begin with thirteen Canadian cities in three leagues within Organized Baseball on a wartime footing. Canada, along with the rest of the British Empire, had joined the conflict in support of the Crown.

Although the war was still more than three-thousand miles away, the torpedoing of the British Cunard liner *Lusitania* on May 7, sending to their deaths nearly two-thousand people, including 129 Americans, brought widespread condemnation of Germany's "barbaric" submarine warfare and prompted strong protests from Washington. It marked the beginning of deteriorating relations between the Woodrow Wilson administration and the Imperial German government, as well as growing public feeling in favor of Britain and France, if not the autocratic regime of Russia's Czar Nicholas II. The sinking of the *Lusitania* would have been particularly poignant for the big-league players and others who had made the global baseball expedition in the 1913–1914 offseason. The *Lusitania* was the ship that had brought them home to New York from Liverpool.

However ominous the news from Europe might be, for many millions of Americans the immediate concern was the approaching new baseball season. For Boston baseball fans, there was the added excitement of ground-breaking for the city's second new major-league baseball park. In March, Jim Gaffney directed that work start at a site about a mile to the west of Fenway Park, on what had been the Allston golf course. For $100,000, Gaffney had purchased the western part of the golf course, but reserved the frontage on Commonwealth Avenue for future commercial development by the Commonwealth Realty Company, which Gaffney had formed with local banker Robert H. Davis and others. Thus the ballpark would be built on the back end of the property, up against the tracks of the Albany Railroad and a bend in the Charles River. Osborn Engineering of Cleveland, Ohio, the same firm that had built Fenway Park and several other new baseball facilities, would be the prime contractor. Gaffney wanted to have the park ready before the end of the season, in time, he and Braves' fans confidently expected, for the World Series. Some two-hundred men went to work at the site, putting in ten-hour, six-day weeks in mostly disagreeable weather.

Following the usual exhibition games against minor-league teams on the way north from Macon and a couple more tune-ups in Washington, the Braves began defense of their world championship. On April 14, 1915, for the first and only time, Fenway Park was the venue for the opening game of a National League season, with the Philadelphia Phillies as the opposition. The three-year-old ballpark had been returned to its pre–World Series configuration; gone were the extra box seats along the first- and third-base lines and the bleachers on Duffy's Cliff below the left-field fence and in center and right field. Also gone was the barrier in front of the right-field bleachers with its inexplicable lateral eighteen-inch gap.

The game would be the managerial debut of Pat Moran, who for fourteen years had been mostly a backup catcher with the Boston, Chicago, and Philadelphia National League clubs. The 1914 Phillies, having lost two of their three best pitchers as well as their shortstop and third baseman to the Federal League, had dropped from second to sixth and cost Red Dooin his job. With Sherwood Magee and third-baseman John "Hans" Lobert now also gone, most observers thought Moran's team would be fortunate to finish as high as sixth again.[1] That discounted the acquisition of George Whitted to replace Magee in center field, plus Al Demaree, a capable right-hander (and skilled cartoonist), and Milton Stock, an adequate third baseman, both of whom came to the Phillies from the New York Giants for Lobert.

The Phillies also had the major-leagues' foremost power hitter in outfielder Clifford Cravath (called either "Gavvy" or "Cactus"), who had finally made it to the majors to stay in 1911, at age twenty-nine. Like Sherwood Magee, the right-hand-batting Californian quickly learned to slice fly balls toward the short, high right-field wall in his home ballpark. Over the past three years, Cravath had totaled forty-nine home runs, an extraordinarily number in the so-called Dead Ball Era. And then there was Grover Cleveland Alexander, who had won ninety-six games since coming into the league in 1911, but who still hadn't reached his peak.

In pregame doings, Stallings presented gifts on behalf of their former teammates to Whitted and Oscar Dugey. The 9th Regiment Band serenaded the crowd of 20,000 or so; Mayor Curley threw out the first ball. Then Dick Rudolph squared off against Alexander, who was his usual dominating self, shutting out the Braves on six hits. The Phillies got to Rudolph for three runs, with Whitted's single and double doing much of the damage. Sherwood Magee sat out the opener, while Dave Bancroft, a flashy if erratic shortstop William F. Baker had purchased from Portland's Pacific Coast League champions, played the first of his 1,913 big-league games.

On Thursday, in periods of rain, snow flurries, and hail, the Braves lost again. Magee was in the lineup and hit a double, but that didn't help much. Erskine Mayer gave up one run while the Phillies smacked Tom Hughes for nine hits and seven runs. Boston fans might have wondered why Bill James hadn't followed Rudolph, which had been Stallings's usual pitching order in 1914. But after reporting late and in bad humor, James hadn't looked good at Macon. He threw with little zip on his fastball and complained of soreness in his right shoulder. Stallings must have wondered whether pitching in various different climates on last fall's two-month tour hadn't affected James's arm, although obviously the tour hadn't affected Alexander's effectiveness.

Even worse weather wiped out Friday's game with Philadelphia. On Saturday the Braves broke into the winning column by beating Brooklyn, 5–1, Dick Crutcher getting the win with help from Paul Strand. But the game brought more bad news for Stallings. In the midst of a three-run eighth-inning rally, Johnny Evers's persistently bad luck struck again. On a slide into second base, he broke the same ankle he broke in 1910.

As he was carried from the field, the hopes of Evers's teammates and Boston's fandom for a repeat pennant-winner sagged.

Evers returned to Troy with his ankle in a plaster cast. The cast came off a month later, but his ankle was still weak; his physician said it would probably be another month before he would be ready to play. Meanwhile, with Eddie Fitzpatrick at second base, the Braves went on to win four times in the five-game series with the team now increasingly called the "Robins," after manager Wilbert Robinson. Monday the 19th was Patriot's Day, the New England holiday when whichever Boston team was at home always played a morning-afternoon doubleheader. Strand worked a complete game to beat Brooklyn, 7–2, in the morning; with Hank Gowdy making four hits; Rudolph was the afternoon winner, 6–4. The next day, with the score 3–3 in the tenth inning, Red Smith won it on a double to the Fenway Park scoreboard, sending in Fitzpatrick and handing the decision to Hughes. Brooklyn took the series finale, 8–4.

With Evers out indefinitely and James and Tyler slow in coming around, Stallings sought help. In a deal no doubt negotiated while the Brooklyn team was in Boston, the Braves bought Dick Eagan for additional infield insurance. George Tyler's trouble was something of a mystery. He wasn't unhappy with his salary, and he had spent the offseason in New Hampshire instead of going on the baseball tour with James and the other National Leaguers. He just wasn't throwing well, so six days after obtaining Eagan, Stallings spent some more of Jim Gaffney's money to add Pat Ragan to his pitching staff. Gene Cocreham had had his year of shared glory in 1914; he and Adolfo Luque were both released to Toronto. A few weeks later Boston gave Otto Hess his outright release to get down to the twenty-one man limit, which Stallings abominated.[2]

For once, a Boston team managed by Stallings had made a decent start. Despite Evers's injury, Magee's bum shoulder, and uncertainty regarding how James and Tyler would do, Stallings still thought well of his team's prospects. "We're not going to wait until July this year," he declared.[3] Although Les Mann and George Whitted were gone and he had to manage within the twenty-one player limit, Stallings continued to shuffle his outfielders according to the opposition's pitching. Magee would be his everyday center fielder, but Joe Connolly and Herbie Moran would be his regulars in left field and right field against right-handers, and Ted Cather and Eddie Fitzgerald would play against left-handers.

Dick Eagan would be at second base until Evers's return. Larry Gilbert would substitute for Connolly or Moran in twenty-seven games and pinch hit in fourteen.

After winning four of their first seven games, the Braves went to Philadelphia and lost three out of four games. The Braves' 10–2 pounding of Erskine Mayer in the third game, with Hughes coasting to the win and also homering, was the Phillies' first loss after eight wins. In the final game of the series, Alexander gave up ten hits but struck out ten and hung on for a 7–4 victory, Strand taking the loss. The turning point in the game came in the eighth inning, when Gowdy tried to pick Cravath off third base, the ball hit Cravath, and he and another runner scored. Claiming Cravath had interfered with Gowdy's throw, the Braves protested so protractedly to umpire Ernie Quigley that he ejected Gowdy, Red Smith, Butch Schmidt, and Lefty Tyler. Many years later, Gowdy remembered how Stallings took to scolding his players after such losses with references to the automobiles they had bought. So, for example, Rabbit Maranville was an "Apperson jack rabbit bonehead"; others might be a "Packard dunce" or a "Stanley Steamer clown."[4]

That series in Philadelphia was a harbinger of the hard time the Braves were going to have with Pat Moran's team. But in the two games that followed in the Polo Grounds, McGraw's Giants, who Stallings thought would again be his main competition, were already in last place and looked like anything but contenders. The Braves took both games, outscoring the New Yorkers twenty-five to thirteen. On Tuesday, April 27, Bill James, who had pitched two hitless innings in relief a few days earlier, made his first start and won with help from Otto Hess (in his last game with Boston) and Dick Crutcher, 12–5. Butch Schmidt and Red Smith hit home runs in the battering of Bill "Pol" Perritt and Hank Ritter. Wednesday's game was rained out. The game on Thursday was officially recorded as a Braves victory, but it began and ended in total confusion.

John McGraw knew he had an aging team that included several disgruntled players, with Marquard, unhappy about having to miss out on the bigger money Robert Ward had offered him, being the foremost malcontent. Christy Mathewson had lost most of his effectiveness; Jeff Tesreau, twenty-six, had become the mainstay of a suddenly mediocre staff. With Fred Snodgrass slumping badly, McGraw wanted twenty-three-year-old Benny Kauff, reigning star of the Federal League, for his center fielder.

Although the National Commission had ruled against American and National League teams signing or re-signing players who were under contract to the Federals, McGraw claimed Ban Johnson and John Tener had encouraged him to sign Kauff, which he did, for $10,000 plus a $5,000 signing bonus. So Kauff was in center field at the start of the April 29 game, whereupon Jim Gaffney, who was present, ordered Stallings to refuse to play. Base umpire Mal Eason called Tener's office from the Polo Grounds to ask what to do; Tener affirmed that Kauff, under contract to the Brooklyn Federals, couldn't play for the Giants. Meanwhile head umpire Ernie Quigley gave Stallings ten minutes to get his team back on the field and, when that didn't happen, announced the game forfeited to Boston. Stallings agreed to go ahead with the game, but as an exhibition; supposedly McGraw also agreed to that. Played loosely on both sides, it was called after seven innings with the Braves ahead, 13–8. The next day the National Commission—Tener, Ban Johnson, and Cincinnati president Garry Herrmann—upheld Tener's instruction to Eason and went on to declare yesterday's game a regular-season Boston victory. McGraw now claimed he hadn't agreed to the exhibition. Having had had previous troubles with both Tener and Johnson, he was predictably furious, but there was nothing he could do about the situation. Kauff returned to the Brooklyn lineup and went on to lead the Federal League in batting and base-stealing again.

After that head-scratching stay in the Polo Grounds, the Braves went over to Ebbets Field and won two of three, with the Friday, May 2, game another rainout. Hughes pitched a three-hitter on the 1st for a 4–1 win; after Brooklyn won 3–2 on the 3rd, James pitched like his old self, limiting the Robins to one run on six hits and striking out six. Three singles and Cather's triple off Aitchison produced four runs in the fifth inning; Gowdy doubled in two more in the ninth. That made Boston's record 9–7, in a tie with for second with Roger Bresnahan's Chicago team. Philadelphia led at 13–5.

Three Boston wins from New York in four games in Fenway Park left the Giants, at 6–12, even deeper in last place. So far George Tyler had only pitched in an exhibition game on an off day in Bridgeport, Connecticut, although he had managed to bump Ernie Quigley in the

April 26 ruckus in Philadelphia. Tyler made his first regular-season start on May 6 in the opening game of the New York series and pitched well in a 3–1 loss to Tesreau. On the 7th, Ragan relieved Rudolph to get the decision in an 11–7 slugfest; Hughes out-dueled Marquard the next day, 4–3; and on the 10th Tyler and Tesreau were both battered, although Lefty survived for his first win, 14–9.

For their part in the Philadelphia disturbance, John Tener fined Tyler $25 and Gowdy $50. Stallings announced that he was through criticizing the umpires, and that he had told his players to stop their "kicking." Sportswriters took that with a hefty grain of salt. Stallings probably said what he did at Gaffney's direction. The Boston president was getting impatient with the Braves' unruly on-field behavior (even though as yet Johnny Evers wasn't able to contribute to it). He told the *New York Evening Sun's* William MacBeth that it was the prevailing practice for club owners to pay a player's fine; then the money was supposed to be deducted from his next paycheck. That was a joke, said Gaffney, because the deductions usually weren't made. But he was through paying fines, and if the other club owners cooperated, "rowdyism" could be ended. Gaffney may already have begun to have some doubts about keeping his money in baseball. "Why, the license and privilege of the present day ball player are unendurable," he groused. "I know of one National League club that has to pay the laundry and pressing bills of its players in spring training."[5]

The first western team to visit Fenway Park was Miller Huggins's St. Louis Cardinals, who began a four-game series on May 14. At that point the Braves had won twelve games and lost eight; Boston scribes expected them to fatten their record against teams that, with the exception of Chicago, were thought to be weaker than those in the east. Besides losing Lee Magee to the Federals, the Cardinals had traded to the Giants Pol Perritt, one of their best pitchers.

The Braves proceeded to lose three of four to the Cardinals, although the single win, 6–2 over Hub Perdue, was another capable pitching performance by James. Boston also dropped three of four to Pittsburgh, losing the series-opener 10–6 when Tyler, in relief of Rudolph, gave up six ninth-inning runs. Except for a dreary 9–1 finale defeat, the four games with Chicago were all close, but the Braves lost all four to fall to 14–16 and sixth place. With the Phillies having cooled off the past couple of weeks, the Cubs left Boston in first place at 20–

12. The Braves finished with the western clubs by splitting two games with Cincinnati, with another rained out.

But on Friday, May 28, following nine losses in twelve games against the westerners, they swept a doubleheader in Fenway Park from Philadelphia. In the wearying opener, Tyler walked eleven men but held the Phillies to two runs, while the Braves scored five, three on Sherwood Magee's bases-loaded double off Alexander. Between games a band led the players of both teams to the center field flagpole for the raising of the 1914 pennant, with Tener and other dignitaries on hand for the ceremony. In the second game, James gave up fifteen hits, including a home run by Gavvy Cravath over the left-field fence, but still got the decision over George Chalmers, 5–4. Boston won again the next day, 9–4, although in the eighth inning Rudolph hurt his leg running to first base and had to give way to Crutcher. After the Sunday off day, the teams divided their Decoration Day morning-afternoon doubleheader. With Maranville doubling and Schmidt and Fitzpatrick tripling, Hughes out-dueled Chalmers in the morning, 2–1. Schmidt hit another triple in the afternoon, but Tyler lost to Erskine Mayer, 5–2. With the league's standings almost constantly in flux, Boston was back in third place at 19–18.

The Braves concluded their nearly month-long home stand with a win, a tie, and a loss to the Giants. They hit six doubles and drove out the fading Mathewson in a 7–0 shutout by Hughes, who made his second start in two days. After a 5–5 tie, the Giants hammered James, Tyler, and Crutcher for sixteen hits and ten runs; Marquard, though reached for thirteen hits, held the Braves to only three runs. After that unfortunate performance, the Boston team left on its first western tour, now in fourth place with a 20–19 record. On the way to Cincinnati, the Braves stopped in Toronto and lost an exhibition to the International Leaguers. Stallings and his players couldn't have helped being struck by the number of young men in military attire and generally by the different ambience in a city and nation at war.

Before the Braves left for the west, Stallings had predicted his team would be in first place by July 1 and would stay there. Gaffney promised his daughter a little two-seat "runabout" motor car if the Braves came home in the lead; when she passed that along to Stallings, he assured her the car was already as good as hers. That's not the way things worked out.

The trip began favorably enough with two wins in three games in

Redland Field, but that was followed by two defeats in the three games played in Pittsburgh, although in the last game at Forbes Field, Ragan had another good outing. He limited Honus Wagner and his fellow–Pirates to two runs while the Braves scored all eight of their runs in the seventh inning on Charles "Babe" Adams. In West Side Park in Chicago, the Braves again failed twice in three games, Hippo Vaughn shutting them out in the middle game. That left them at the .500 mark, 24–24. Bill James, his arm ailing, couldn't be relied on regularly, and Tyler's work was inconsistent. From here on, Stallings would increasingly depend on Ragan and Hughes, using Hughes as both starter and reliever.

What followed in the four-game series in Robison Field in St. Louis that ended the Braves' western sojourn was downright disheartening. On Thursday, June 17, they couldn't score on Hank Robinson; Rudolph lost his game on a two-run pinch-hit single by Robert "Ham" Hyatt. Friday's game went twelve innings before the Cardinals ended it, 3–2, and on Saturday Hughes surrendered five runs in the eighth inning and lost it, 6–1. The Boston batters could do little with left-hander Slim Sallee's slow curveballs. Stallings went with Crutcher on Sunday, but the Cardinals scored five times on him, while rookie Lee Meadows, one of the earliest bespectacled major-leaguers, checked the Braves with two runs. After that sweep, Boston was in fifth place with 24 wins, 28 losses. St. Louis had improved to 29–26, three games behind Philadelphia and three and a half back of the Cubs.

Although Sherwood Magee had been in the lineup every day, sore shoulder and all, and was leading the team in batting, he hadn't played well in the St. Louis series. He also got on the bad side (temporarily) of Stallings and captain Evers (still disabled but traveling with the team) "for a bit of indiscretion in St. Louis," according to the *Sporting News's* "National League Notes."[6] What happened was that the members of the St. Louis Press Club hosted a dinner for the Boston ballplayers at one of the city's downtown hotels. Although Stallings usually left his players to look after themselves as long as they were ready to play the next day, on this occasion he and Evers had agreed that everybody ought to be in bed no later than 1:00 the next morning. Magee stayed out considerably later. No fine was assessed (or at least not made public), but the incident further aggravated the collectively disagreeable mood that usually goes with consistent losing.

A *Sporting News* contributor who watched the games at Robison Field reported that throughout the series "the umpires [had] to use their authority to the limit to keep the crabbing Braves in check." Despite his earlier pledge, Stallings was back to blaming the umpires for losses. In *Baseball Magazine*, Bill Phelon observed of the Braves' stumbles, "the frantic bawlings and wailings of George Stallings do not appear to spur them on."[7] The rosy prediction Stallings made before the team left Boston had come to naught; one also supposes Gaffney's daughter wouldn't get her runabout.

Having lost nine of thirteen decisions in the west, the Braves returned home on Wednesday, June 21, to begin a three-game set the next day with Brooklyn. They righted themselves (temporarily) by sweeping the series on three well-pitched games, the best of which was Tyler's 6–0 whitewash on the 24th. But in a six-game series in the Polo Grounds, including two doubleheaders, they resumed their slump. On Friday, June 26, Pol Perritt shut them out, 5–0. Before a crowd of about 20,000, they won Saturday's game, 7–5, by scoring five ninth-inning runs on Marquard, aided by a two-run single by Rudolph and wild throws by center fielder Fred Snodgrass and first-baseman Fred Merkle. Monday's doubleheader was a double loss. With only a day's rest, Rudolph yielded two runs in the bottom of the ninth to blow the opener, 3–2. The first game of the Tuesday doubleheader was one of Christy Mathewson's few good outings in 1915, a 3–2 decision over Ragan. Boston did salvage the nightcap finale of the stay in the Polo Grounds. Perritt allowed only two runs, but Hughes pitched a six-hit shutout. After a ten-week absence, Johnny Evers returned to the lineup in a big way, singling, doubling, lining one of Perritt's pitches into the right-field bleachers, and making an acrobatic play to tag out Chief Meyers's attempt to stretch his single into a double.

Matters didn't improve in Philadelphia, where the Braves lost three games before winning the last one. In the series-opener on Wednesday, June 30, Evers's ankle gave him so much pain he had to take himself out, and Cravath's drive into left field took a bad bounce, knocked Joe Connolly unconscious, and went for a triple. George Davis, having again joined the team at the end of the Harvard law school term, made his first start and got slapped around, 8–5. The next day, in the bottom of the ninth inning, Cravath hit what would later be called a "walk-off homer" off Ragan to win it 2–1 for newlywed Mayer, whose bride was in the stands. The teams played a doubleheader on Saturday. The first game was still another defeat, 4–1; the nightcap was still another salvage operation, won 5–3. That left the defending champions in seventh place at 30–35.

On Monday, July 5, the Braves were scheduled to play an Independence Day doubleheader in Brooklyn (delayed a day, of course, by the proscription on Sabbath commercial amusements). The morning game was rained out; that afternoon Hughes was unable to stop the slide. Boston lost for the eighth time in its last eleven games, falling 6–3 to Jeff Pfeffer. Back-to-back doubleheaders followed on Tuesday and Wednesday. Both Tuesday games were defeats, 3–2 and 4–3, absorbed, respectively by Rudolph and Ragan. Wednesday's first game matched a pair of left-handers, Tyler and Sherrod "Sherry" Smith. It ended in Boston's third-straight one-run loss, 4–3. The nightcap was something of an epic. James pitched five innings and left for a pinch hitter, complaining of a hurting arm. Davis took the mound with the game scoreless and, though touched for nine hits, matched Phil Douglas (recently purchased from Cincinnati) for eleven frames, at which point the umpires decided it was too dark to continue. Douglas, a hard-to-beat spitballer when he was sober, allowed only four hits and struck out eight.

That night, July 6, the defending National League champions, with a 30–39 record, found themselves where they had stood a year earlier—in last place. Contrary to what Stallings had declared in April, the Braves again seemed to be waiting until July (or later) to start contending for the pennant. As one writer put it, "This year the Braves have at no time shown anything in the way of championship form."[8]

Yet at that juncture, the National League teams were even more tightly bunched than they had been a year earlier; Boston was still only ten and a half games behind first-place Chicago. In his syndicated column, Hugh Fullerton quoted the opinion of an unnamed National League club owner that the league was weaker than at any time since the raids of the fledgling American League "wrecked it" in 1901–1902. No present National League club, the owner believed, could have finished in the first division in 1913, before the Federal League began its raids on the league's rosters. Yet Fullerton thought that weak or not, the current National League race "promises to be more interesting than any we have had in years."[9]

Stallings decided the team needed shaking up. Larry Gilbert, batting .151 in forty-five games, and Ted Cather, batting .206 in forty games, were sent to Toronto. That left Stallings with only four outfielders, including utility man Fitzgerald. Dick Crutcher, with a 2–2 record in fourteen appearances, went to Jersey City. Paul Strand had pitched in only six games, losing one and losing one. He had complained all season of a hurting pitching arm. Stallings evidently didn't sympathize with the young left-hander, because he drew an indefinite suspension "on account of failure to get in condition"—that period's euphemism for being too much of a nocturnal good-timer.[10] Stallings reinstated him shortly, but he pitched only a few innings over the rest of the season.

With his team in last place, and with Butch Schmidt injured and Evers in and out of the lineup, Stallings didn't feel much like smiling. But that week's issue of the *Sporting News* carried a big advertisement for Coca-Cola, with a beaming likeness of the Boston manager. The accompanying text explained that while Stallings had never before endorsed anything, "The genuine goodness of Coca-Cola induced him to break this rule."[11]

Back in Fenway Park, the Braves broke their losing streak in the first of five games versus third-place St. Louis. Trailing 3–2, they won the game ingloriously in the tenth inning, when Bill Doak issued consecutive bases-loaded walks. On Saturday, July 10, only about 7,500 were on hand for a double-header split, Hughes losing the opener, 7–1, Davis outpitching Lee Meadows in the nightcap, 3–1. Another doubleheader on Monday ended in two defeats. Slim Sallee won a fine duel with Rudolph, 2–1; Hub Perdue, in relief of Doak, got the second-game decision when the Cardinals scored in the top of the tenth inning to beat Tyler, 4–3.

Evers replaced Fitzpatrick for that game and got into a wrangle with his old nemesis, Cy Rigler. According to what was reported in the *Boston American*, when Rigler called Bob Bescher safe at the plate, Evers shouted to Rigler that he was giving Boston the worst of it on orders from Tener, who wanted to keep the league race close. Of course such an accusation would have made absolutely no sense, inasmuch as the Braves were trailing everybody else. After traveling up to Boston to talk with Rigler and base umpire Bill Hart, Tener dismissed the story. But Chandler D. Richter, associate editor of *Sporting Life*, accepted the *Amer-*

ican's account of what happened and insisted that "Evers should have been suspended or heavily fined."[12]

On Tuesday, July 13, the Braves hosted Pittsburgh in their third-straight doubleheader and lost the opener, 3–1, to drop eleven games below .500. Since their June 26 victory over New York, they had won only four times in eighteen games, with one tie. The pitchers had generally performed well, but with the team batting only .233, lowest in the league, they usually received sparse run support. Over that nineteen-game span, the Braves had averaged 2.3 runs per game. But in the second game of the Pittsburgh doubleheader on the 13th, their bats finally awakened for seven runs, one more than the Pirates scored on Davis.

That game marked the beginning of the Braves' revival. They took the remaining two games from the Pirates, although to win the last one they had to play fifteen innings before scoring the winning run on Babe Adams and giving the victory to Tyler (who, like Adams, was pitching in relief). Seventh-place Cincinnati came into Fenway Park on July 17 and lost a doubleheader, Boston winning both games by 3–2 scores, with Evers playing a doubleheader for the first time. Butch Schmidt's two-run double in the ninth inning gave the decision to James, who had relieved Hughes, who in turn had relieved Ragan. Rudolph took over for Davis in the second game and gained the victory when the Braves scored three times in the seventh inning. After winning two of the remaining three games with the Reds, the Braves improved to 39–44 and ceded the cellar to Buck Herzog's club. Boston now trailed Philadelphia, which had displaced Chicago in the lead, by only eight games. In St. Louis, W. J. O'Connor was predicting the Braves were ready for a pennant drive.

The Braves ended their home stand in grand style, sweeping four games from Roger Bresnahan's Cubs and dropping them to third place behind Philadelphia and a hot Brooklyn club that was getting consistently strong pitching from Jeff Pfeffer, Sherry Smith, and a revitalized Jack Coombs. Meanwhile St. Louis, experiencing a disastrous stay in the east, had fallen into the second division.

The first game of the Chicago series, on Thursday, July 22, was a boisterous affair. Boston won 4–3, scoring the winning run when left-hander George Pierce threw wildly during an effort to catch Maranville in a rundown. Heinie Zimmerman protested so vigorously to base umpire

Bob Emslie, claiming he had tagged Maranville, that Emslie ordered him out of the game; subsequently Tener fined him $100. Earlier in the game Evers drew a walk but lingered at home plate, taunting Ernie Quigley and tossing sand around the batter's box. Quigley thumbed him out of the game, whereupon Evers stepped on the umpire' toes, and Quigley hit Evers in the chest. Tener made another trip to Boston, talked to the umpires, fined Evers $100, and, in an unusual act, fined Quigley a like amount. He also ordered the two to shake hands before the next day's game.

On Friday, with Tener staying over to see how things went, Evers and Quigley first sat together in the visitors' dugout for a photographer, then, like obedient little boys, shook hands at home plate. After that display of good feeling, Tyler pitched an eleven-inning game, which the Braves won, 2–1, on Maranville's single over second base past Bert Humphries, who had relieved Hippo Vaughn. With that they improved to 41–44 and moved up to sixth place, ahead of New York (for which little was going right) and to within six games of Philadelphia. On Saturday, Rudolph pitched a masterful two-hitter to beat Jimmy Lavender. Evers's fifth-inning single brought home Herbie Moran with the game's only run. The last game of the series was another one-run shutout. Magee drove in Connolly in the fourth inning; Hughes saved Ragan's game in the eighth, retiring the Cubs with the bases loaded.

Stallings had been working with only five effective pitchers. Bill James's shoulder gave him so much pain he had to be used sparingly; Paul Strand was also of little use. So Stallings reached all the way down to the Class B leagues for some pitching help. Gaffney bought two youngsters: Left-hander Art Nehf, who had already won nineteen games in the Central League for Terre Haute, his hometown, and right-hander Jesse Barnes, a Kansas native obtained from Davenport of the Three-I League. Both would join the Braves in Cincinnati.

Before heading west, the Braves made a one-game stopover in Brooklyn on Tuesday, the 27th. Evers's fifth-inning error led to three Robins runs, which seemed to be enough for big Phil Douglas. In the top of the ninth, however, with the Ebbets Field crowd jeering him, Evers singled and, still favoring his ankle, gave way to pinch-runner Fitzgerald. Fitzgerald went to third base on Connolly's hit; Magee's double brought in both runs to win it for Tyler, 4–3. After eleven victories in their last twelve games, the Braves had finally made it back to .500.

Sixteen days later, when they arrived in Philadelphia from the west, the Braves were playing above .500, but just barely. They began the trip in Cincinnati with a tidy 3–1 performance from Rudolph, then swept a doubleheader the next day, Ragan cruising 10–1 in the opener and relieving Davis in the nightcap to pick up another win, 7–6. With at least six teams still crowding each other, the Braves had climbed to third place. Although the lowly Reds took the last two games of the series, Boston remained in third place. In the finale, Pete Schneider bested James, who made his first start in weeks, 5–3.

After a Saturday rainout and an idle Sunday (in force in Pittsburgh as in Philadelphia under Pennsylvania law), the Braves swept a doubleheader from Fred Clarke's Pirates by scores of 5–4 and 7–2, Hughes and Tyler doing the honors. The one-sided nightcap wasn't noteworthy except for a rare scrap between a player and an opposing manager. In the fourth inning, Bob Emslie ruled that Pittsburgh's John "Zip" Collins had beaten Butch Schmidt to first base as Schmidt tried for an unassisted putout. Evers and Schmidt ranted at length, with Evers getting up in Emslie's face and punching a finger in his ribs, until the umpire had enough and ordered him out of the game. On his way out through the home dugout, the Braves' captain stopped for a drink of water.

Clarke—an old enemy of Evers going back to their fierce pennant battles of the previous decade—yelled for the umpires to get him off the field, whereupon Evers, by one account, called the Pirates' manager "yellow" and cursed him. By another account, he "playfully threw some of the water at Clarke." Enraged, Clarke grabbed Evers, threw him against the dugout wall, and started choking him. Evers broke away and exited the dugout. At that point, according to still another account, the umpires also ordered Clarke to leave, and he and Evers resumed their confrontation under the grandstand. Policemen intervened and escorted Evers to the visitors' clubhouse, while players from both teams milled around the Pittsburgh dugout and fans jumped on its roof.[13]

John Tener notified Evers he was suspended for three days—oddly enough, not for his fight with Clarke but for what he had said to Bob Emslie. Pittsburgh owner Barney Dreyfuss called for Evers to be banned from baseball; in *Sporting Life*, Chandler Richter condemned Evers but also Tener for his leniency. He thought Evers should have been given a long suspension after his July 22 clash with Cy Rigler; what happened in Pittsburgh, Richter editorialized, was another instance when "Evers brought disgrace upon the game." John E. Wray, sports editor of the *St. Louis Post-Dispatch* and a longtime Evers critic, would have settled for a month's suspension. "Johnny tramples on everything from the umpire's toes to the rules of common decency," Wray inveighed, "and is punished with a three-days' rest for his weak ankle." Two days later, though, Wray offered a different perspective on the Boston captain, describing him as "a torch, flitting here and there, igniting the other and more passive spirits in the game until they flash and flame as brilliantly as himself." Wray identified "the main trouble with Evers' make-up [as] that he mistakes assault for aggressiveness and abuse for argument."[14]

With Evers sitting in the Forbes Field grandstand, the Braves also won the third and last game of the series with Pittsburgh, 5–1. Hughes, who had become Stallings's workhorse, pitched a seven-hit, one-run game, while the Braves scored five times on Al Mamaux, the Pirates' young ace right-hander. Now 50–46, they moved to within one game of second-place Brooklyn and three and a half of Philadelphia.

While the team was in Pittsburgh, Bill James left for an appointment in nearby Youngstown, Ohio, with James "Bonesetter" Reese, a Welsh immigrant who, without much formal medical training, had made a wide reputation for treating athletes' muscle and joint ailments. Pitchers frequently went to Reese, who used manipulative techniques that were supposed to put life back into "dead arms." As David Jones has suggested, "in all likelihood James suffered a torn rotator cuff, a condition that the medicine of the day was powerless to correct."[15] James would rejoin the team and continue to draw his $333.33 bi-monthly pay checks, but he was finished for the season.

From Pittsburgh, the Braves went into West Side Park in Chicago and lost three games in three days. Fred "Cy" Williams slammed a triple off Hughes in the bottom of the ninth inning to decide the third game, 3–2. That dropped the Braves into fourth place, behind the Cubs and just ahead of Pittsburgh.

In Chicago, Evers told reporters that after the upcoming series in St. Louis, he intended to quit for the season and go out to Colorado or California to rest and restore his health. Describing his fight with Fred Clarke as "a harmless run-in," he went on to complain, "These attacks upon my character hurt. If I try to stick it out until October I'm afraid

I'll be one of those 'complete wrecks.'" Last winter's pneumonia and the broken ankle, he said, had worn him down. He hadn't been able to get to sleep before 3 a. m. He also thought he "suffered from heart attacks." (They were most likely anxiety attacks.) As for his penchant for getting himself ejected and suspended, he explained tersely, "I can't play ball unless I crab."[16]

By the time the Boston team reached St. Louis on its last western stop, Evers had changed his mind. Now he said he would do nothing until he saw Jim Gaffney in Philadelphia. By telephone from his home in Cedarhurst, Long Island, Gaffney told the *Sporting News*, "They're not going to ride Johnny Evers out of baseball so long as I am president of the club. John, you know, is excitable and high strung" and felt he was being "picked on" by the press and umpires.[17]

In St. Louis, Evers returned to the lineup in time for the Braves' fourth loss in a row, 7–2. The next afternoon Rudolph held the Cardinals to two runs while his mates scored six. After a rainout, Boston beat St. Louis in the first game of a doubleheader by the same score but had to settle for a 2–2 tie in the second game. Having won seven and lost six in the west, the Braves were in fifth place, behind Chicago, Pittsburgh, Brooklyn, and Philadelphia. But at that point every National League team except St. Louis and Cincinnati was playing above .500.

On Friday, August 13, the Braves opened a three-game series in Philadelphia. Presumably Evers and Gaffney had their talk; if so, the Boston president may have told the team's cantankerous captain to take a rest. In any case, Evers was in Troy for a couple of days while the Braves were defeated in all three games, twice by shutouts. Art Nehf pitched respectably in his big-league debut but lost to Alexander, 5–3; first-baseman Fred Luderus hit a home run, triple, and double in Al Demaree's 9–0 shutout; and on Monday, Eppa Rixey blanked the Braves again, 5–0. Boston again fell below .500, at 52–53. At that point, Philadelphia's record was 55–45, Brooklyn's 57–49, and Chicago's 53–51. Pittsburgh, New York, St. Louis, and Cincinnati made up the second division, in that order.

After three weeks on the road, the Braves arrived home to find their new ballpark, already named "Braves Field," ready two weeks ahead of schedule. On Tuesday the 17th, Jim Gaffney's close friend Clark Griffith joined Gaffney, John Tener, and Robert H. Davis for a final inspection

119

of what was, at that juncture in baseball history, the biggest thing of its kind, both in seating capacity and playing-field dimensions.

The field was laid out seventeen feet below street level, in a natural amphitheater formed from a valley in the former Allston golf course. The outfield dimensions were enormous. Gaffney, Bob Ruzzo has noted, "rejected the anomalies of geometry that characterized many competing venues." He didn't like the short fences in left field in Fenway Park and right field in the Phillies' ballpark, and he probably thought the same way about the inviting left- and right-field corners in the Polo Grounds. Gaffney believed (rightly so) that the game's most exciting play was the inside-the-park home run, and assumed his customers felt likewise. Although as yet the distances to various outfield points weren't painted on ballpark fences, as calculated at the time, the distances were 402.5' down the left-field line, the same to left-center field, 461' to the scoreboard in straightaway center field, 542' to the deepest point in the right-center-field corner, 400' to right-center, and 375' down the right-field line. Ty Cobb took one look at the outfield expanses and predicted nobody would ever hit a ball out of the park. F. C. Lane could hardly believe the size of the place: "As the observer stands on the diamond and gazes into the vast ocean of seats that swarm about him, he is lost in the immensity of the scene."[18]

Constructed entirely in steel and concrete (unlike Fenway Park, which had wooden sections), Braves Field had a seating capacity of about 41,000, which at that time exceeded the Polo Grounds by some 7,000. The single-decked grandstand, extending from first base around to third, seated 18,000; open pavilions flanked the grandstand, seating 10,000 and 9,000; and a smaller bleacher section (which came to be called the "Jury Box') was in right field, seating 4,500 at 25 cents per space. Each section of the stands had toilets (referred to as "retiring rooms") for both men and women. To make it as easy as possible for people to reach Braves Field, Gaffney got the Boston Elevated Railway System to run a rail spur from the Commonwealth Avenue station into a 600'–long concrete enclosure right at the entrance to the ballpark. When the game was over, fans could board one of the twenty trolley cars waiting for them on the spur and speedily return to the city's center.

On Wednesday, August 18, Governor David I. Walsh, Mayor James F. Curley, and the mayors of thirteen other New England cities were

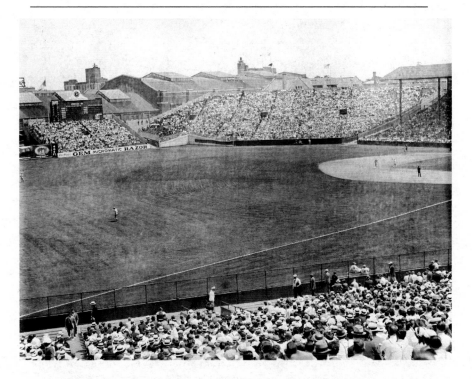

Braves Field. Although this photograph dates from 1932, and various modifications had been made to the outfield fences, the big right-field pavilion and the free-standing right-field bleachers (which became known as the "Jury Box") were as they looked when Braves Field opened in August 1915 (courtesy Boston Public Library).

present for Braves Field's inaugural game, along with some 4,000 other sufficiently prominent citizens and 10,000 or so Boston school children, let in free as guests of the ballclub. The paid attendance was around 32,000. *Sporting Life* called it "the biggest crowd that ever witnessed a baseball game."[19] Pregame ceremonies included the raising of the World Series championship flag, after which Clark Griffith threw out the first ball to Stallings, who played catcher, while Cardinals manager Miller Huggins stood at the plate and feigned a futile swing. After that, the first game in the history of Braves Field got underway.

St. Louis was in town for a three-game set. After a strong first-half showing, the Cardinals had fallen to seventh place. The inaugural game was the kind of low-scoring, closely played contest one could expect in such spacious surroundings. St. Louis mustered a single run on Dick Rudolph, while the Braves managed three on Slim Sallee. Playing his first game for Boston was outfielder Pete Compton. Compton had recently been the subject of litigation between the St. Louis Federals and Kansas City of the American Association. When financially strapped Kansas City couldn't meet its payroll, Compton claimed to be a free agent and jumped to the "Terriers." Kansas City's owner went into court and secured an injunction prohibiting Compton from playing for the Federals, then sold him to Boston.[20] Stallings also signed the veteran Fred Snodgrass, released by the Giants, and made him his regular center fielder, with Magee moving to left. Now the Braves' manager's only outfield rotation would be his three left-hand batting right fielders: Moran, Connolly, and Compton.

After Red Ames won the next day's game for St. Louis, 4–1, Tom Hughes had another fine outing, blanking the Cardinals and Lee Meadows on five hits, 1–0, to put the Braves back at .500. On Saturday the Braves met Pittsburgh in a doubleheader and got more good pitching from Rudolph, who topped left-hander Erv Kantlehner, 3–1, and even better pitching in the nightcap from Nehf, who shut out the Pirates and Al Mamaux, 2–0. After the idle Sunday, the Braves won again when Snodgrass, in his first game as a Brave, doubled in the deciding run in the eighth inning off Babe Adams. Hughes got the victory, 3–2, in relief of Tyler. The last game of the series was a 10–0 walkover and another shutout for Ragan. With Chicago having just dropped three of five games in Philadelphia, the Braves had taken over third place with a 58–54 mark, well within reach of Brooklyn (61–53) and the Phillies (60–50).

On the 25th, Rudolph and Chicago ace Hippo Vaughn met in still another tough matchup. The big left-hander surrendered only two runs, but that was more than enough for Rudolph, who recorded the Braves' third shutout in five days. A 4–4 rain-shortened tie set up a doubleheader on the 27th, which the teams divided. Having lost four of their last seven decisions, the Cubs left Boston all but out of pennant contention.

The Braves ended their stand against the western teams with four meetings with tail-end Cincinnati. The games were notable in that each was a shutout, and that Boston won the first three by identical 2–0 scores. On Saturday the 28th, Rudolph blanked the Reds, 2–0; in Monday's doubleheader, Nehf and Hughes did the same. But on Tuesday, Fred Toney held the Braves scoreless while the Reds got to Tyler for four runs. With the Red Sox in a tight pennant battle with Detroit in the American League, local baseball enthusiasts were getting excited about the prospect of an all–Boston World Series.

The Braves next entertained Brooklyn for three games, which gave them a ripe opportunity to dislodge the Robins from second place. In the series opener, on Thursday, September 2, the Braves made four first-inning errors, and the Robins sent six runners across the plate on Rudolph. It ended 10–1, an easy victory for Pfeffer. In that one-sided loss, Evers again got into hot water with the league president, and this time with his employer as well. In the sixth inning, with the score 9–0, Bill Byron, another old adversary, called Snodgrass out on strikes for the third out. Evers argued the call with Byron, then thumbed his nose at the umpire on his way to second base and, when Byron put him out of the game, kept up his nose-thumbing on his way to the dugout. Eddie Fitzpatrick jogged out to replace Evers and said something to Byron, who tossed him as well. Then Butch Schmidt got into it with the umpire and joined his teammates in the clubhouse.

That night Evers received Tener's telegram informing him of a five-day suspension. Gaffney supported Evers a month earlier after the fracas with Bob Emslie and Fred Clarke in Pittsburgh, but now he had run out of patience with a team captain whose irresponsible antics had cost the team his services, right when it stood a good chance at another pennant. Evers simply wouldn't be paid for those five days, Gaffney told the press.[21]

Having hardly exerted himself in the previous day's rout, Rudolph went back to the mound on the 3rd and held the Robins to three runs, while the Braves scored six. They gained second place the next day on Nehf's one-hit shutout, 6–0, with all the Boston runs scoring in the second inning on Jack Coombs. The young left-hander would have had a no-hitter if Pete Compton hadn't lost Otto Miller's fly ball to right field in the sun. The next man up hit into a double play, so Nehf ended up facing the minimum twenty-seven batters. The Braves left for a Labor Day doubleheader in New York, in second place by one percentage point but still four games behind Philadelphia.

A double defeat by the sixth-place Giants hurt badly, because in Brooklyn, the Phillies also lost both games to the Robins. In the Polo Grounds, Boston dropped the morning game, 5–2, Rube Benton (recently bought from Cincinnati) outpitching Hughes. In the afternoon, Tesreau received four-run support; Rudolph received nothing. The Braves came back on Tuesday to score seven runs on Perritt and Mathewson, while Ragan held New York to two. Brooklyn defeated the Phillies again on Phil Douglas's three-hitter, so that at dusk on September 7, Brooklyn trailed Philadelphia by only one game; the Braves were now three out of first.

His suspension served, Evers was back at second base when the Braves crossed the East River to Brooklyn for a doubleheader and a single game. Rube Marquard, discarded by New York a week earlier for the waiver price, started the first game and endured a bombardment that ended 12–1. Nehf was credited with the win, although he succumbed to the intense heat and gave way in the fifth inning to Hughes. The second game, matching young Jesse Barnes against the veteran Nap Rucker, also went to the Braves, 4–1, although Fitzgerald had to take over at shortstop after Maranville was spiked. The single game on Thursday the 9th was a stinging defeat. Tyler pitched one of the best games of his career but still lost to Pfeffer, 1–0. The lone run scored on an infield single on the one hit Tyler gave up. Meanwhile, the Phillies, back home, were in the process of sweeping four games from the Giants and putting them in the league cellar.

After Tyler's 1–0 loss, the Boston players dressed quickly, grabbed their already packed bags, and jumped into taxis to catch a train for Pittsburgh. Usually they would have had a travel day before starting play in the western cities, but on this occasion they had to make a 400–mile, 10–12 hour overnight trip—and play a doubleheader the next afternoon. Whereas in September 1914 the Braves had played twenty-six home games, this September their schedule had them on the road for the next fifteen days. Moreover, they began the western trip under strength. Various players were troubled by injuries. With Schmidt unable to play because of a spike wound, Snodgrass had moved to first base. Ragan was hampered by a sore finger on his pitching hand; Compton was hobbled by a sore leg. Maranville's spike wound was serious enough to keep him of the lineup for a week.

By the time the Braves arrived in Pittsburgh, Fred Clarke had announced that effective at season's end, he was resigning as Pirates manager, after a twenty-one-year National League career as player and player-manager.[22] Although Stallings and his players couldn't have been much rested for the doubleheader, they managed a split, then, presumably after a good night's sleep, won again the next day. From the "Smoky City," the Braves went to Chicago for four games.

Hughes was the winner in the opener, 8–1, while Philadelphia won in Pittsburgh. Brooklyn lost in St. Louis and dropped into a virtual tie for second place with Boston. On Sunday, September 12, the Braves lost 6–3 and again fell behind Brooklyn, which won in St. Louis. The Phillies, rained out in Pittsburgh, gained a half-game on Boston. All three contenders won on Monday, but on Tuesday, St. Louis rookie left-hander Charlie Boardman, in his only start of the season, downed Brooklyn's Marquard, 6–3; the Braves beat the Cubs, 7–1, behind Rudolph and occupied second place.[23] In Pittsburgh, the Phillies won their seventh game in a row, 4–3, on Cravath's home run over Forbes Field's left-field wall. On the 15th, the Pirates' Kantlehner shut out the Phillies on four hits to end their winning streak, but in Chicago, Phil Douglas, acquired from Brooklyn for cash a week earlier, baffled the Braves with his spitball. Pitching for his third National League team in 1915, Douglas threw a three-hit shutout and struck out ten. Lefty Tyler again pitched in tough luck, allowing only five hits but losing the decision 1–0 on Frank Schulte's eighth-inning home run over the right-field screen. Brooklyn had an off day, so that night the pennant race stood at Philadelphia, 76–57; Brooklyn, 73–62; Boston, 73–63.

At the end of that final game in West Side Park, Red Smith lived up to the reputation for hot-headedness that went with being red-haired. Having gone hitless, Smith accosted plate umpire Byron and exchanged angry words with him. Other players got between the two, but Byron dodged around them and took a couple of wild swings at Smith, whereupon Bill James pinned the arms of the much smaller Byron. Smith took some wild swings of his own before Al Orth, the other umpire, grabbed him. Smith was ready to fight Orth, too, until several teammates steered him to the visitors' dressing room through the home dugout. The few hundred people who lingered to watch the fray applauded Byron. He received more applause the next day, when he stood at the grandstand railing before the Cubs' game with Brooklyn and apologized to the spectators for his behavior.

Restraining Byron was about the most-useful thing Bill James had done for the Braves for months. Stallings decided there was no point in keeping him with the team, so he told him to go home to California and gave him train fare from St. Louis. A week or so later, in Cincinnati, Stallings received an itemized bill from James, asking reimbursement for $15 he had spent for meals en route. (Whether the Boston manager responded to the pitcher's meticulous accounting isn't known.)

In St. Louis, Maranville returned to the lineup for what was scheduled as a doubleheader and a single game. In the first game of the twin bill, on the 17th, the Braves were shut out, 1–0, for the second day in a row, wasting another scintillating performance by Art Nehf. The second game was called with the score 2–2. Gowdy wasn't around at the end, having been banished by Ernie Quigley sometime earlier.

In those two games, the Braves got their first look at a nineteen-year-old Texan purchased a couple of weeks earlier for $600 from Denison in the Class D Western Association. Nearly six feet tall but weighing only 135 pounds, Rogers Hornsby would be at shortstop for the remainder of the Cardinals' games, but he fielded erratically and was generally overmatched by big-league pitching. Next season, though, would be another story for the youngster.

Because of the tie, another doubleheader had to be played on Saturday the 18th. In the opener the Braves' bats broke loose in their biggest offensive outburst of the year, hammering Dan Griner and four successors for twenty runs on twenty-two hits, including three doubles and three triples. In the third inning, with Rudolph on the mound with an 11–0 lead, Bob Bescher grounded out to Sherwood Magee (now substituting for Schmidt at first base). Bescher wasn't happy about Rudolph's "quick" pitching—delivering the ball before the batter had reset himself from the previous pitch—a trick with which Rudolph had struck out four Cardinals in the first two innings.

Bescher, who was nearly four inches taller and thirty pounds heavier, charged Rudolph; the pair grappled and tumbled into the dirt until Hank O'Day, back to umpiring since the previous month, ordered both from the game. As was usually the case in baseball fights, nobody was hurt. Three Boston players escorted Rudolph to the visitors' clubhouse, where a couple of policemen took over to ensure he and Bescher didn't go at it again. Barnes pitched the rest of the way, giving up one run. Ragan worked the nightcap and defeated Sallee, 6–3. The Braves had gained a half-game on Brooklyn and Philadelphia, which won their games in Chicago and Cincinnati, respectively.

Again the behavior of Stallings and his men brought censure from foreign quarters. The *Sporting News*, by way of editorially condemning the ugly conduct of the crowds at Fenway Park in the recent Red Sox–Detroit series, also took a swipe at the Braves: "Most of the season—to say nothing of last season—the Boston Nationals have been in bad odor[,] and perhaps no more unpopular team has been seen upon the field than the obstreperous Braves, with their billingsgate for opposing players and their bickering with umpires." From Chicago, Sy Sanborn partly blamed Red Sox manager Bill Carrigan for the hostile atmosphere that met visiting teams in Fenway Park, but he blamed Stallings even more. "The addition of Stallings' personality," Sanborn wrote, "made the Braves the most obnoxious aggregation of players that has performed before the public in recent years. At the start of the season the Braves were such a chesty lot they tried to ride roughshod over every opponent and all the umpires." Sanborn quoted Roger Bresnahan that all it took to beat the Braves was for pitchers to keep the ball low. They couldn't see it below their waists "because their chests stick out so far."[24]

The Braves played three games in Cincinnati, winning two, losing one. Rudolph came back from his tussle with Bescher to pitch well, topping Pete Schneider, 3–2. That put the Braves in a tie for second place with idle Brooklyn. In St. Louis, the Phillies split a doubleheader, Alexander winning for the third time in the past week in the opener. On the 20th, Fred Toney defeated the Braves on three hits, 4–1. Hughes left with the score 2–1; Barnes gave up the other two runs, aided by Evers's muff of Buck Herzog's line drive. The Phillies were rained out in St. Louis; Brooklyn lost, 1–0, in Pittsburgh. Stallings started Barnes the next day; the young right-hander came through with a 4–2 win. In St. Louis, the Phillies swept a doubleheader; rain prevented Brooklyn's game in Pittsburgh. Philadelphia was now 81–59, Boston was 76–65, and Brooklyn was 75–65.

The Braves wound up their western trip with a second stop in Pittsburgh, this time for three games. They could ill afford the 8–4 drubbing they took on September 23 in the first of the series. Brooklyn won in Cincinnati, while in Chicago the Phillies won their second doubleheader in a row, with Alexander notching his thirtieth victory and thus earning a $1,000 bonus Philadelphia president Baker had promised him. Boston won the other two games in Pittsburgh. Nehf continued his remarkable work, shutting out the Pirates, 2–0, both runs scoring in the top of the ninth inning on Kantlehner. The Braves won the series finale by scoring five runs in the first five innings on Bob Harmon. Tyler left in the third inning after giving up four hits and a run; Hughes relieved him and held the Pirates to one run the rest of the way. Philadelphia won its remaining two games in Chicago; Brooklyn won and lost in its last two in Cincinnati, leaving the standings Philadelphia, 85–60; Boston, 78–66; Brooklyn, 78–68. So as the three contenders headed back east to close the season, the Phillies led the Braves by a comfortable six and a half games, the Robins by a half-game more. Philadelphia had seven games remaining, Boston eight, Brooklyn 6.

Rain across the east kept the Braves idle for two days. The Phillies and Robins got in one game, at Ebbets Field, which Philadelphia won, 6–4, with George Chalmers benefitting from four Brooklyn errors. That was the twenty-sixth victory in the last thirty-six games for Pat Moran's team, and put them one win and one Boston loss from the pennant. That would happen the next day in Braves Field.

Appropriately enough, Thursday, September 29, was Pat Moran Day, arranged by people from his home town of Fitchburg, Massachusetts. Governor Walsh was also on hand to honor his old Fitchburg schoolmate with the customary floral horseshoe. Several Red Sox players, having all but clinched the American League pennant, were in the Braves Field grandstand looking over their presumed World Series opponents. With the ceremonies out of the way, the Phillies won the pennant-clincher. Alexander shut out the defending champions on one hit, 5–0, for his thirty-first victory of the season. The game was effectively decided in the top of the first inning, when Cravath slammed a three-run home run to the distant outfield expanses off Dick Rudolph. That evening the city of Philadelphia could celebrate its first-ever National League pennant; Boston could forget about an all–Boston World Series.

As he left the field late that afternoon, Sherwood Magee must have considered his ill fortune. Had he remained at Philadelphia, he could have fulfilled his ambition to play on a pennant-winner, and could also look forward to a nice World Series check. By contrast, George Whitted, who had put in a solid year as the Phillies' regular center fielder, must

Grover Cleveland Alexander. The greatest National League pitcher of his time (George Bantham Bain Collection, Library of Congress).

have considered his good fortune. He hadn't wanted to leave the Braves, but he was about to get his second Series check. Oscar Dugey must have considered himself even more fortunate. Although he had played sparingly and done little at bat when he did play, he also was in line for a hefty addition to his season's salary.

In his report on the game in the *Sporting News,* Tim Murnane was whimsical: "The Braves were present, of course, like the turkey was on Thanksgiving. They looked like a much different team from what they did last fall at this time. They showed no pepper, and went down and out without a kick."[25] The Braves still had seven games to play, all in Braves Field, including two with Philadelphia and five with the Giants. Three years later, the National Commission would direct that the second-, third-, and fourth-place teams would share proportionately in the World Series money (changed to second and third in 1919), but in 1915 it was second place and nothing else at stake for the Braves. At least for George Stallings, that was enough. As always, he intended to keep his players hustling.

While the Phillies were clinching the pennant in Braves Field, Brooklyn was also winning in New York. The next day the Braves drove out Eppa Rixey and gained an 8–2 win for Hughes; in the Polo Grounds, Jeff Tesreau shut out the Robins. On Saturday, October 1, Nehf finally had a bad game, losing 9–2 to Erskine Mayer, while the game in New York was rained out. Two days of rain prevented the Braves and Giants from playing in Boston; three rainy days kept Brooklyn off the field in Philadelphia.

When the four teams finally got to play on Monday the 4th, Jeff Pfeffer outdueled the Phillies' Hugh McQuillan, 3–2, in a game taking only an hour and three minutes, while the Braves beat the Giants in both games of a doubleheader. Tyler pitched a nice 4–1 game to top Pol Perritt; in the nightcap, Rudolph and Rube Benton battled for twelve innings, each giving up four runs, until Moran scored when catcher Bobby Schang's attempted pickoff throw hit him in the back.[26] John McGraw sat in the Braves Field grandstand during both games. After watching another dreary afternoon of baseball, he got into an altercation with a spectator named Walter E. Jackson. When Jackson called a policeman, McGraw retreated to the Braves' clubhouse, where the officer of the law found him but declined to arrest him.

More rain in Boston and Philadelphia washed out the Tuesday games. On Wednesday the Phillies ended their season on a high note, sweeping two games from Brooklyn. The Braves also took two quickly played games from New York, both by 1–0 scores. Hughes won over Emilio Palmero, a slender, twenty-year-old Cuban left-hander McGraw was giving a trial; Ragan shut out the Giants and Tesreau. On October 7, a sparse crowd scattered around the 40,000–plus seats of Braves Field watched the Giants win 15–8, with both managers playing several substitutes. Ralph Stroud and George Davis pitched all the way, Stroud giving up seventeen hits, Davis twenty-four. Larry Doyle, the Giants' veteran second baseman, collected four hits to claim the National League batting title at .320, the lowest winning average in any major league up to then.

Final standings: Philadelphia 90–62, Boston 83–69, Brooklyn 80–72. The Phillies' ninety wins were the fewest for a National League champion since both major leagues adopted a 154–game schedule in 1904. The other five teams finished in a tight cluster: Chicago (73–80),

Pittsburgh (73–81), St. Louis (72–81), Cincinnati (71–83), New York (69–83).

From July 9, when the Braves began a home stand with St. Louis, they played at a .612 pace, which would have been good enough to win another pennant if they hadn't gone through that slump in June and the beginning of July and, despite Stallings's assurance, waited until July to get really started. Of course two years earlier, a second-place finish would have delighted Boston's National League fandom, but after the spectacular 1914 season, and given preponderant preseason opinion (Bill Phelon's being an exception) that the Braves would repeat, it was a deep disappointment for people who had been quickly spoiled to having a winner.

Boston finished in second place as a consequence of a 14–8 record versus Brooklyn, but against Philadelphia they won only seven of twenty-one games and, oddly, lost nine of twenty-one to St. Louis. The Braves' .240 team batting average was the lowest in the National League, although only St. Louis and Philadelphia scored more runs. Joe Connolly's .298 again led the team, but he batted officially only 303 times. Sherwood Magee had the most official at bats (571), hit a respectable .280 with 87 runs driven in, and had 34 doubles, but he hit only two home runs. Red Smith's average fell to .264, although he tied Magee in doubles.

Rudolph pitched 341 innings (to Alexander's 376), had 30 complete games (to Alexander's 36), and won 22 times; but he also led the league in losses (19). Tom Hughes led the majors in mound appearances (50) and posted a 16–14 record; Pat Ragan's record was 15–12; Tyler's was a mediocre 10–9 in just over 200 innings. Art Nehf's record was 5–4 in his ten starts; Jesse Barnes started three games, completed two, relieved in six, and finished with a perfect 4–0 record. Bill James pitched thirteen times, winning five and losing four before leaving for home.

At the end of the season, Stallings had only twelve players who had been with him a year earlier: Evers, Maranville, Smith, Connolly, Moran, Gowdy, Rudolph, Tyler, Davis, Hughes, Schmidt (who played little the last month of the season), and Bert Whaling (who did much of the late-season catching in place of the slumping Gowdy). Of course the previous winter the National League owners had voted to lop off four roster positions per team, and a couple of Braves defected to the Federal League. Still, for a World Series winner, the attrition had been extraordinary.

Tim Murnane offered a tongue-in-cheek explanation for the Braves' comedown: "I found the Braves were not liked by the other teams in the National League and this was bound to handicap their chances, which it did." The *Pittsburgh Press*' Ralph Davis explained it more straightforwardly, in terms of James's debility and "the failure of Evers to quit his senseless kicking and keep himself in the lineup." Bill Phelon agreed that, coming when it did, Evers's five-day suspension in September was critical, as was James's failure to contribute much. But Phelon put more emphasis on Evers's absence from the lineup for more than half the season, Tyler's frequent unreliability, Eddie Fitzpatrick's inability to hit better than .221 in the 105 games he divided between the infield and the outfield, and the Braves' doubleheader loss to the Giants on Labor Day.[27]

Evers's broken ankle and his various suspensions kept him out of the lineup for eighty-three of the team's 157 games (which included five ties). But the Trojan was never one to apologize for his erratic and often outrageous behavior on the ball field and his self-absorbed, sometimes neurotic behavior away from it. Nor was he reluctant to speak his mind on whatever occurred to him.

After the Phillies clinched the pennant, Evers quickly attributed their success to his old teammate Pat Moran. A couple of writers submitted that Moran had learned his baseball from Frank Chance; in response to that, Evers took a gratuitous swipe at his former manager, with whom his relations at Chicago had become increasingly strained. "When it comes down to brass tacks," he told an interviewer, "the idea of anyone learning baseball from Frank Chance is foolish enough, but for a man of Moran's baseball brains it is preposterous…. I don't give Chance the credit for any managerial ability because I don't think he has any."[28] So much for a man who had led Evers and the Cubs to four pennants and two World Series victories in five seasons.

For John McGraw, it had been a bad year all around. Although three and a half games from the first division might look like a respectable last-place, it was still last place—the first time a McGraw team had finished there in a full season.[29] Moreover, on the morning of October 6, before the second doubleheader with Boston that afternoon, several Giants players had to testify in justice of the peace court in suburban Brighton, where Walter E. Jackson had filed a complaint claiming McGraw had threatened him with a pen knife during their set-to at the end of the games on the 4th. The magistrate listened to the players and, perhaps taking into consideration that McGraw's weapon had been less than lethal, refused to issue an order for his arrest.

In the offseason McGraw would seek to add enough talent to bring the New York team back to its former eminence. George Stallings would do the same in an effort to recapture the glory of 1914. But whatever McGraw and Stallings were doing between October and March was overshadowed by maneuverings culminating in the restoration of the pre–Federal League baseball order, as well as by the fact that in 1916, Stallings and his players would be working for different people.

7

1915–1916: "Come on; start the Percycution"

The 1915 Philadelphia Phillies were a good team, featuring the National League's finest pitcher in Grover Cleveland Alexander, whose thirty-one wins were the most in the major leagues that year and the most in his league since Christy Mathewson's thirty-seven in 1908. The Phillies batted only .247 as a team, but Alexander and the rest of the staff allowed the fewest runs (463) in either major league and pitched twenty shutouts, twelve by the man now inevitably referred to as "Alexander the Great." In Gavvy Cravath, the Phillies also had the foremost power hitter in the game. Cravath's twenty-four home runs were the most anybody had hit so far in the century, and he also drove in a majors-best 114 runs. But the Boston Red Sox possessed a superb outfield trio in Duffy Lewis, Harry Hooper, and the incomparable Tris Speaker; and Boston's pitching was deeper and mostly younger, including twenty-year-old Babe Ruth, who won eighteen games in his first full big-league season. The Braves' sweep of the Athletics a year earlier had broken a run of four-consecutive American League World Series victories, but in 1915 things returned to form.

As Joseph Lannin had made Fenway Park available to the Braves for the Series games in Boston, so now Jim Gaffney (no doubt for a nice percentage of the gate) returned the favor to the Red Sox. The capacity crowds for the games in Braves Field would be the largest in the history of the October spectacle up to that time. Alexander pitched beautifully to win the Series opener, 3–1, played in Philadelphia on Friday, October 8, but that would be it for the National League champions. With President Woodrow Wilson in attendance for the second game, Boston won by the same score on George Foster's three-hitter. The Red Sox won the next two games, in Braves Field, then finished off the Series back in

134

Philadelphia, winning 5–4 on Harry Hooper's ninth-inning home run, his second of the game, off Eppa Rixey.

Meanwhile Frank Bancroft organized another post-season exhibition tour of National and American Leaguers, which this time Evers joined. Prominent National Leaguers who went along for the second time included Philadelphia's Alexander, Brooklyn's Jeff Pfeffer, and Pittsburgh's Max Carey. Sherwood Magee also made the tour, as did such American Leaguers as Philadelphia's Amos Strunk and Wally Schang, Boston's Dick Hoblitzell and Heinie Wagner, and again the other Bill James, now with Detroit. It was a less-ambitious venture than the one the previous fall. The teams again traveled north, northwest, and then down through California, but they didn't make it to Hawaii again. While they were riding trains and playing in little places and big places, back east momentous changes were brewing.

In its second season, the Federal League had produced an even tighter pennant race than the Chicago-Indianapolis battle in 1914. Chicago won by the narrowest margin any pennant has ever been won in any league billing itself as "major." The "Whales," as Joe Tinker's team was called, finished with an 86–56 (.5657) record to St. Louis's 87–57 (.5649) and Pittsburgh's 86–57 (.562). Chicago's George McConnell, a thirty-eight-year-old spitballer and former American League journeyman, paced the league's pitchers with twenty-five wins; for St. Louis, former Cardinal Dave Davenport won twenty-two; former Giant Otis Crandall, twenty-one; and the venerable Eddie Plank, a like number. For Pittsburgh, former Brooklyn moundsmen Frank Allen and Elmer Knetzer had twenty-one and eighteen wins, respectively. Yet for all the drama of the pennant race, most Federal League clubs ended the season in even worse financial condition than a year earlier.

Things might have worked out differently if the Federal League had landed Walter Johnson—to stay. Although Johnson was manifestly underpaid and heavily courted by the Federal agents, he remained with Washington during the 1914 season, winning twenty-eight games and, as usual, leading all hurlers in strikeouts and innings pitched. But after that season Johnson finally succumbed to Charles Weeghman's blandishments and signed with the Chicago Federals for a big increase. Then, accompanied by a torrent of publicity, he jumped back to his old club and stayed there (with the National Commission obviously making an exception to its rule against re-signing players under contract in the Federal League). Johnson's decision to return to Organized Baseball, Bob Ruzzo has contended, was a critical factor in the ultimate failure of the Federal League enterprise. Another factor Ruzzo cites was the untimely death in the fall of 1914 of Robert B. Ward, who was not only co-owner of the Brooklyn Federals but the financial benefactor of various other teams in the league. Still another was bitter opposition to the Federal League on the part of J. G. Taylor Spink, publisher of the influential *Sporting News*.[1]

Although aggregate attendance in the National and American leagues had improved over 1914 by about 300,000, that was still 1.5 million below 1913. Eight lower minor leagues had disbanded during the season. The four American Association and International League clubs that had to compete with the Federals continued to suffer at the gate; matters got so bad in Baltimore that the team moved to Richmond, Virginia, to play out its schedule. So by the fall of 1915 just about everybody—even Ban Johnson, who had called for a fight to the death with the "invaders"— was ready to cut losses and settle baseball's sixth "war" since 1882.[2]

Preliminary talks took place during the World Series between the three members of the National Commission and Federal League president James Gilmore, plus Harry Sinclair, owner of the Newark Federals, and Phil Ball, who held a majority of stock in the St. Louis Federals. The Federal owners then got Kenesaw Mountain Landis, judge for the federal district of northern Illinois, to dismiss their antitrust suit against Organized Baseball. Landis was happy to oblige, inasmuch as he had sat on the case for a year and a half in anticipation that baseball's bigwigs would eventually come to terms.

The deal was made in meetings in New York at the Waldorf Hotel in mid–December and tidied up a little later in Cincinnati. Sinclair, who had more money than anybody else, kept things moving in the right direction. The final agreement—signed for Organized Baseball by the three members of the National Commission and for the Federal League by Gilmore, Weeghman, Sinclair, and Pittsburgh's Edward Gwinner— provided that Ball could buy out Robert Hedges, owner of the St. Louis Browns, and Weeghman could purchase Charles P. Taft's 90 percent interest in the Chicago Cubs. Always a high roller, Weeghman had to borrow most of the $500,000 he paid Taft.

The Federal League dissolved in exchange for a payment from Organized Baseball of close to $500,000, to be divided among the league's eight groups of investors. Kansas City, Newark, Buffalo, and Baltimore reverted to being solely minor-league towns. Organized Baseball abandoned its threat to black-list players who had jumped to the Federals and, at least implicitly, recognized the validity of Federal League contracts by stipulating its clubs could sell players to whoever was willing to buy them. But the players would sign with their new teams for what their Federal League contracts—in some cases long-term ones—specified they were to be paid. The National and American league owners ended up paying $129,500 for those contracts.

Sinclair purchased the contracts of the Kansas City, Buffalo, and Brooklyn players and sold the long-sought-after Benny Kauff and others to the New York Giants for $48,500. Weeghman and Ball simply amalgamated their Chicago and St. Louis rosters and also kept Joe Tinker and Fielder Jones, their Federal League managers.[3] Additionally, the club owners in each league agreed to lift the roster limits (twenty-five in the

Federal League president James Gilmore and Chicago Whales owner Charles Weeghman. Although their enterprise failed, Weeghman, builder of what became Wrigley Field, ended up owning the Chicago Cubs (George Bantham Bain Collection, Library of Congress).

American League, still twenty-one in the National League) for the Chicago and St. Louis teams, on the assumption that Tinker and Jones needed in-season time to sort out their players. The Browns would continue to play in Sportsman's Park, which Phil Ball also purchased from Robert Hedges, while Weeghman announced the Cubs would abandon aging West Side Park for his two-year-old steel-and-concrete ballpark on Chicago's north side.

The Baltimore group wanted to buy the penurious St. Louis Cardinals; Helene Robison Britton, who had inherited the franchise from her uncle, was ready to unload it. But opposition from the National Commission, especially from Garry Herrmann, and from Edward G. Barrow, president of the International League, closed them out. The angry Baltimore investors spurned their share of the buyout money and filed their own antitrust suit against Organized Baseball. After successive verdicts and appeals in the lower federal courts, the case reached the U.S. Supreme Court, which in 1922 ruled against the Baltimore suit and handed down its historic judgment exempting Organized Baseball from the antitrust laws.

In the early fall, George Stallings, again probably at Jim Gaffney's direction, sent a letter to all Braves players under reserve, admonishing them against continuing their on-field rowdiness during the coming season. Whether or not Gaffney had stopped the practice in 1915, Stallings advised his players that the club would pay no more fines; the money would be deducted from their paychecks. He may have known a settlement with the Federal League was in the offing, and that a substantial number of that league's players would be on the market. So he began making changes in his personnel, sending Herbie Moran and Bert Whaling to the Pacific Coast League's Vernon club in exchange for Joe Wilhoit, a thirty-year-old outfielder who had batted .325 the past season. In 1916, he said, there would be many new faces on the Braves, which prompted Eddie Fitzgerald to quip: "All right, I'll grow a beard during the winter."[4]

From the annual major-league meetings in New York (where of course the big news was the settlement with the Federals), Stallings went to Boston. There he made the surprising statement that he would like to trade Rabbit Maranville for Cincinnati player-manager Buck Herzog. Stallings may have been joking, although if so, he didn't explain that. If he was serious, then what he said didn't make a great deal of sense. Thirty years old and a veteran of eight National League seasons with the Giants, Boston, and Cincinnati, Herzog could play shortstop, second and third base, and even some outfield. He was also a better hitter than Maranville, who in three full seasons hadn't batted above .247 (which he did in 1913). Yet Maranville, still only twenty-two, was generally regarded as the best shortstop in the National League if not in both leagues; two years earlier Stallings had even proclaimed him (with more than a modicum of exaggeration) the greatest player to come into the majors since Ty Cobb. Rabbit was also the favorite of the Braves' fans. Whatever Stallings had meant when he talked about trading Maranville, nothing came of it. Come Opening Day, Maranville would still be the Braves' shortstop; Herzog would again be trying to get the Reds out of the league's nether region.

A couple of weeks later, on January 8, 1916, the second big baseball story of the winter broke. Jim Gaffney was ready to get out of the baseball business. The Braves' 1915 home attendance of 376,283, though about six-thousand short of 1914's, was still the second-highest total in the forty-year history of the Boston National League franchise and the third-highest in the league.[5] Gaffney must have made at least a modest profit. Yet he knew that to continue to be competitive, the Braves would have to take on some ex–Federal Leaguers and pay them at the inflated levels their contracts called for. Gaffney was first and last a business man, not a "sportsman," as other baseball investors liked to see themselves. Offered a good deal, he took it.

When the sale was announced, Gaffney posed for the press with Percy Haughton, the celebrated Harvard football coach; Gaffney's partner Robert H. Davis; and Arthur Wise, the banker who had arranged financing for the construction of Braves Field, and who now became the club's vice president. Haughton would be its president, but he was only part of a syndicate that included Governor David I. Walsh and various other prominent politicians and bankers. Stallings retained his small amount of stock, as did Walter P. Hapgood, who had become the club's business manager the previous summer after Herman Nickerson went back to sports-writing. Six days later, the final papers were signed. Although Gaffney never publicly disclosed how much money he received, according to Harold Kaese, "He admitted selling the Braves for a lot more than the $187,000 he had paid for the team four years earlier."[6] Estimates of the amount in the baseball press ranged as high as $500,000. The sale didn't include Braves Field, which continued to be owned by the Commonwealth Realty Trust. Gaffney's thirty-three-year lease on the ballpark was transferred to Haughton and associates.

Although Percy Haughton had also coached the Harvard baseball squad a year earlier, his renown was in college football; he had no previous connection to professional baseball. Yet "in Boston," Kaese has written, "it was taken for granted that anything he tackled would be a success." A writer for the *Chicago Herald*, however, poked fun at the Braves' new president, asking "What ought to be the name of a big league ball team owned by a magnate whose first name is Percy?" He urged "Chicago bugs" to send suggestions for re-naming the Braves to the sports editor of the *Herald*. "Come on; start the Percycution."[7]

On January 17, while National League officials and owners convened in New York to celebrate the fiftieth anniversary of the league's founding, Stallings and Haughton talked over things at Braves Field before going to lunch at the Copley Plaza hotel. Afterward Haughton told newsmen he agreed with Stallings's plans for bringing in new players. In his syndicated column, Christy Mathewson related that Johnny Evers had come down from Troy to meet the Braves new president. At Haughton's and Stallings's request, Evers agreed to sell the minority interest in the Troy New York State club he had acquired a couple of years earlier.

Evers's assessment of Haughton, as Mathewson quoted him, was that "He hasn't any Harvard manners," which the Trojan intended as a compliment. After observing Haughton eating an onion sandwich in Garry Herrmann's hotel room at three in the morning, Evers said, "I don't believe he is a real Harvard guy." On the same occasion, Mathewson asked Stallings, "Is he [Haughton] going to let you run the club?" Stallings replied in his usual blunt manner: "When they start to tell me what to do, I quit. That was the trouble with Frank Farrell and Hal Chase when I was trying to manage the Yankees to a championship."[8]

Stallings claimed he had made $300,000 for Gaffney, yet he hadn't heard a word from him since he sold the ball club. (If Stallings referred to gross receipts, the figure was probably pretty accurate; if he meant clear profits, he greatly exaggerated.) The Braves' manager added he wasn't happy that before the sale, Gaffney had made arrangements for the team to move from Macon, close to Stallings's plantation, and do its spring training in faraway Miami. But if he was miffed about the new training site, he was no doubt mollified when, after returning to Boston from Haddock for more talks with Haughton, he revealed he had received a five-year extension on his manager's contract and a boost to $15,000 per year. He was also made a member of the Braves' new board of directors. During a stopover in New York, he said he was after several ex–Federal Leaguers.

Then he got the bad news that Butch Schmidt, at twenty-nine, was retiring from baseball to give full attention to the Baltimore butcher shop he owned, and where he had worked since the age of thirteen. A profile of Schmidt as "the player-worker," written by John J. Ward, proved ill-timed. It appeared in *Baseball Magazine* in March.[9] Although Schmidt told Ward he considered the grind of the baseball season a "vacation" from his off-season schedule—getting up at 4 a.m. six days a week to open the shop and get it ready for customers—he knew his baseball days were numbered. The 1916 season would have been the last under his two-year contract for $5,000 per year. The big Marylander said he was worried about a salary cut after the contract ended, adding that he wanted to be a full-time husband and full-time father to his young son. Although injuries had kept Schmidt out of thirty games in 1915, Stallings had been counting on him to be at first base on Opening Day, thus keeping intact the infield the Braves had fielded since August 1914.

So Stallings needed a first baseman. Early in February, he phoned Edward Gwinner in Pittsburgh to talk about buying Ed Konetchy, who had put in seven years in the National League with St. Louis before being traded to Pittsburgh in 1914. After winning fifteen of their first seventeen games that season, the Pirates had finished in seventh place. That infuriated owner Barney Dreyfuss, who blamed courting Federal League agents and also Konetchy and his slump to .249. Facing a salary cut or another trade, Konetchy had jumped from the Pirates to play in the same city for Gwinner's "Rebels."

Almost invariably referred to as "Big Ed," the 6'2½" inch, 200–pound Konetchy, a right-handed batter and fielder, had been one of the most-productive hitters in the Federal League in 1915, with a .314 batting average, ten home runs, thirty one doubles, eighteen triples, and ninety-three runs driven in. He had two more years to go on a contract that paid him $7,500 per year. Gwinner put his price for "Koney" (as he was abbreviated in box scores) at $15,000, which was too rich for Stallings. The Boston manager made another call to Schmidt, asking him to come to New York to talk about playing one more season. No, Schmidt replied, his decision was final.

Two weeks later Gwinner and Stallings met in New York and came to terms. Gwinner agreed to sell Konetchy, plus pitchers Elmer Knetzer and Frank Allen, for a total of $18,000. Percy Haughton and associates would have to honor Konetchy's Federal League contract through 1917, but Allen's contract for $5,500 and Knetzer's for $4,500 would expire at the end of the 1916 season.

In his syndicated column, Grantland Rice reported Stallings had ordered his players to stay out of automobiles until the coming season ended. Rice himself was convinced "automobiling" was bad for baseball players, because they rode around at night and visited roadhouses, and because driving into the wind (in the open vehicles of the time) affected their eyesight. (Meanwhile, Maranville acceded to Haughton's plea that he not join a touring basketball team, as he had in previous off-seasons.)

Rice also quoted Stallings as saying he now had six good pitchers, and he thought the 1916 Braves would be the best team he had ever managed. In Rice's view, the infield of Konetchy, Evers, Maranville, and Red Smith was preeminent in the major leagues. At that point, according to Rice, the betting odds were 11–5 on the Braves to win the pennant. But Tim Murnane was skeptical of the Braves' chances. For one thing, Murnane didn't think Konetchy was in a class with Butch Schmidt. As for the rest of the team, "I know of no one but Stallings ... that could hope to develop a winner out of the material the Braves have at hand."[10]

Frederick G. Lieb of the *New York Press* pointed out that the Braves were a different outfit from the team that won it all in 1914. Among the outfielders, only Joe Connolly remained. All of that season's pitchers were now in the minor leagues, with the exception of Dick Rudolph, George Tyler, and Bill James and Paul Strand—the last two being of doubtful status. Stallings expected George Davis, who was finishing his Harvard law degree, to report late in June, as usual. Davis, though, decided to retire from baseball and pursue a legal career full time. After his sensational World Series performance, Hank Gowdy had returned

Charles "Butch" Schmidt. The 1914 Braves' stalwart first baseman, Schmidt would quit baseball a year later at twenty-nine (George Bantham Bain Collection, Library of Congress).

to his normal output, batting .247, one point higher than in 1914, in 118 games. Lieb didn't think much of the lanky backstop, remarking sarcastically, "Gowdy, the wonderful maskman of last winter, now is regarded so high that Haughton and Stallings are running amuck trying to get a catcher."[11]

Stallings spent the early part of March at Haddock. A year and a half earlier, he had hired Bayard "Bud" Sharpe—whom he had managed in the minors between Sharpe's stints as an outfielder in 1906 and 1910 with Boston and Pittsburgh—to live on the plantation with his wife Bertha and generally run things for him. Stallings's guest at Haddock on this occasion was Sam Crane, a sixty-one-year-old, onetime major-leaguer, who wrote for William Randolph Hearst's *New York Evening Journal*. Crane watched as Stallings and Sharpe supervised the loading and carting of five-hundred bales of cotton that had been stored over the winter, until Stallings got the price he wanted.

Crane was a native of Massachusetts, but as with the "Frolic of the Braves" playlet staged in Boston in the fall of 1914, what he reported from Haddock invoked the stereotypes of black Americans then common among white Americans, regardless of one's background. Crane wrote that Stallings considered all the black people on his plantation as "'his children' and looks after the welfare of the happy-go-lucky darkies as if they were not paid employees." When the work was done that night, Crane witnessed "a negro frolic," with "old Aunt Josephine," born a slave, joining in the dancing. A wedding between a young man and woman also took place; Crane described "the dusky beaus, matrons and maidens," all decked in their finest apparel.[12]

After winding up his business at Haddock and notifying all the married Braves not to bring their wives to Miami, Stallings left for the southernmost site where any team had done spring training up to then. Stallings traveled most of the nearly six-hundred miles from Macon to Miami on the Florida East Coast Railroad, the extension of which to Miami had been financed by Henry Flagler, John D. Rockefeller's partner in Standard Oil, and completed in 1896. The draining of much of the Everglades swamp and the construction of various canals connecting to the Miami River had created a small-scale land boom. Having grown to about seven thousand people, Miami had already become a winter destination for affluent northerners, who stayed at Flagler's posh Royal Palm Hotel. The five-story hotel had 450 guest rooms and suites, one hundred of which were furnished with private baths—an impressive number in those days. Haughton and associates intended to follow Gaffney's policy of putting up the Braves in the best accommodations available, so that's also where they lodged in Miami.

Otherwise Miami wasn't yet much of a town. Twelfth (later Flagler) Street was lined with business establishments, including five-story Burdine's Department Store; but many of the streets were unpaved, especially in the black "quarter." Miami had no professional baseball; white and black semipro teams provided the local baseball entertainment. The baseball field on which the Braves practiced had a skinned diamond and a rough outfield, with spectator accommodations consisting of a couple of rickety bleachers. So apart from climate and lodging, Miami didn't offer much to a major-league baseball team.

Most of the Braves had come down by steamer to Savannah, then to Miami. It had been a rough passage; much of the way the vessel was buffeted by storms, which made for general seasickness. So the players were pretty worn down when, as ordered by Stallings, they took the practice field the morning after their arrival. Bill James, whose contract still had a year to run, made the long trip from California and tried to pitch, but he could put nothing on the ball. "His arm is gone," Johnny Evers said. "Bill knows it and we know it."[13]

Inasmuch as he couldn't depend on James, Stallings eventually filled out his pitching staff with thirty-three-year-old Ed Reulbach. Released by Brooklyn owner Charles Ebbets after the 1914 season, Reulbach had signed with the Newark Federals and posted twenty wins for a fifth-place team. Failing to come to terms with Reulbach, Pittsburgh's Barney Dreyfuss returned his contract to Harry Sinclair. Learning that Stallings wanted him, Reulbach joined the Braves in Miami and began rounding into shape, although it wasn't until Opening Day that Reulbach's status was finally settled. John Tener, Dreyfuss, Haughton, and Pat T. Powers, Sinclair's partner in the Newark franchise, met in Tener's New York office and reached an agreement that the Braves could have the pitcher.

Throughout 1915, Imperial Germany's Atlantic submarine campaign—which involved the sinking not only of British and French warships but merchant and passenger ships and more deaths of U.S. citizens—kept tensions between Washington and Berlin at a high level. At the same time, the Wilson administration repeatedly protested the British navy's interference in U.S. trade with European neutral countries. By the spring of 1916, Germany had agreed to restrict its submarine attacks to British and French warships, thereby somewhat moderating its relations with the U.S.—for the time being. His Majesty's government continued to inspect and delay cargoes bound for the Continent from U.S. ports, at the same time that U.S. agricultural, industrial, and financial interests acquired a bigger and bigger stake in a British and French victory.

Now, however, the United States found itself close to war with Mexico, which had been in turmoil since the overthrow of the dictator Porfirio Diaz in 1910. Various armed bands battled government troops as well as each other. In the north, a private army led by the bandit *caudillo* Francisco "Pancho" Villa raided towns along the U.S.–Mexican border and killed American citizens. On March 18, 1916, President Wilson ordered General John J. Pershing to lead an expeditionary force into northern Mexico, with the objective of capturing Villa. After penetrating three-hundred miles into the country, Pershing's force still hadn't found Villa, but in the confused circumstances in the region, it fought several small engagements with Mexican army troops (*"Federales"*). By then Mexican President Venustiano Carranza was denouncing Pershing's expedition as an invasion. Fearing a full-scale conflict, the Wilson administration ordered Pershing to pull his troops back near the border. While Miami was a long way from what was happening in northern Mexico, in the state of Texas, where the Cardinals, Giants, Browns, White Sox, and Tigers were all training, plenty of people stayed anxious about the situation.[14]

Chandler Richter, touring the southern training camps for *Sporting Life*, hailed the Braves as being in better condition than any he had seen that spring. "Johnny Evers is in wonderful shape," Richter reported. "We have never seen the Trojan in such good health and good humor." Richter compared newcomer Joe Wilhoit to the Cubs hard-hitting Cy Williams, observing that he was as tall as Williams but faster. Wilhoit and Sherwood Magee, thought Richter, would be Stallings's everyday outfielders, while Fred Snodgrass, Joe Connolly, Pete Compton, and Zip Collins (who had appeared in five games in September after being picked up from Pittsburgh for cash) would compete for the third outfield position. After watching the Braves win three in a row from the hapless Athletics, who had come all the way down from their training base at Jacksonville, Richter enthused, "The team is playing August ball in March." Harry Davis, Connie Mack's right-hand man, predicted, "You might just as well get ready to count the Braves in on the next World's Series." "All things considered," Richter concluded, "the Braves look like a wonderful outfit."[15]

Late in March the Braves "broke camp" in Miami and, after playing more games with the Athletics in Jacksonville, embarked on a series of exhibition stops with minor-league teams in Georgia, the Carolinas, and Virginia scheduled by Walter Hapgood. It became something of an ordeal. Stallings missed some of it, having left Evers in charge of the team and detoured for a final visit to see that everything was in good order at his plantation. Most of the time the players weren't in one place long enough to put up at a hotel, but had to sleep on trains, some of which lacked diners. After several days of enduring such hardship, Maranville organized a protest. While they continued to play their scheduled dates, they stopped shaving and took to wearing clownish caps and work shirts. That went on until the team reached Washington, despite demands and then entreaties from Stallings and Hapgood, perhaps also from Evers in his capacity as team captain.

In Washington, where they split two exhibition games with the American Leaguers, Congressman W. H. Carter of Needham, Massachusetts, arranged for them to meet President Wilson in the White House. Though a baseball fan, Wilson had a lot more important matters on his mind and gave the players only a few minutes. After that, it was on to Brooklyn to start the 1916 season, with Hugh Fullerton predicting an all–Boston World Series, and Johnny Evers again prompting amused disbelief by announcing from here on he intended to stay off the umpires. Bill Phelon predicted, "Boston will win out if everybody keeps his health."[16] Everybody wouldn't.

8

1916: "The Miracle Man is set for a big drive"

The 1916 season began with eighteen ex–Federal Leaguers (not including pitchers) in major-league lineups: twelve players in the National League but only six in the American League, four of whom were with the St. Louis Browns. Among the National League teams, only defending champion Philadelphia and St. Louis had nobody from the Federal League in the Opening Day lineup, although the Phillies had added Chief Bender to their pitching staff. Besides Bender, a dozen or so pitchers from the Federal League were also on big-league rosters, mainly with the amalgamated Browns and Chicago Cubs. Hal Chase, perhaps the most highly regarded everyday player who had deserted to the Federal League, signed with Cincinnati after hitting a league-leading seventeen home runs with Buffalo. The relatively small number of ex–Federals could be taken as confirmation the league had offered an inferior brand of baseball. But one might also argue that both major leagues and especially the National would offer a better brand in 1916. In any case, with the Federal League now history and with the economy prospering again, the general expectation was that it would be a banner season.

On Wednesday, April 12, in chilly but crowded Ebbets Field, Brooklyn, the Braves began their fourth season under the direction of George Stallings. Having settled the Reulbach matter, John Tener and Barney Dreyfuss, joined by National League secretary John Heydler, came over from Manhattan for the event. Stallings's Opening Day lineup had Ed Konetchy, Johnny Evers, Rabbit Maranville, and Red Smith in the infield; Sherwood Magee in left field; Pete Compton in center; and Joe Wilhoit in right. Regardless of what Frederick W. Lieb had written a few weeks earlier, Hank Gowdy was still Stallings's regular catcher; Walt Tragesser, who had joined the Braves at the end of the past two seasons, was his backup. Haughton and Stallings had decided to abandon the blue-flannel road uniforms worn since 1913, in favor of the gray flannels most teams wore away from home.

Again Dick Rudolph was Stallings's Opening Day pitcher; Wilbert Robinson countered with right-hander Larry Cheney, who had won sixty-seven games in three seasons for the Cubs before faltering in 1915 and, in August, coming to Brooklyn in exchange for a run-of-the-mill outfielder and cash. With his curves and spitballs as effective as ever, Rudolph held the Robins to six hits and one run, while the Braves hit Cheney hard. Rudolph himself contributed a double to Boston's nine hits; Maranville also had a double; Magee hit two singles and a triple. It ended 5–1, a promising start for Stallings—unless he still held to his superstition about Opening Day wins.

Then, as usual, rain set in. The Braves and Robins got to play again on the 15th, Boston winning 4–2 when Magee sent one of Sherry Smith's pitches over Hy Myers in center field to drive in two runs. Tom Hughes pitched well for the win. More rain limited the Braves to two games in Philadelphia. They lost both, the first to Grover Cleveland Alexander, who worked a five-hit, 4–0 shutout, Rudolph taking the loss. On the 19th, in a 6–5 defeat, both Stallings and Pat Moran used an unusual number of pitchers for that period. The Phillies drove out Hughes, who was succeeded by Elmer Knetzer, Lefty Tyler, and Ed Reulbach. Erskine Mayer started for the Phillies and gave way to Eppa Rixey. In the top of the ninth inning, Chief Bender took the mound, seeking to hold the one-run lead. That he did, but he also threw an inside pitch that hit Magee on the left wrist. Self-professed medical man Stallings figured the wrist would heal itself, but an x-ray, ordered by Haughton, revealed a bad break. So Magee's tough luck continued: first a shoulder injury the previous spring, now a broken wrist that would keep him sidelined for more than month.

Complaining that even the usually even-tempered Alexander had thrown at them in Philadelphia, the Braves returned to Boston for their home opener with Brooklyn. On Thursday, April 20, only about eight-thousand New Englanders paid their way into Braves Field for the first home game of the season. They shivered through a sterling performance by Jesse Barnes, who threw a seven-hit shutout, while the Braves bombarded Jack Coombs for seven runs in the first two innings. It ended

8–0. Before the game members of the Harvard class of 1899 lent a touch of gentility to the event by honoring classmate Percy Haughton with (yes) a floral horseshoe.

But there was nothing genteel about Friday's game, a 10–3 trouncing in which Art Nehf and Knetzer surrendered twelve hits; the Braves committed ten errors (two by Evers, four by Red Smith); and Maranville and Brooklyn third-baseman Ivan "Ivy" Olson exchanged punches. After that sloppy exhibition, Stallings sold Knetzer to Cincinnati for an undisclosed amount of cash. He also sent Paul Strand, who hadn't pitched at all so far, to Roger Bresnahan's Toledo club, with the option to recall him. The recall never came.

The Giants came into town for a scheduled four-game series and had to sit around the hotel lobby while two games were called off because of mixed rain and snow. The Braves won the remaining two games— sandwiched around another bad-weather cancelation—by 3–1 and 3–2 scores, getting good pitching from Rudolph and from Tyler, in his first start. In New York's second defeat on the 27th, plate umpire Bill Klem got tired of harassment from the Giants' dugout and ordered John McGraw and everybody to the showers except those at their positions in the field. Under the grandstand at game's end, McGraw yelled curses at Klem as he headed for the umpires' dressing room. Klem went at McGraw but was pulled away by Bob Emslie. It was still another memorable run-in between two men whose set-tos would stretch over more than a quarter-century.

After another rain-idled day, the Braves dropped another game to the Phillies and Alexander, 5–2. On Saturday, April 30, Haughton and associates had to call off the game on what was typically the best attendance day of the week. Having played only nine games since the start of the season, Boston was in fourth place with a 5–4 record. The Giants, limited to the same number of games, had won only once. Herman Nickerson, now *Sporting Life's* Boston correspondent, criticized the schedulemakers for having the Braves play at home in typically cold and wet April weather (although he neglected to note the games all the other eastern teams had lost to bad weather).[1] Ahead loomed numerous doubleheaders, always bad news for managers, who would have to cope with overworked pitching staffs.

After the Sunday off day, Rudolph topped Philadelphia's Mayer,

Umpire Bill Klem, 1914. Klem was one of the best of all time, but he got no love from either the Braves or John McGraw (George Bantham Bain Collection, Library of Congress).

5–2; on Tuesday, Hughes relieved Reulbach in the ninth inning and struck out Dave Bancroft, Dode Paskert, and Gavvy Cravath to preserve Reulbach's first victory as a Brave, 4–2. But in the series finale, Alexander scored his second shutout and third win over the Braves, 3–0; Barnes was the loser. Then the Braves left town for their first visit to the Polo Grounds, intending to play four games before embarking on their first western trip. Bill James was left behind. He hadn't pitched an inning so far, and he wouldn't pitch an inning over the rest of the season. He asked to be placed on the voluntarily retired list and was.

The Braves got to play three games in New York, with the Friday, May 5, date rained out. On the 4th, Rudolph was socked for six first-inning runs, then shut out the Giants the rest of the way as the Braves hacked away for seven on Jeff Tesreau. They won by the same 7–6 score on Saturday, collecting fourteen hits off Christy Mathewson, who nonetheless endured until, in the top of the tenth inning, Benny Kauff's error put the Braves ahead. Emilio Palmero, the young Cuban left-hander, pitched a bit better on Monday, but only a bit. Boston won, 6–2, behind Pat Ragan. That night the Braves left for Chicago in second place, a half-game behind Brooklyn. They had won ten of their first fifteen games, which was the best showing to that point any of Stallings's Boston teams had made. The Giants, at 2–13 (both wins by Tesreau), looked even worse than last-year's tail-enders. But the Giants' 1916 season was about to turn into the most bizarrely streaky any major-league team ever had.

So far, apart from Evers's tiff with Ivy Olson on April 21 and a few minor protests to umpires, the Braves had been astonishingly well behaved, so much so that Herman Nickerson lamented the timidity of Evers and the players generally. That he blamed on the National League's new policy of assessing fines for ejections and requiring fines to be paid directly to the league office. But John Tener was so pleased that on May 4, following Boston's opening win in New York, he sent Percy Haughton a telegram praising the team's conduct: "Judging by the position your club holds in the race" [with the Braves temporarily in the lead], "the ... policy has not militated against the team's success. I congratulate you and Manager Stallings on the splendid behavior of the boys."[2] Time would tell in that matter.

The Braves took two out of three from the Cubs, in their first appearance in Charles Weeghman's showplace North Side ballpark (now known as either "Weeghman Park," "Cubs Park," or "National League Park"). In their two wins, they scored twenty runs on Joe Tinker's pitchers, including an 11–10 slugging match in which Evers doubled and singled twice. But the western trip started to go wrong in Pittsburgh, where Haughton joined the team. On Saturday, May 13, he watched his employees commit three errors and Hughes, in relief of Reulbach, walk two men with the bases loaded in the sixth inning to give the Pirates a 5–3 victory. On Monday, Boston lost again in a free-hitting game, 8–7. The Boston Globe's James C. O'Leary, traveling with the team, criticized Bill Klem for bad calls on the bases and, at game's end, for cursing out Maranville as Rabbit left the field and "mildly chided" the umpire.[3] O'Leary complained that Klem consistently made calls against the Braves, and that for some reason the league office assigned him to more Boston games than any other umpire (which was doubtful).

Following a rainout on Tuesday, the Braves moved on to Cincinnati for four-games, where the trip really went bad. The series in Redland Field started well. Boston won the opener, Hughes holding the Reds to one run while the Braves scored seven on Gene Dale, an eighteen-game winner in 1915 who had suddenly lost his effectiveness.[4] At this point in the season, against right-handers, Stallings was using a left-hand-batting outfield of Zip Collins in left, Pete Compton or Joe Connolly in center, and Joe Wilhoit in right.

On Thursday, the 18th, Pete Schneider edged Reulbach, 3–2. In the fifth inning, Evers insisted that Klem discard a discolored ball, which Klem refused to do. After hitting into a double play, Evers lingered to pursue his case and received an ejection for his troubles. Klem kept the ball in question in play for the rest of the game. So much for the "splendid behavior" Tener had commended. After Nehf and Ragan took 3–2 and 6–1 losses in the final two games in Cincinnati, the Braves went to St. Louis for four games, playing only a little better than .500 ball.

W. J. O'Connor expected a good crowd at Robison Field on Sunday the 21st for the series opener, "because there are some belligerent bleacherites who live for the chance to fight Evers." Lefty Tyler, who hadn't pitched much so far, threw a two-hit, 2–0 shutout in the opener, beating Red Ames. O'Connor joked that the outcome of the game "was incidental to the monumental disappointment of the rooters who found Evers playing only a thinking part." O'Connor also thought Evers was being "muzzled," but then he hadn't been at that game in Cincinnati a few days earlier.[5]

No doubt the Boston players who remembered Rogers Hornsby from the previous September as an underweight, choke-hitting, plate-crowding kid were surprised at his changed appearance and batting style. Over the winter Hornsby had gained thirty pounds, and now he stood nearly erect in the batter's box, gripped his bat at its end, positioned himself in the far back corner of the box, stepped into the pitch at an angle, and lined the ball all over the field. Hornsby did little against Tyler that day, but he was on his way to a .313 batting average in his first full season. Soon he was being hailed by the *Sporting News* as the "best youngster in the National League" and "a star of the first water."[6]

On Monday, Hughes struggled to a 9–5 win, but the Cardinals won the third and fourth games of the set: Slim Sallee's 3–0 shutout, Ragan taking the loss; Lee Meadows's 5–4 win over Rudolph, with Hornsby starring at bat and afield. The Braves started home having won five and lost eight in the western cities. Brooklyn had won seven of eleven in the west and slipped to second, while Philadelphia had won ten of fourteen. Meanwhile, the Giants had gone on a sensational run, sweeping all thirteen games they played in Pittsburgh, Chicago, St. Louis, and Cincinnati, and vaulting into a third-place tie with Boston.

Unfortunately, the Braves had to open their home stand with McGraw's red-hot ball club. McGraw had largely rebuilt the Giants. From the team that lost the 1913 World Series, only pitchers Christy Mathewson and Jeff Tesreau; infielders Fred Merkle, Larry Doyle, and Art Fletcher; and outfielder George Burns remained. The previous February, Chief Meyers had been sold to Brooklyn, where he reunited with his old battery mate Rube Marquard. From Harry Sinclair's collection of Federal Leaguers, the Giants had added not only Benny Kauff but spitballer Fred Anderson and former Braves catcher Bill Rariden; trades the previous season had secured pitchers Pol Perritt and Al Benton, while Ferdie Schupp, a slightly built left-hander given brief trials the previous three years, had finally made the team.

The Giants continued their streak in Braves Field, sweeping all four games, beginning with a 12–1 drubbing on Thursday, May 26. On Friday, New York won a well-pitched doubleheader, 4–3 and 3–1, Anderson and Benton defeating Hughes and Ragan. And on Monday, the 29th, Mathewson was masterful for the last time in his storied career, throttling the Braves, 3–0. New York's seventeenth consecutive victory—all achieved on the road—put them in second place (19–13); the Braves dropped to fifth (15–17), behind Chicago. After Mathewson's shutout, Percy Haughton took a train to New York to complain in person to John Tener about Mal Eason's umpiring. As always, Tener backed up his umpire.

In Brooklyn, the Braves had to play two doubleheaders, divided by a single game. With a healed Sherwood Magee back in the lineup, they ended their six-game losing streak in the morning of the Decoration Day doubleheader, 5–3, behind Tyler. But they lost the nightcap, 1–0, Sherry Smith shutting out the Braves and getting Brooklyn's one run in the seventh inning on Hy Myers single. The Giants' winning streak came to an end in their morning loss in Philadelphia. On Tuesday, Jeff Pfeffer, with whom the Braves usually had trouble, beat them, 3–2, wasting a good outing by Barnes. That made it eight losses in Boston's last nine games. But on Wednesday, Ragan and Rudolph both pitched fine games, Ragan defeating Larry Cheney, 6–1, on a four-hitter, Rudolph topping Jack Coombs on a five-hitter, 3–1. Brooklyn was in first place at 22–14 to 21–17 for the Phillies, who lost a single game to New York. The Giants, after splitting four games in Philadelphia, were still third; the Braves were back in fourth.

With Chicago coming into Braves Field for three games, Stallings left the team and traveled to West Chester, Pennsylvania, for the funeral of Bud Sharpe, who, only thirty-five, had died suddenly a few days earlier at the Meadows. Evers was in charge of the team, but when the Braves' manager returned, he took a leave of absence and went home to Troy. He had a cold and a sore right elbow; besides, he complained, he was being gagged by Tener and the club's (unnamed) management. Sportswriters around the league observed that the man who claimed he couldn't play unless he "crabbed" hadn't been showing his usual fire and hustle. Dick Eagan took over second base.

For the next two weeks the Braves continued at a mediocre pace and continued to have trouble putting numbers on the scoreboard. At first, Magee's return added little to their offense; so far Konetchy hadn't hit as he had been expected to do. Since their 8–5 win in St. Louis on May 22, the Braves had played eleven games, won only three, and averaged slightly more than two runs per game. The offensive woes continued against the Cubs. They lost two games and won one, Frank Allen's well-turned 3–2 victory over Hippo Vaughn. The series opener was a 2–1 defeat, and in the third game, left-hander Gene Packard, a twenty-game winner in two seasons with the Kansas City Federals, shut them out, 1–0.

During the Chicago series, a truly wacky episode occurred. The small right-field bleachers section in Braves Field was well known as a gathering place for gamblers. In the middle of the game, two of them got into a quarrel; one man pulled a small pistol and supposedly shot the other in the leg. The umpires stopped the game for ten minutes while the victim was ministered to, before he was taken to a local hospital to have his wound treated. Some of the bleacher-sitters who had been near the shooting told police they thought the wounded man might actually have accidentally shot himself! In any case, no charges were filed.

The Braves and Cardinals were able to play two games, which they split, before two more games were rained out. Slim Sallee edged Rudolph, 2–1; Ragan won the next day, 3–2. With a 20–22 record, Boston was still in fifth place. The rain persisted for the next three days, washing out two meetings with Cincinnati. When the teams finally got to play, they pretty much made up for their idleness. On June 13 neither team could score for sixteen innings, until the game was called. The next day's game lasted twelve innings, Ragan and left-hander Clarence Mitchell both going the route. Magee first saved the game in the top of the twelfth with a running, bare-handed catch of Fritz Mollowitz's drive in in the left-field corner, then lined a single past first base to win it, 4–3.

The home stand concluded with a series versus Pittsburgh. Magee had injured his shoulder again when he hit the concrete barrier in front of the third-base pavilion after making the game-saving catch the previous day, and missed the opener with the Pirates. Pittsburgh won, 2–1, dropping

Tom L. Hughes. In 1915 and 1916, Hughes was invaluable to Stallings as both starter and reliever (George Bantham Bain Collection, Library of Congress).

Boston two games below .500. Magee was back in the lineup the next day, Friday, June 16, in time for Tom Hughes to make baseball history by pitching a no-hit game, defeating the Pirates, 2–0. Hughes walked two batters and struck out seven, the seventh victim being Honus Wagner, whom Bill Klem called out on a three-two count to end the game. The Braves won as they had won many times—by pressing the opponent's defense. They scored in the first inning, when pitcher Erv Kantlehner threw wildly past second trying to double up Maranville, and their other run in the eighth on catcher Walter Schmidt's throw over Wagner's head on a double-steal attempt, Maranville coming home again.

The history-making aspect of the game was that Hughes became the first pitcher to hurl a no-hit game in each major league. On August 30, 1910, when he was with Stallings's New York American Leaguers, the lanky right-hander held Cleveland hitless for ten innings before giving up five hits in the eleventh and losing, 5–0.

Besides Hughes, Tyler and Barnes were also pitching well, which was a good thing, inasmuch as Rudolph was nursing a sore leg, the same one he had injured running to first base in 1915. Saturday, June 17, was Bunker Hill Day, a traditional holiday in the Boston area to commemorate the first real battle of the Revolutionary War. The scheduled doubleheader would undoubtedly have drawn a big crowd to Braves Field, but it was another rainout in what continued to be an extraordinarily wet baseball season in the northeast. The rains continued and caused cancelation of the first game of a scheduled five-game set in New York. The Giants had cooled off after their seventeen-game run, losing six of ten meetings with Cincinnati, Chicago, and St. Louis, although they still held third place.

On Tuesday, the 20th, before a fine Polo Grounds turnout of 23,000, the Giants won the first game of the makeup doubleheader, 4–3, reaching Tyler for three runs in the first inning and scoring what turned out to be the winning run in the fourth on a double steal. Anderson was the winner. In the second game, Ragan held the Giants to five hits and no runs. Although he was still complaining of what he said was neuritis in his elbow and arm, Evers had rejoined the team and was in the lineup for the nightcap. Besides singling in Maranville in the sixth inning with the game's only run, he made a fine stop and throw to keep New York from scoring in the eighth.

On Wednesday, the Braves won in ten innings, 5–4, with Evers again driving in the winning run. It was a rain-plagued game that Bill Byron refused to call, despite protests from both Stallings and McGraw. Hughes continued his heroics, relieving Allen in the bottom of the eighth inning with the score 4–4 and two runners on the soggy baselines. He got the third out and held the Giants runless to secure the victory, after Maranville scored on Evers's single in the top of the tenth on Mathewson, pitching in relief of Perritt. All the other games were rained out. On Thursday, Boston made it three wins in four games from the slumping New Yorkers with a 3–1 victory, to advance a game over the .500 mark. Meanwhile Brooklyn swept a doubleheader from Philadelphia to restore its two-game lead.

In Philadelphia, where the Braves were to play five games, they again faced Alexander, with the usual result. The Phillies pushed across a run in the eleventh inning to beat the unlucky Barnes, 2–1. But on Saturday, Konetchy bounced a two-run home run into the center-field bleachers in a 4–2 win for Ragan over Al Demaree.[7] Thereby the Braves displaced New York in third place, because at Ebbets Field the Robins delighted an overflow crowd estimated at 35,000 by taking both games of a doubleheader from the Giants and padding their lead over Philadelphia. The Braves also won their remaining three games in Philadelphia. They swept a doubleheader on the 26th, in the nightcap of which they won 9–5, scoring the most runs they had put across since that 11–10 shootout in Chicago nearly seven weeks earlier. In the series finale they finally beat Alexander, bunching four hits and a base on balls for three fourth-inning runs. Barnes worked another outstanding game, a five-hit shutout. With eight wins in their last ten games, Boston held third place by two and a half games over New York, and were a game and a half behind Philadelphia, three and a half behind Brooklyn.

Returning home, the Braves met Brooklyn in five games, losing the first two but winning a single game. In the second game of the series, Hank O'Day called a fourth ball on Art Nehf with the bases loaded to force in what proved the winning run. From the dugout, where he had to remain in street clothes, Stallings gave O'Day some of his choicest invective, then, after talking with Haughton, left the dugout and took a seat in the grandstand behind home plate to judge O'Day's calls. The Braves' manager didn't care for Mal Eason's work on the bases, either.

He offered to pay $50 to any local fan who could remember when Eason had made a call in the Braves' favor. He got no takers.

The next issue of the *Sporting News* pictured Evers and Stallings on the front page, above a caption reading: "Johnny Evers has forgotten that he misplaced his nerve and is playing ball like the Evers of old. Stallings smiles and is at his best—he is accusing the umpires of trying to throw games to his rivals, a sure indication that the Miracle Man is set for a big drive."[8]

On Saturday, July 1, a doubleheader drew some 21,000 to Braves Field, the season's biggest turnout so far. Everybody except Wilbert Robinson and his players left happy after two Boston victories. Snodgrass, Gowdy, and Magee hit doubles off Pfeffer in the 7–4 opener; Allen got the win in relief. The Braves made two runs each in the fifth, sixth, and seventh innings, with the two in the sixth scoring on a perfect squeeze bunt dropped by Snodgrass. Both Zip Collins and Eddie Fitzpatrick (subbing for Wilhoit, out with a bad leg) crossed the plate, as Pfeffer had trouble fielding the ball. The second game was a pitchers' battle between Ragan and Rube Marquard, won in the seventh on a passed ball and an outfield muff. Magee hit four singles in four times at bat. The Phillies beat the Giants, so at the end of the day, the standings were: Brooklyn, 36–25; Philadelphia, 34–28; Boston, 32–27. New York, at 30–30, seemed to be slipping out of the race.

As the pennant race tightened, tempers shortened. At the end of the Brooklyn series, Stallings was in high dudgeon, hotly denying Charles Ebbets's accusations that Boston's pitchers were deliberately throwing at Brooklyn's batters. That was "a squeal that does not come with good grace from the president of the Brooklyn club." When the Braves played in Brooklyn a few weeks earlier, retorted Stallings, Pfeffer kept Magee, Maranville, and Smith ducking and hit Konetchy. In turn, Ebbets filed a formal protest with John Tener over remarks Evers and Stallings had made to him during the games in Braves Field.[9] Meanwhile rumors circulated of dissension among the Braves. Evers and Red Smith weren't speaking to each other, Evers and Maranville were griping about Konetchy's failure to bat up to expectations, and the Braves infielders didn't like the way the outfielders were playing!

After the Sunday layover, the Braves were scheduled to end their stay in the east with three home games versus Philadelphia. They got to play two, winning one and losing one. On Monday, July 3, they beat the Phillies, 5–1; then their Independence Day doubleheader was rained out, another financial setback for Haughton and associates. The teams were supposed to play a makeup doubleheader the next day but got in only one game, because with rain falling in the morning, Haughton and Stallings called off the first game, occasioning howls from fans who had waited an hour for the ballpark to open. Later that afternoon, the skies cleared sufficiently for the teams to play. It was another tough defeat for Barnes, Eppa Rixey outdueling him, 2–1.

At one point in the game, Bill Byron called a third strike on Evers, who threw his bat high in the air, whereupon Byron thumbed him out of the game. Tener was sitting at field level, within earshot of Evers, who, as he left the field, made a weird wisecrack to Byron about certain players being criticized by "the wife of the president of the league." Whatever Evers meant by that, the whole episode was too much for Tener, who laid a ten-day suspension on the Boston captain. Evers wired a futile apology to the league president, pleading that he was "grievously at fault."[10] Tener was unmoved. Remembering his telegram back in May congratulating Haughton on the Braves' good behavior, he must have been shaking his head in dismay.

In St. Louis, W. J. O'Connor took issue with Tener's form of punishment, arguing that suspending a player hurt his whole team, whereas a stiff fine hurt the player, not the team. O'Connor compared Evers's ten-day suspension to the three-day suspension Ban Johnson had given Ty Cobb for throwing his bat, which came down in the grandstand in Chicago. What should have been done in Evers's case, O'Connor wrote, was a fine equivalent to ten days' salary. In effect that's what happened, because Haughton and Stallings agreed that the obstreperous Boston captain's pay would be withheld during his suspension.

Hoping for drier weather, the Braves team left for Chicago with a 33–28 record to Brooklyn's 39–25 and Philadelphia's 35–29—by far the Boston team's best position in the standings at that point under Stallings (or any manager for a long time). The Braves arrived after a stopover for an exhibition game in Buffalo, scene of their humiliating loss two years earlier.[11] Evidently Haughton and Stallings had run out of patience with Evers's on-field tantrums and suspensions, as well as his complaints about aches and pains. Whatever the situation may have been, the

Boston manager left the team in Chicago and traveled to Cincinnati, where, according to an anonymous report, he and Garry Herrmann discussed swapping Evers for player-manager Buck Herzog.[12] Another report had it that Charles Weeghman had offered the Braves $50,000 for Maranville, but Haughton and Stallings refused that when the Evers-Herzog negotiations fell through. It turned out such dealings did actually take place; no less a figure than Arthur Wise, Haughton's chief partner in the Boston franchise and its treasurer, confirmed them.

So on Friday, July 7, Maranville was at shortstop, Dick Eagan played second base, and Evers sat in the grandstand as the Braves began a four-game series with Joe Tinker's Cubs, who had settled into fifth place. In a duel of left-handers, Frank Allen pitched his best game of the season in vain; for the second time, Gene Packard shut out the Braves, 1–0, and this time on one hit. But before a good Saturday crowd, Tyler and George McConnell staged another pitching duel, which Boston won, 2–1.

That was the beginning of another successful tour of the western cities. The Braves won the remaining two games in Chicago and two of three in Pittsburgh (with one rainout). On the 15th, with Rudolph taking the mound for the first time in three weeks, they opened a four-game set in Cincinnati and, in a rare offensive outburst, won, 9–2. That put them in a virtual tie with the Phillies for second place. They won again the next day but lost, 9–2, on the 15th, with a large number of Rotarians, who were in Cincinnati for their

Percy Haughton. He discovered big-league baseball wasn't at all like the Ivy League (George Bantham Bain Collection, Library of Congress).

national convention, in attendance at Redland Field. They also dropped the series finale to the Reds, 6–4.

Those two Cincinnati victories weren't enough to save Buck Herzog's job as Cincinnati's manager. Although he remained under a player contract, Garry Herrmann relieved him as manager and put catcher Ivy Wingo in charge—for two games. Where Stallings had failed in his efforts to trade Evers for Herzog, John McGraw worked out a deal with Herrmann whereby Herzog and outfielder Wade Killefer would go to the Giants in exchange for outfielder Edd Roush, infielder Bill McKechnie, and Christy Mathewson.[13] At the age of thirty-six, the great Matty had 372 major-league victories to his credit, including eighty-three shutouts, although in the current season he had won only three times in six starts.[14] Now he would become the Reds' manager, a position for which he was thought to be eminently suited.

The Cincinnati–New York trade was concluded on July 20, by which time the Braves were in St. Louis, sweating through a five-game series in even hotter weather than in Cincinnati. Evers returned to the lineup on Wednesday the 19th for the first game with the Cardinals, a 10–1 walkover, Rudolph again getting an abundance of runs. Brooklyn lost a doubleheader in Pittsburgh; Philadelphia was rained out in Cincinnati. Evers demanded that he be paid all the money he hadn't received during his suspension and had a nasty quarrel with his manager and the club president, who wouldn't relent.

Evers hadn't reformed. On Thursday, Lee Meadows defeated Barnes, 5–2, in a game in which the Braves did more clowning than effective ball-playing. Throughout, they gave plate umpire Cy Rigler a hard time. When a St. Louis batter wanted Rigler to examine the ball, Gowdy tossed it to Smith, and the whole Braves infield pretended to scrutinize it. After the third out and the ball in question was dropped near the mound, Evers crawled to it and, after peering at it for a few moments, announced, "I don't think there's a period after Tener's name." Evers also picked a quarrel with Miller Huggins, inexplicably calling him a "double-crosser." The whole business left W. J. O'Connor disgusted.[15]

Friday the 21st was the twenty-first straight day of temperatures in the nineties in St. Louis. Despite Rogers Hornsby's inside-the-park home run that bounced off the center-field gate, nearly five-hundred feet from home plate, the Braves won, 4–3, Tyler helping himself with a home run of his own. On Saturday, Bill Doak outlasted Ragan, 6–4, but Rudolph closed the road trip with his third win since coming back from his injury, edging left-hander Bob Steele, 2–1. Philadelphia won in Cincinnati; Brooklyn was en route east from Pittsburgh. Having won ten of fifteen games in the western cities, the Braves left St. Louis's heat in second place by two percentage points over the Phillies (43–34 to 44–35). Brooklyn, which had gone 8–7 in the west, seemed to have a fairly comfortable lead (48–32).

The Braves began an eighteen-day home stand, during which twenty-four games were scheduled. Although they opened on Tuesday, July 25, with a 3–2 loss to Chicago in eleven innings, they would thrive hosting the western outfits, as they had thrived on their recent western trip. Early in the game of the 25th, plate umpire Mal Eason tossed Evers when he went into a characteristic rant following a called third strike. As Cubs first-baseman Rollie Zeider was leaving the field, he bumped into Evers, who hit him on the shins with his bat. They clinched, Eason got between them, Evers left, and Zeider stayed in the game. The Cubs' winning run scored when Fitzpatrick, subbing for Evers, threw the ball into the visitors' dugout, and Eason allowed the base runner to come all the way around from first to score. Boston officially protested Eason's call to the league office but got no satisfaction.

After that inauspicious opening, the Braves beat the Cubs twice; in between, they played a rain-soaked, 2–2 tie called after eleven innings. On the 26th, Hippo Vaughn held the Braves hitless for eight innings, until Eagan drove in Allen with the game's only run. Vaughn kicked so loudly about plate umpire Al Orth's calls that Orth put him out of the game. Mike Prendergast replaced him to get the final out; Hughes finished up for Allen in the ninth. In the last game of the Chicago series, Art Nehf was the winner, 2–1, losing his shutout on Maranville's error. Meanwhile Brooklyn won three of four from St. Louis; Philadelphia did the same against Cincinnati. The Braves lost half-a-game to each.

The *Boston Journal's* Ralph McMillin roasted both Eason and Orth for their work in the Boston-Chicago series, not only for bad calls but for tolerating the foul language of Joe Tinker and Heinie Zimmerman, which, he wrote, could be heard all over Braves Field. For once, by McMillin's account, the Braves players were the targets rather than the instigators of the billingsgate.

As usual, Stallings's pitchers were carrying the club. They threw four shutouts in July, three by Pat Ragan. None of the Braves was hitting much. Gowdy was batting .238, Magee a disappointing .227, Evers .212 in sixty-three games (of the eighty-three the Braves had played). Brooklyn's Nap Rucker—a veteran left-hander in his last year in the majors—told *Baseball Magazine's* F. C. Lane that Boston's pitchers weren't "naturally great, but Stallings is the smartest manager in the big leagues. He has studied baseball until he knows it from A to Z.... He has something on every player in the league.... It is Stallings who has made a finished machine out of the Braves' pitching staff."[16]

St. Louis followed Chicago into Braves Field for six games, including doubleheaders on Saturday, July 29, and Monday, the 31st. The Saturday twin bill drew some 25,000. Rudolph won again, defeating Red Ames, 4–3, despite Hornsby's four base hits in four times at bat. The Braves pounded out eight runs on Lee Meadows and successors in the nightcap; Hughes was shaky but came out with the victory, 8–5. Bill Doak won the first game on Monday, 4–3; in the second game, Rudolph was the winner in relief of Allen, 2–1. Allen had to leave after he and Walt Tragesser, who had come into the game when Gowdy suffered a split finger, collided going after a ball tapped between home plate and the mound. The catcher was knocked cold; Allen was also shaken up. Rudolph started the next day and shut out the Cardinals, 1–0, Meadows taking the loss. Following the Braves' 5–3 defeat in the last game of the series, Stallings cornered Cy Rigler and told him (as related by Harold Kaese), "After your exhibition of umpiring this afternoon, you ought to be put in prison."[17] For that the hot-tempered Georgian drew a three-day suspension. A group of Boston fans started a petition to Tener protesting Rigler's and Bob Emslie's umpiring.

Meanwhile the Phillies also split six games with Chicago; Brooklyn won five of six from Cincinnati. So with two months of the season remaining, Brooklyn held first place with 56 wins, 34 losses, to Boston's 49–37 and Philadelphia's 51–39. New York, now 46–44, was still fourth.

Against Christy Mathewson's Cincinnati ball club, Boston had to play seven games in four days, including three doubleheaders. With both Boston catchers disabled, Stallings had hurriedly signed young Arthur Rico, a Boston sandlot catcher, and recalled Earl Blackburn from Providence, where he been sent on option in the spring.[18] On Thursday,

August 3, the Braves and Reds split a doubleheader, Boston losing the first, 3–1, winning the second, 5–2. Evers, in charge of the team in Stallings's absence, sat out the first game. In the fourth inning, Bill Byron ruled that Red Smith had interfered with a Cincinnati runner at third base, and waved the runner in to score. Evers and Smith had been on bad terms for some time; now Evers shouted from the dugout (again as related by Kaese), "What alibi are you going to give now for your dirty ball playing?" The Trojan may have been joking, but even if he was, it was a peculiar thing for a teammate to say, let alone the captain and acting manager. In any case, Smith didn't take it as a joke. When he got to the dugout, he took a couple of swings at Evers, until Byron intervened and ordered Evers to the clubhouse, with Smith yelling for Evers to wait for him after the game. That Evers did, and the two put on a genuine fist fight. After teammates separated them, Evers left the ballpark, saying he was "disgusted" and about ready to quit the Braves. The next day he apologized to everybody concerned.[19]

Whatever the reason—whether he was too upset to play or nursing cuts and bruises inflicted by Smith—Evers also sat out the remaining five games with Cincinnati, then, pleading a sore arm, again went home to Troy. W. J. O'Connor was as tired of Evers's shenanigans as most other people were, suggesting that if the National League "could fire him bodily out of baseball, without arousing certain of the fans, they would do it."[20]

Boston won all of the other five games with the Reds. In the third and last doubleheader, on Monday, August 7, Barnes shut out the Reds, 1–0, on five hits; Allen scattered ten hits in the nightcap in hurling a 6–0 shutout. Three days of rain kept the Braves and Pittsburgh idle. They were able to play a doubleheader on the 11th, which they split, closing the Braves' home stand with a 13–5–1 record. Then it was to Brooklyn to play a doubleheader and two single games before they left on their last western trip.

On Saturday the 12th, before an Ebbets Field crowd that heckled them for four hours, the Braves swept two from the league leaders, winning both games by 5–4 scores. Stallings used sixteen players in the first game; Rudolph wasn't at his best in the nightcap, but Snodgrass's three-run home run won his game. On Monday, Larry Cheney quelled the Braves, 5–2, but on Tuesday they made it three out of four over the league leaders, 4–1, Rudolph winning his second game in the series.

That put Boston's record at 59–40 to Philadelphia's 61–42 and Brooklyn's 63–38. New York was still fourth at 52–50, as McGraw continued to reconstitute his team.

Three weeks earlier, the Giants had paid a bargain $10,000 to St. Louis for Slim Sallee; McGraw immediately put the lean left-hander into his rotation. Now McGraw installed Walter Holke at first base and traded Fred Merkle to Brooklyn for catcher Lew McCarty. A week later, on August 28, McGraw made a transaction that was something of a dazzler: The popular Larry Doyle and two substitute outfielders went to Chicago for shortstop Mickey Doolan and the frequently sought-after Heinie Zimmerman. McGraw now had his Giants positioned for a "big drive" of their own.

After a two-week absence, Evers rejoined the team before it left for the west. With two open days before the Braves had to be in St. Louis, Walter Hapgood arranged for Stallings to split his players into two squads for exhibition games in Jamestown, New York; Toledo, Ohio; and Terre Haute and Lafayette, Indiana, the last two stops being the home towns, respectively, of Art Nehf and Walt Tragesser. Hapgood wasn't the players' favorite person after the fiasco of the spring trip north; no doubt (perhaps with the exception of Nehf and Tragesser) they would have liked to travel directly to St. Louis and enjoy a full day's rest in their hotel, instead of having to sleep two nights in Pullmans. Ralph McMillin wrote critically of what the Braves' were doing, wondering why a ball club in the midst of a pennant race would schedule meaningless exhibitions, denying its players needed respite and also risking injuries. But as always, the Braves management—like that of all the other big-league teams, including the wealthier ones such as the Giants and Cubs—used such dates to defray travel, hotel, and meal costs.

Meanwhile, at Percy Haughton's behest, the National League club owners convened in New York to consider the petition signed by a large number of Boston fans, calling upon the league to do something about the umpiring in general but especially that of Cy Rigler and Bob Emslie. The owners considered the petition and dismissed it, although they did agree to try to curb dugout yammering at umpires and the opposition. Then Tener issued an order that "players are not to be allowed to address remarks to or about umpires, opposing players or spectators. The umpires are to be treated with more respect, and their decisions are to be final. Also, there are to be no more verbal attacks on the visiting players by the white-clad players."[21] It was, of course, one thing to issue an order, another to have it obeyed. Besides, what about "verbal attacks" by the visiting players? The Braves were good at that, too.

On August 18 and 19, the Braves' pennant chances took a setback in the only two games scheduled in St. Louis, when they lost 4–3 in eleven innings and 7–4 the next day. One might have thought the Boston captain, having been away from the team for two weeks, would have tried to be on his best behavior. Instead Evers gave the umpires so much trouble in St. Louis that Tener suspended him still again, for two days. Schuyler Britton, husband of the Cardinals' owner, had his own grievance, wiring Tener to complain that Tyler, Maranville, and Smith had used abusive language when, before the game, he wouldn't open the particular gate onto the playing field they wanted opened. Tener took that under advisement and decided to fine Tyler $75 and Maranville and Smith $50 apiece.

As in past campaigns, the antics of the Braves and their manager brought reproach from the press in opposition cities. The *New York Morning Sun's* Joe Vila (never known for his balanced views) chided not only Stallings and Evers, but also the Boston writers for supporting the Braves' rowdiness. All around the National League, Vila claimed, "there is bitter hostility for Stallings and Evers." "Stallings," a reporter in the *Cincinnati Post* scolded, "has sanctioned a repetition of the goat-getting tactics that won the 1914 world's championship." According to that city's *Enquirer*, ill feeling toward the Braves was even more widespread than Joe Vila thought: "The fans all over the country are sick and tired of the unsportsmanlike tactics of the Braves and their owners, who have done all they could to injure the umpire staff of the league and make themselves unpopular in many ways." And in *Baseball Magazine*, Bill Phelon wrote that outside of Boston, the Braves' "popularity has all but evaporated.... Their own conduct, their methods on and off the field—and their querulous complaints during the regular season have alienated the support of the fans, and the crowds have turned enthusiastically to the Brooklyn team."[22]

Unfazed by press criticism—if any of them even read it—the Braves swept a three-game series in Cincinnati, with Evers again occupying a grandstand seat for two of the three and again talking about quitting baseball. Hughes bailed out Allen in a 4–3 win on Sunday, August 20; Rudolph topped Pete Schneider on Monday, with Konetchy driving in both Boston runs; and Magee's running catch in left field ended Tuesday's game, called after six innings in the rain—a 1–0 victory for Tyler, the single run scoring on an infield out.

The universally admired Christy Mathewson had the hearts of Cincinnati fandom. Moreover, he and Hal Chase, on his way to his only batting title, seemed to be on equitable terms. But the Reds were a bad team, although in Edd Roush, the Reds had acquired a young center fielder who would quickly become one of the finest all-around players of his time.

On Wednesday, while the Braves were en route to Chicago for a four-game series, Brooklyn lost to the Cubs and Philadelphia was beaten in Pittsburgh. That loss, the Phillies' fourth in five games in Pittsburgh, put them two behind Boston and four and a half from Brooklyn. At that point Pat Moran's team seemed to be fading, but then the Phillies tightened things up again by sweeping three games in St. Louis. The Braves swept their four games with the Cubs, one of which was Rudolph's two-hit shutout, his tenth straight win. They gained a couple of lengths on Brooklyn, which split four games in Cincinnati.

Boston's western tour ended in Pittsburgh with seven games: a grueling three-straight doubleheaders and a single game. Stallings must have wondered how his hard-worked pitchers would stand up. They did all right. Boston split the first doubleheader, on Tuesday, August 28, losing 5–1, winning 8–2. The next day they took both games, Tyler getting a 6–1 decision in the opener and also gaining the victory in the nightcap in relief, as the Braves rallied late. They split the third twin bill, Rudolph winning the first game, 1–0, his eleventh time in a row. The Pirates drove out Nehf to take the second game, 7–6. The series finale also went to Pittsburgh, 3–2.

While the Braves were struggling through their stay in Pittsburgh, Brooklyn was winning two of three in St. Louis; Philadelphia was doing the same in Chicago. So as the Braves headed back to Boston, having won twenty-one times against ten losses in August, their record was 69–46. Philadelphia's was 67–49, Brooklyn's 72–44. New York, having lost four straight games in Philadelphia and won only four of sixteen in the west, had fallen to 56–59 and appeared to be out of the race.

Joe Connolly hadn't hit well all season, and Stallings had relegated him to pinch-hitting duties (which he did twenty-five times, with little success). On Hank Gowdy's recommendation, Boston purchased outfielder Larry Chappell, a left-handed outfielder, from Columbus of the American Association. Stallings put him in left field and moved Magee to right, keeping Snodgrass in center most of the time and benching Joe Wilhoit, who had been a general disappointment at the plate. Chappell would do little better. In search of more runs, the Boston manager had pretty much abandoned the alternating lefty-righty outfield he had employed with such success two years earlier.

As in 1914, the Braves would play a long September home stand, but again there would be a lot of doubleheaders. On Friday, September 1, they began a six-game set with the new-edition New York Giants. Heinie Zimmerman was at third base, Buck Herzog was at second, Walter Holke was at first, Benny Kauff was in center field, and Bill Rariden was the catcher. Only George Burns in left field, Art Fletcher at shortstop, and Dave Robertson in right field remained from the 1915 Giants' regular lineup. Boston won, 3–1, on a fine outing by Pat Ragan. In Philadelphia, Alexander won his twenty-sixth game and pitched his twelfth shutout, as the Phillies swept a doubleheader from Brooklyn. Now the Braves were only a game out of first place. In the opener of the Saturday doubleheader, Slim Sallee was in command, 4–1; the nightcap was called with the score 5–5. The Labor Day doubleheader drew the Braves' biggest home crowd, some thirty-thousand. It was a split, the Braves winning, 3–2, in the morning, the Giants taking the afternoon game, 8–3. The Phillies swept Brooklyn again, their fifth in a row over the Robins, so at nightfall on Labor Day, Philadelphia had tied Brooklyn for the lead at 72–49; the Braves were a game behind. New York, 58–60, still didn't look to be going anywhere.

Then the Braves entered a stretch where they all but blew their season. The Phillies came into town and beat them three times in four games, with one tie, to run their winning streak to eight games. On September 5, Alexander overcame Barnes, 4–2, in the first game of a scheduled doubleheader; the nightcap was scoreless when it was rained out after five innings. After the next day's game was also rained out, the Phillies won both games of a doubleheader. Eppa Rixey subdued the Braves, 4–2, in the opener; Erskine Mayer shut them out, 2–0, in the second game. Philadelphia took a game-and-half lead over Brooklyn, which lost the finale of a four-game series with the Giants. That particular game would be the beginning of something history-making.

The Braves' bad stretch continued in a four-game set with Brooklyn, of which they won only the final game. On the 8th, Jeff Pfeffer and Sherry Smith checked them in a doubleheader, 6–2 and 4–0. They were shut out again, 5–0, on the 9th by Larry Cheney, who received the only run he needed in the first inning when Jake Daubert's hit to center field got away from Snodgrass, and the Brooklyn first baseman made it all the way home. That made it seven straight losses, during which the Boston team had scored six runs. Ragan finally got some run support on the 11th and defeated Marquard, 5–1. In New York, the Giants won four straight from the Phillies and improved to 64–62, versus Boston's 72–54, Philadelphia's 75–53, and Brooklyn's 77–52. Recently Percy Haughton had Walter Hapgood place an advertisement in Boston's newspapers for advance World Series tickets. But Tom Hughes had been put out of action for the rest of the season after taking a drive off his pitching hand; Evers was back in Troy seeing his personal dentist to get an infected tooth removed (the infection supposedly the cause of his neuritis); and Maranville missed a few games with a broken nose and sore thumb. Advance Series sales no longer seemed a good idea. Herman Nickerson wrote of his old employers: "The Braves have about as much chance to win the pennant as the snow ball on the hot stove."[23]

Nickerson's judgment proved premature, because at that juncture, the Braves were fortunate to host the Cubs, against whom they had fared well most of the season. They got back in the race by winning and tying a doubleheader and taking both games of the next day's doubleheader, before being shut out on the 14th. The Braves gave Rudolph only one run in the first game of the series-opening doubleheader, but he pitched a shutout. The smallish but sturdy right-hander also started the nightcap and worked nine innings before leaving in favor of Tyler, who pitched four innings before the game was called at 3–3. On the 13th the Braves finally scored in bunches, winning 7–3 and 11–6, with Red Smith collecting five hits in five at bats in the opener and Magee hitting a base-loaded home run in the nightcap. Reulbach was the winning pitcher in both games, going the route in the opener and relieving Barnes in the second game. On the 14th, however, they were shut out, 2–0. Philadelphia split four games with St. Louis; Brooklyn won three of five from Pittsburgh; and New York ran its winning streak to eight with a four-game sweep of Cincinnati.

At the start of three games with St. Louis, the Braves' record was 75–55. Philadelphia's was 77–55; Brooklyn's, 80–54; New York's, 68–62. The series with the Cardinals was a three-game Boston sweep—by scores of 7–1, 2–0, and 6–3, Tyler pitching the shutout. But Brooklyn won four of five from Cincinnati; Philadelphia took three of four from Chicago. Alexander, trying for his thirtieth victory, lost 2–0 to Hippo Vaughn in the last game of that series. The Giants won three-consecutive double-headers from Pittsburgh; suddenly their fourteen-game streak had become as big a story as the three-corned pennant race.

Having rallied against the Cubs and Cardinals, the Braves proceeded to drop three games to Cincinnati, which was in a tight fight with St. Louis for seventh place. On Wednesday, September 20, Rudolph took the mound with little to offer except hittable pitches. He and successors were battered for seventeen hits and twelve runs, while the Braves managed five off Clarence Mitchell. Hal Chase had four hits, including two doubles; Henry "Heine" Groh, the Reds' little third baseman, also hit a pair of doubles. On Thursday, the Reds made fourteen more hits but could put across only five runs, although that was enough for Pete Schneider, who outpitched Tyler, 5–4. On Friday the Reds pounded Art Nehf and others for another twelve hits, to win 8–5. Ex-Brave Elmer Knetzer was the beneficiary of the barrage. Chase collected another pair of hits, for a total of eight in the series. In the three games, Cincinnati's batters connected for forty-four base hits, good for sixty-six total bases.

That debacle left the Braves five and a half games behind Brooklyn, which won all three of its games with St. Louis; two and a half behind Philadelphia, which took three of four from Pittsburgh; and only three in front of the Giants, whose streak had reached seventeen in a row. The Braves appeared all but done for.

"The astounding success of some of [his] supposedly weaker opponents," the *Sporting News* commented derisively, "jarred Stallings into several near fits." Ralph McMillin, in an I-told-you-so mode, ascribed Boston's letdown to "its ill-advised barnstorming trip just after the club had defeated the Dodgers three out of four in that series in Brooklyn."

According to McMillin, Stallings's divided squads "arrived in St. Louis in anything but a happy frame of mind and with travel-tired bodies," with the consequence that they lost their first two games to the Cardinals.[24]

George Stallings in 1916. No more miracles for the "Miracle Man" (George Bantham Bain Collection, Library of Congress).

The Giants were too far behind to entertain pennant hopes, but the journalist and syndicated cartoonist Thomas "Tad" Dorgan had the perfect metaphor for them: "The Giants remind me of a fighter who has been knocked out going down the aisle licking everybody in the house." Ralph McMillin wasn't happy about the Giants' surge, denouncing the player deals with the Giants by Cincinnati, St. Louis, and Chicago as intended "to keep New York on the map this year."[25] McMillin had no use for the commonly held notion that a winning team in New York was good for the financial health of the National League as a whole.

But just when everybody had the Braves written off, they played three doubleheaders and a single game with Pittsburgh in five days, won six times, and tied the other contest. Boston's pitching was outstanding throughout the series. On Saturday the 23rd, Rudolph won the opener of the first doubleheader, 4–2; Ragan and Wilbur Cooper persevered to a thirteen-inning, 1–1 tied in the nightcap. On Monday, Tyler pitched a 5–0 shutout; Reulbach followed with a fine game of his own, winning 3–2. Nehf and Allen were the victors the next day, 3–0 and 2–1; and the Braves wound up the series with Tyler's second shutout, the unlucky Cooper taking a 1–0 loss. Brooklyn won four of six from Chicago. In Philadelphia, Alexander pitched both games of the Saturday doubleheader with Cincinnati, winning his thirtieth and thirty-first decisions; the Phillies also captured two single games from the Reds. The Giants continued their phenomenal play, extending their streak to twenty-three by taking two doubleheaders and two single matches from St. Louis.

So on Thursday morning, September 28, the National League's standings looked like this: Brooklyn, 90–57; Philadelphia, 87–58; Boston, 84–58; New York, 82–62. With more games left to play than Brooklyn, the Braves still had an outside chance for the pennant, although Walter Hapgood was refunding the money Boston's faithful had mailed in for World Series tickets.

The Giants took care of the Braves' outside chance by winning the first three games of a four-game series in New York. On Thursday, afternoon, a throng of some 35,000 filled the Polo Grounds for a doubleheader. It went badly for Stallings's stalwarts. Rudolph absorbed a tough 2–0 defeat in the opener, Jeff Tesreau blanking the Braves on six hits. Right fielder Dave Robertson's home run over the fence in the right-field corner (257' from the plate) was all the offense Tesreau needed.

Boston's troubles with Cy Rigler continued. In the top of the ninth inning, Rigler called out Red Smith for interference at second base, when Herzog, after dropping the ball, apparently interfered with Smith—"a palpably erroneous decision," according to James C. O'Leary. In the nightcap, Benny Kauff connected for a bases-loaded homer into the same area where Robertson's landed, accounting for four of the seven runs the Giants scored on Ragan; again the Braves failed to score, this time on Ferdie Schupp.

Across the East River in Brooklyn, the Robins and Phillies began a three-game series, which everybody assumed would effectively determine the National League's pennant-winner. On Thursday, the Phillies knocked out Pfeffer with eight runs in support of Alexander, who cruised to his thirty-second victory. That moved the Philadelphia team to within two games of the leaders. On Friday, rain all around the New York area forced cancelation of the games in both Manhattan and Brooklyn, setting up big attendance dates for two Saturday doubleheaders.

In the opening game in the Polo Grounds, the Giants continued their domination of the Braves (and everybody else). Rube Benton kept the Boston team from scoring for the third game in a row; Rudolph was the losing pitcher, 4–0, in New York's twenty-sixth straight victory. In the second game, Benton went back to the mound in an effort to give the rest of Giants' staff a break, but his effort was in vain. The Braves' bats finally came alive to produce eight runs and bring the streak to an end. Red Smith and Magee homered into the left-field bleachers in an easy 8–3 outing for Tyler. It had been a breath-taking run of victories, one that, nearly a century later, would remain unequaled in major-league history

Over in Ebbets Field, the Robins and Phillies played the first game of their doubleheader in the morning, Charles Ebbets having received permission from the league to do that, inasmuch as all the reserved seats had been sold for yesterday's rained-out game. The Phillies hit Pfeffer hard again, winning, 7–2, behind Rixey. That was Brooklyn's sixth-consecutive defeat by Philadelphia. In the afternoon, Alexander, like Pfeffer, went to the mound for the second time in three days, but on this occasion he couldn't do the job, giving up six runs while Rube Marquard held the Phillies to one. That left the teams still two games apart; in fact, the presumably decisive series had really settled nothing. Brooklyn would remain at home to end the season with four single games versus New York, while the Braves would finish with six games in Philadelphia, beginning with two doubleheaders. The Phillies could still win the pennant, or Boston could beat out the Phillies for second place, or New York could edge Boston for third.

On Monday, October 2, before an overflow crowd, Alexander won for the thirty-third time and recorded his sixteenth shutout, 2–0, over Ragan. The Braves grabbed the second game, 4–1, scoring late on Chief Bender, who had relieved Al Demaree. Allen relieved Reulbach to gain the decision.[26] In Brooklyn, Jack Coombs shut out the Giants and Ferdie Schupp, 2–0, to increase the Robins' lead by half-a-game. John McGraw wanted to win—he always did, even the most obscure exhibition contests. Moreover, word had got around that he bet a large sum of money at the beginning of the season that the Giants, a last-place outfit in 1915, would finish no lower than third. (The respected sportswriter J. Ed Grillo put the figure at $15,000, which seems unrealistically high.) But at least one reporter in the Ebbets Field press box that Monday thought McGraw's players, "now that their streak is busted, seem to have lost heart. The interest is gone from their playing. … It wouldn't surprise anybody here if Brooklyn won three straight."[27]

Uncle Robbie's men didn't do that, although the next day they clinched Brooklyn's first twentieth-century pennant, beating the Giants, 9–6, while the Braves won both games in Philadelphia. Rudolph defeated Rixey in the first game, 6–3, two Phillies errors contributing to Boston's five-run seventh inning. Mayer was victimized by five more errors (including one of his own) in the 6–1 nightcap. The Braves played errorlessly behind Tyler.

Brooklyn's pennant-clinching victory was tainted by controversy—something that had often been associated with McGraw's teams, as would continue to be the case in the years ahead. Benton and Sherry Smith started the game, but neither was effective. Perritt and Pfeffer relieved them, Pfeffer ending up the winning pitcher. It was a sloppy game in which the teams combined to commit seven errors. New York's infielders let ground balls they could have fielded get by them, runners ran the bases carelessly, Perritt took a long, slow windup with runners on base, and in general the Giants played indifferent baseball.

Brooklyn was ahead 6–5 at the end of the fifth inning, when

McGraw suddenly disappeared from the dugout and wasn't seen again. In interviews over the next two days, he first said he wasn't accusing his players of not trying to win, but then he went on to claim they ignored his signals, showed "miserable judgment in every department of play, and almost turned the game into a farce." "Such baseball disgusted me, and I left the bench…. I refused to be connected with it."[28]

Amid vehement denials by the New York players that they had given less than their best, the baseball press produced a shower of speculations on why the Giants played as they did, and why McGraw did and said what he did. Some writers suggested a natural letdown after the record-breaking winning streak; others, frayed nerves after the team's exhausting pace; still others, sentiment in favor of Uncle Robbie on the part of the New York players who had been on the team when he was McGraw's coach. And then there was McGraw's alleged bet on third place. For the record, Robinson said, "McGraw's suspicions in this matter are ridiculous." Off the record, he growled, "He pissed on my pennant."[29]

Meanwhile everybody had to play out the string. McGraw put Herzog in charge of the Giants for their remaining two games, which they won and then lost. McGraw spent one day watching a Washington–New York game in the Polo Grounds, then left with his wife for Baltimore and the Laurel race track. The Braves lost to the Phillies, 7–5, before closing the season with a good performance by Nehf, who gained a 4–1 decision over two Philadelphia youngsters.

The final National League standings for 1916 were: Brooklyn 94–60, Philadelphia, 91–62; Boston 89–63, New York, 86–66, Chicago, 67–86, Pittsburgh, 65–89, Cincinnati, 60–93, St. Louis, 60–93. So while the Braves ended up a notch lower than in 1915, they actually won six more games and finished a couple of games closer to the pennant-winner. One could look back over the season and see that what probably kept them from the pennant were their 11–15 record in May and those seven-straight losses in September. With the exception of May, they had a winning margin in every month and were particularly strong in August. They also had a winning record against every team in the league except the Phillies, with whom they split twenty-two games.

The Braves' main difficulty was lack of offense. Their .233 team batting average was the lowest in the majors. Konetchy led in average (.260) and runs driven in (70), while Magee, limited to 120 games, mostly because of his broken arm, slumped to .241. Maranville batted only .235. Wilhoit, who was expected to boost offensive output, batted only .240. Evers never returned to the lineup after leaving to get his infected tooth taken care of. Of Boston's 158 games (which included six ties), he played in only seventy-one, calling into question whether he was any longer of much value to the team.

Again the Braves' strength was their pitching—but then pitchers continued to have the upper hand in both major circuits, especially in the National League. Boston's pitchers allowed the fewest runs in either league (453) and had a collective earned-run average of 2.19, bettered only by Brooklyn's 2.12, which was the best in the majors. Rudolph's 19–12 record again led the staff; Tyler's was 17–9, with a staff's best 2.02 earned-run average. Hughes probably would have won twenty games if his broken hand hadn't finished him with a month to go in the season. As it was, he won sixteen, lost only three, and saved five for others. Jesse Barnes consistently pitched in bad luck and ended with a 6–13 record and a 2.37 earned-run average.

By pre–1914 standards, it had been a successful season, although after the "miracle" of that year, anything else had to be a disappointment. Home attendance suffered from holiday and Saturday rainouts, although the 313,495 people who paid for seats in Braves Field was still the third-highest total in

Wilbert Robinson. "Uncle Robbie" was also unhappy with McGraw after the 1916 season, for reasons different from Moran's (George Bantham Bain Collection, Library of Congress).

franchise history. The Braves actually drew better on the road—449,400 by the calculation of the *Boston Globe's* Melville E. Webb. Things still looked pretty promising for the once-downtrodden Boston National Leaguers. But in fact Bay State fans had already seen the best of times for the Braves—for a long time. Ahead, moreover, was the ghastly European war, which the Wilson administration would finally fail to keep the United States from entering. For baseball, as for nearly everything else, big changes were in the offing.

9

1917 and After:
"A shadow of the rapid
stuff that won a flag"

On the eve of the World Series, Bill Phelon acclaimed the 1916 pennant races "the greatest in baseball history."[1] "Wild Bill" had been around for a long time, but he evidently forgot what happened in 1908, when Detroit won the American League pennant by a half-game over Cleveland and two and a half over Chicago; and the Cubs won a pennant-deciding replay game with the Giants, while Pittsburgh ended up tying the Giants for second place.

Yet the 1916 races had provided about as much drama as any fan could want. The outcome in the National League wasn't decided until the last days of the season. Even without Tris Speaker, the Boston Red Sox won again with the premier pitching staff in baseball, now headed by Babe Ruth, a twenty-three-game winner. But whereas they had barely edged Detroit in 1915, this season they had to fight off both Chicago, which had added the stellar Joe Jackson to its outfield, and Ty Cobb's Tigers. Boston finished two games ahead of the White Sox, four ahead of Detroit.

Once again the Braves' management made Braves Field available to the Red Sox for their World Series home games. If it was different National League competition in 1916, the outcome was the same. Like Philadelphia a year earlier, Brooklyn could win only one game, as Ernie Shore beat Uncle Robbie's outfit in the first and fifth games, Ruth overcame Sherry Smith in fourteen innings in game two, and Hubert "Dutch" Leonard won the other decision. The Series had gone to the American League in six of the past seven years; that one National League victory, as Grantland Rice put it, "was won by an inspired ball club in a delirium."

In four of the National League's Series defeats, its entry could win only one game. Rice thought Brooklyn would have finished no better than fifth in the American League. Part of the trouble was that the National League had handicapped itself with its twenty-one-man roster limit. But Rice might also have noted that the league lacked everyday performers of the stature of Cobb, Speaker, Jackson, and Eddie Collins, and had fewer emerging young stars such as Ruth and George Sisler.

As expected, with the Federal League out of the way, and especially with the Federals' competition eliminated in four big-league cities, attendance improved substantially in both leagues. National League clubs drew about 620,000 more than in 1915; the American League's increase was a bit above one million. The minor leagues also fared better; of the twenty-six beginning the season only three—all in Class D—failed to complete their schedules.

But thanks to John McGraw, an aggravating bit of business hung over the National League after the World Series. Jack Kofoed, a nineteen-year old sportswriter for the Philadelphia *Public Ledger*, might proclaim, "Baseball is honest to the core, and you know it!" Yet enough questions had been raised about McGraw's conduct and the Giants' play in that October 3 game—including a demand by Phillies manager Moran for a thorough investigation—that John Tener and the league's board of director seemingly had to do something.

Although Tener first said he would just as soon forget the whole issue, he then announced the league's board of directors would take it up at the National League' annual meeting in New York in December. When Tener met with the directors—Charles Ebbets, Percy Haughton, and Barney Dreyfuss (with Giants owner Harry Hempstead recusing himself)—nothing at all happened. *Sporting Life* editorialized, "Not a word was mentioned about the uprising of Manager John J. McGraw in Brooklyn when he accused his players of indifference in their work.... Those club owners who were highly incensed over the reflection on the game have since cooled off and the league has decided to call it a closed incident." Ban Johnson—who had earlier compared McGraw's behavior to a captain deserting his ship—said when he heard the news, he "exploded." Tener retorted that whatever Johnson had to say was "buncombe."[2] So that was the end of that.

The National League club owners did do a couple of significant

John McGraw and Pat Moran, the Polo Grounds, New York. They look friendly here, but Moran was furious with McGraw at the end of the 1916 season (George Bantham Bain Collection, Library of Congress).

things at their December meeting. They voted six to two to raise the roster limit by one man, while the American League kept its twenty-five man rosters. And in concert with the National Commission and the American Leaguers, they voted to abrogate the "Cincinnati Agreement"

181

made early in 1914 with the Players Fraternity. Percy Haughton made two proposals designed to create more offense: three balls for a walk and only one strike on foul balls. Neither proposal got anywhere.

The other big news coming out of the National League's meeting was the naming of a new manager for the Chicago Cubs. Although Joe Tinker had managed Charles Weeghman's Chicago Federals to a pennant in 1915, Weeghman expected the 1916 Cubs, combining the cream of his Federal League champions with a team that tied for fourth in 1915, to do better than a poor fifth place. So Tinker was out, and Weeghman's first choice to replace him was none other than George Stallings, who was still under contract to the Braves through 1920. According to Tim Murnane, Stallings was anxious to go to Chicago for the big increase Weeghman had mentioned. Haughton put a prohibitive price on Stallings's contract: $50,000. That was too steep even for the free-spending lunch-room king, who then put a hypothetical question to Haughton: If he had been able to get Stallings, would Haughton have replaced him with Fred Mitchell? The Boston president replied, yes, he would. "If Mitchell is good enough for the Braves," said Weeghman, "he's good enough for me."[3]

Mitchell had coached Harvard's baseball team the past two springs. Late in the 1916 season, he had signed with the Braves as assistant manager (whereas in 1913–1914 he was under a player contract). Stallings highly valued Mitchell's services and demanded a player from Chicago in return for the man he referred to as "my right eye." What he got was Joe Kelly, a thirty-year-old journeyman outfielder, who had batted .254 in fifty-two games the previous season. According to various sources, an undisclosed amount of cash also changed hands. Murnane's final comment on the deal: "Pres. Haughton blocked Chicago's great desire for the services of Stallings and sent him back to the cotton fields a much-disappointed man."[4]

That was also one of the last columns contributed by the *Boston Globe*'s sports editor and the man widely regarded as the dean of baseball writers. Two months later, at age sixty-three, Murnane suffered a fatal heart attack in the Shubert Theatre in Boston.

Outside the meeting rooms at the Waldorf Hotel, the lobby and corridors buzzed with talk about cutting expenses in the time-honored way employers did it—by cutting their employees' pay. With the multi-year contracts players had signed—either to lure them into the Federal League or to keep them from jumping—now expiring, the owners were determined on a policy of retrenchment. The National League owners even reduced their president's salary. Bill Phelon wrote that he expected "quite a house cleaning" among the Braves, and that as contracts expired, Stallings and Haughton could slash about $23,000 from the club's payroll.[5]

Fred Snodgrass made it easy for them. When he was offered $4,000, half of what he had reportedly been paid, he announced his retirement and, at twenty-nine, went into banking in his native California, later becoming a city councilman and mayor in Oxnard. For the past two years, the Boston club had carried Bill James's salary; now it didn't have to pay him anything. Rabbit Maranville's two-year contract, under which he had

Fred Snodgrass. Snodgrass ended his solid nine-year National League career with the Braves, after being released by John McGraw (George Bantham Bain Collection, Library of Congress).

reportedly been paid $6,000, had expired; according to Bill Phelon, he wanted $9,000, but if that were true, Haughton had no intention of giving it to him. He held out until early March before signing; if he got any kind of increase, it wasn't much. Supposedly Dick Rudolph's contract was for the same $7,500 he had received in 1916, but he wanted a two-year contract and didn't sign for 1917 until February.

Lefty Tyler, Ed Konetchy, Sherry Magee, and various other Braves were also unhappy with the terms offered them for 1917; Magee was saying he wanted to be traded. But under the hold of baseball's reserve clause, they all ended up having to sign for what their new contracts specified. Except for Joe Connolly, who went to bat only 110 times in 1916 and batted .227. Connolly wouldn't sign a contract that contained a fifty percent cut. Stallings sold him to Indianapolis, whereupon he decided to retire to his farm at North Smithfield, Rhode Island. All around the two major leagues, players not only had to accept less money but also, in cases where the ten-day clause had been omitted from contracts, accept restoration of that hated provision. As for Johnny Evers, he said 1917, the final year of his contract with Boston, would be his last as a player. Quite a lot of people would have agreed it was about time.

If the end of the period of big pay increases and multi-year contracts meant the club owners had regained the advantage in dealing with their hired hands, that winter they were also relieved of what they had always considered a fundamental threat to owner-player relations. The Baseball Players' Fraternity had never accomplished a great deal, but when the Cincinnati Agreement was abrogated, Fraternity president David Fultz called for players throughout Organized Baseball to refuse to sign their contracts, which would amount to a general strike. Many players had already signed for 1917, but about seven-hundred—most of them minor-leaguers—pledged not to sign. With the owners talking about suspensions and hiring replacements, few major-leaguers were willing to put their careers in jeopardy for the sake of minor-leaguers. So when the solidarity Fultz had counted on proved illusory, he gave up, canceled the strike plans, and released everybody from their pledges. With that, in effect, the Players' Fraternity self-destructed. Later, ironically, Fultz became part of baseball's executive elite, serving two years as president of the International League.

The Braves again did their spring training in Miami. The previous September, Ralph McMillin, in his column criticizing the in-season trades Cincinnati, Chicago, and St. Louis had made with New York, predicted the Giants had "built a juggernaut car that promises to bust the race of 1917 to smithereens." Bill Phelon also picked the Giants to finish first, followed by Brooklyn, Philadelphia, and Boston.[6]

By the time the Braves and the other teams arrived at their training sites, the United States had moved perilously close to war with Imperial Germany. At the end of January, the German naval command announced a resumption of unrestricted submarine operations, which would inevitably mean the loss of American ships and American lives. Shortly thereafter the Wilson administration, tacitly acknowledging the failure of its incursion into northern Mexico, ordered the withdrawal of General Pershing's force. The final blow to American neutrality was a note the German foreign minister sent to his government's representative in Mexico City, instructing him to inform the Carranza government that if Mexico joined Germany in a war with the United States, Mexico would regain Texas, New Mexico, and Arizona, territory it had lost in the 1830s and 1840s. Intercepted by the British and made public, the "Zimmerman Note" served further to intensify American war feeling.

On April 2, President Wilson addressed a joint session of Congress and asked for a declaration of war against Imperial Germany. Four days later, both houses voted overwhelmingly for war. According to Harold Kaese, when the Braves finished playing their way north from Miami and arrived home to open the season, Maranville, Evers, and Gowdy went to the recruiting stand on Boston Common and tried to enlist, "but the Army wasn't quite ready for them."[7] In fact the U.S. army wasn't ready for any large number of volunteers. Very early it was decided that the army would rely on conscription to realize the millions of soldiers presumed to be necessary to fight in Western Europe. On May 18, Wilson signed the Selective Service Act; June 5 was the day on which all men between the ages of twenty-one and thirty were required to register. Married men with dependents were exempt for the time being.

So on Wednesday, April 11, 1917, for the first time, the professional baseball season began with the nation at war. But not on that day in Boston, because the Braves' opener with the Giants was rained out. On Thursday, besides the usual Opening Day rites—speeches, floral horseshoes, and the like—the Boston management designated the occasion "Soldiers and Sailors Day," and the whole scene took on a patriotic aspect. A portion of the advance ticket sales was pledged to the military recreational fund of the Young Men's Christian Association. The band from the Charlestown Navy Yard provided martial airs, detachments of soldiers and sailors paraded around the field, while overhead an aviator named Walter Bullock performed flying stunts in his biplane. After all that, the game was something of a letdown, a 6–4 loss, Jeff Tesreau defeating Rudolph.

The scheduled Opening Day washout was rather emblematic of the Braves' 1917 season. Not much went right for the team expected at least to be in contention for the pennant. The broken pitching hand Tom Hughes had suffered late the previous season continued to trouble him so much that it was August before he took the mound. He worked in eleven games, winning five, losing three. Used mainly in relief, Pat Ragan pitched with a sore arm and finished with six wins, nine losses. Dick Rudolph's earned-run average jumped from 2.16 to 3.41 as he struggled to a 13–13 record. Lefty Tyler ended with a respectable 14–14 mark, but Jesse Barnes, continuing to receive poor run support, ended up losing a majors-worst twenty-one games, while winning thirteen. Art Nehf emerged as Stallings's ace, with seventeen wins against eight defeats.

Late in July, Haughton and Stallings signed thirty-eight-year-old Ed Walsh, who had been one of the great pitchers of his time with the Chicago White Sox but had appeared in only fourteen games over the past three seasons, before getting his release. Walsh's try at a comeback amounted to four games, eighteen innings, no wins, one loss. Ed Reulbach pitched in five games and also won none and lost one before being released.

Maranville's patriotic zeal must have cooled somewhat after he tried to enlist, because he was still with the Braves on Registration Day and would remain with them the whole season, batting a career high (to that point) .260. But on June 2, Hank Gowdy made himself into something of a national hero by becoming the first major-leaguer to volunteer for military service. Gowdy joined the First Ohio Militia, which was subsequently reorganized as the 166th Regiment of the 42nd Division (known as the "Rainbow Division" because it was made up of men from twenty-six states and the District of Columbia). From the spring of 1918 until the armistice was declared the following November 11, Gowdy and his division would see a great deal of combat in the struggle to repulse Germany's desperate all-out offensive, then to push back the Kaiser's forces and bring the war to an end.

By the start of the season, Larry Chappell was back in the minor leagues. Sherwood Magee, so unhappy over having to take a pay cut that he wanted to leave the Braves, got his wish on August 1, when he was sold to Cincinnati for the waiver price after appearing in seventy-two games and batting .256. Ed Konetchy broke his leg and missed a month of the season. Joe Wilhoit and Eddie Fitzpatrick saw limited action. The outfielders who put in the most playing time were Joe Kelly (who batted only .222) and Ray Powell (.272) and Walter Rehg (.270), both purchased during the season from the minor leagues. After Gowdy's departure, Walt Tragesser (.222) took over regular catching duties.

Johnny Evers was at second base on Opening Day, but after three games he sat down and didn't get back in the lineup until June. During the period when he was on the bench, he gave an interview to *Baseball Magazine*, in which he recounted that his left arm had pained him since the middle of the previous season (although it was his right elbow he complained about in 1916). Evers said besides having his infected tooth removed, he had undergone two months of electric current treatment on the arm, which had eliminated the pain but left the arm dead. But then, he went on, "I have never felt wholly right since I had that severe nervous breakdown some years ago. I don't think anyone ever fully recovers from such an attack."[8]

On July 12, after playing twenty-four games in a Braves uniform, the fiery Trojan, hero of the 1914 pennant drive and the World Series sweep, suffered the indignity of being sold to Philadelphia for the waiver price. There he revived somewhat, playing in fifty-six games, although he batted only .224 for Pat Moran's Phillies. Johnny Rawlings, purchased from Toledo in the offseason, became Stallings's regular second baseman.

The Braves got off to a fairly good start. After two losses to the Giants, they won three games from Philadelphia and another from New York. But after winning in Brooklyn on April 28 and playing the Robins to a 6–6 tie the next day, they never again reached the .500 mark. "For six solid weeks," Bill Phelon observed in June, "the Braves played a game that was but a shadow of the rapid stuff that won a flag three years ago, and took high honors in 1915 and 1916."[9] They didn't get any better after that, finishing in sixth place with a 72–81 record, twenty-five and a half games behind New York. If not the juggernaut Ralph McMillin had predicted they would be in 1917, the Giants had a relatively easy time gaining John McGraw's sixth pennant. At 98–56, they outdistanced Philadelphia by eleven and a half games. St. Louis, Cincinnati, and Chicago also finished ahead of Boston. If it was a drearily disappointing season for the Braves, it was even more so for Brooklyn; the defending league champions were a half-game worse than Boston. Under three managers (including Honus Wagner for one game), Pittsburgh was a dreadful outfit, ending 51–103.

Although the war-production effort was slow in gearing up, by the late summer more and more Americans were working in factories and plants, at longer hours, six days a week. So while their wages grew, fewer people had the opportunity to attend baseball games. Then, too, the absence of tight pennant races—Chicago won in the American League by ten games over Boston—depressed interest and attendance in the last six weeks or so of the season. Overall big-league attendance fell by nearly 1,300,000: 690,000 in the National League, 593,000 in the American League. The Braves' home crowds dwindled to 139,242, a drop of some forty-four percent.

By mid-summer, draft call ups were cutting deeply into minor-league rosters, especially in the lower minors, where players tended to be younger and less likely to have families than in the upper minors and the majors. Of the eighteen minor leagues starting the 1917 season, nine finished it. But if 1917 season was a poor season throughout Organized Baseball, 1918 was going to be worse—a lot worse.

On January 4, the Braves sent Lefty Tyler to the Cubs for Larry Doyle, catcher Art Wilson, and $15,000 in cash (which, given the sickening attendance falloff, the franchise badly needed). Rabbit Maranville, like a number of other major-leaguers, had volunteered for the navy rather than wait to be drafted into the army, so Stallings needed a shortstop. Five days later, Boston traded Doyle and Jesse Barnes to the Giants for Buck Herzog. Doyle was nearing the end of a fine career, but Barnes was a quality young pitcher (although he would pitch only six times in 1918 before entering military service). At thirty-two, Herzog still had some good baseball years ahead of him. But McGraw said later that he had suspected Herzog hadn't played honestly in the World Series, which the White Sox won in six games (handing McGraw his fourth-straight Series defeat).

If the 1917 season had been a big letdown for Braves fans, 1918 was downright dismal. The Braves dropped another notch in the standings, and Stallings, like the other managers, struggled to keep a halfway decent lineup on the field. In July, Secretary of War Newton D. Baker issued his "Work or Fight" order, under which all able-bodied men of draft age (which had been extended from eighteen to forty-five at the end of August 1917), employed in "non-essential" occupations, were subject to the draft—unless they took jobs contributing to the war effort. Secretary

Baker refused to exempt professional baseball from the work-or-fight order, so dozens of ballplayers began leaving their teams to gain employment in munitions plants, steel mills, and particularly shipyards. Most of them actually worked less at their designated jobs than they spent time playing on company-sponsored teams in highly competitive leagues. Major-league teams recruited players from the collapsing minor leagues (of which only the International League survived the season) and carried on as best they could.

At the end of July, Baker gave baseball a reprieve, ruling that the season could continue until Labor Day (September 2), after which the World Series could take place. Fred Mitchell's Chicago ball club easily beat out the Giants. Hippo Vaughn, Lefty Tyler, and Claude Hendrix combined for sixty of the Cubs' eighty-four wins in the truncated season. With Babe Ruth playing much of the time in the outfield and leading the majors with eleven home runs (besides winning thirteen games), Boston won a close race over Cleveland and Washington and then disposed of the Cubs in six games. Given the subtraction of a month of the schedule, everybody, with the possible exception of the Cubs, lost money. The biggest losers were probably the Braves and Brooklyn, who drew 84,938 and 83,831, respectively, the worst attendance figures for any big-league teams in nearly thirty years.

That winter Percy Haughton and other members of his syndicate, tired of losing money, put the Braves on the market. Stallings and Walter Hapgood made an offer, which Haughton rejected as too low. The sale went to John McGraw's friend George Washington Grant, a New Yorker who had made his fortune running a chain of motion-picture theaters in New England. The price was said to be $400,000. Arthur Wise stayed on as a director and club treasurer, as did Hapgood as business manager and secretary. Stallings's contract still had two years to run. He squirmed through another drab season; the Braves finished sixth, thirty-seven and a half games behind first-place Cincinnati (in a 140-game season, which the owners, fearing another bad attendance year and wanting to save two weeks in players' salaries, had foolishly agreed to).

The 1920 Braves finished seventh, only a half-game better than bottom-dog Philadelphia. Stallings gave Bill James, who had been pitching semi-pro ball in California, a try at making a comeback at age twenty-eight. The big right-hander started one game, gave up five hits and two walks in five innings, and left a big-league mound for good. The most memorable day in an otherwise unmemorable season was May 1, when the Braves' Jim Oeschger and Brooklyn's Leon Cadore both pitched all the way to a twenty-six-inning, 1–1 tie. Such heroic pitching would be unthinkable a few decades later, but in those days a pitcher stayed in as long as he was going well. His contract having expired, Stallings didn't ask for another one. Instead, he and Walter Hapgood bought the Rochester International League franchise, and Stallings again became a minor-league manager.

Epilogue:
"Not Stallings baseball"

Boston's representative in the National League had entered upon a long and mostly lackluster period, one in which their aging fans could only think back wistfully on the years 1914–1916, when the Braves were champions and then close contenders. They did finish in fourth place in 1921 under Fred Mitchell, who had been fired by Chicago after a fifth-place showing. But they didn't get back into the first division until the next decade, when they had back-to-back fourth-place finishes in 1933 and 1934, before hitting rock bottom in 1935 with an abysmal 38–115 record. After rising to fourth place again in 1937, they reverted to form, becoming second-division habitués for six years under the less-than-inspiring direction of Casey Stengel and Bob Coleman.

In the early post–World War II years, however, the Braves regained respectability. Under manager Billy Southworth—with scintillating pitching from Johnny Sain and Warren Spahn, and fine performances from everyday players such as Bob Elliott, Alvin Dark, and Tommy Holmes—they rose to fourth in 1946, third in 1947, and a pennant in 1948, although they lost to Cleveland in the World Series. Then, after three years in fourth place, they fell to sixth, attracting only 280,000 or so fans to Braves Field, the smallest total in the majors. In March 1953, with the Braves already in spring training wearing caps with "B" on them, owner Louis Perini moved the team to Milwaukee, where the county government had financed a brand new stadium with acres of parking spaces. An "M" was hurriedly sewn on the players' caps.

* * *

Until the mid–1920s, and the construction of Yankee Stadium and the enlargement of the Polo Grounds and Chicago's Comiskey Park,

Braves Field remained the biggest—and arguably the finest—baseball facility anywhere. In that decade, it underwent the first of numerous modifications in its outfield distances, all intended to transform a playing field designed for triples and inside-the-park home runs into one fitted to the kind of power-oriented baseball Babe Ruth popularized. Within fifteen years or so, Jim Gaffney's innovation of running trolley cars directly into the ballpark complex was obsolescent, as better-off Bostonians increasingly moved to the suburbs and drove to Braves Field in personal automobiles. By the late 1930s, Braves Field (also called the "Beehive" in the few years when the team was known as the "Bees") acquired a rather rundown appearance.

After 1944, when Louis Perini and two partners in a New England construction business gained control of the franchise, they financed various changes in the ballpark, including night games, better sight lines, and a grove of fir trees behind the outfield fence to break the chill wind blowing off the Charles River. Both Braves Field and the team experienced a renaissance; in 1947 the franchise finally topped one million in home attendance, and the next year, when the Braves won the franchise's second twentieth-century pennant, they attracted 1,455,438 customers. After Perini suddenly moved the team to Milwaukee, Boston University purchased Braves Field and tore down the stands except for the huge right-field pavilion, which still serves as the seating area on one side of the university's football and soccer field.

In the winter of 1920, **George Stallings** married for the third time, to Bertha Thorpe Sharpe, widow of Bud Sharpe and the mother of a young daughter named Cecilia. Bertha quickly bore Stallings his third son, whom they named George Stallings, Jr. For a few years, Stallings was quite successful in Rochester. From 1921 to 1923, playing 168-game schedules, his teams won 306 games, which ought to have been enough to dominate the International League. But the upper minors had opted out of the annual major-league players' draft, so that Jack Dunn was able to keep mostly intact his Baltimore powerhouse, which won six consecutive pennants. In 1924, 1925, and 1926, Rochester finished fourth, third, and sixth; in mid-season 1927, with his team deep in the second division, Stallings sold his holdings in the franchise and resigned.

The high-strung Georgian had suffered a pretty bad heart attack in 1923 (although that didn't keep him from engaging in a fist fight the next year in Newark with an umpire named Sullivan). One might have thought he would decide the time had come to give up the grind of riding trains, putting up in the second-class hotels where even upper-minors teams stayed, and being away from his family much of the time. But in 1928, Stallings and Hapgood, together with a group of Montreal investors, obtained an International League franchise and brought the French-speaking city back into the International League after an absence of ten years. The group also financed construction of a new ballpark, called Delorimier Downs. Stallings went back to managing.

That was a mistake; he had a severe heart attack in mid-season in Toronto. Again he survived, quipping to reporters, "Well, boys, the umpire up yonder has two strikes on me but the old man's not out yet."[1] Stallings resigned as Montreal manager and, as advised by physicians, made the long journey home by train. At Haddock he was supposed to follow the prescribed treatment for people recovering from heart attacks: rest, relaxation, avoidance of stress. Stallings had never been good at any of that. After another crisis and stays in hospitals in Macon and Atlanta, he improved enough to return to Haddock. At 6 a. m. on Monday, May 13, 1929, his nurse entered his bedroom and found him dead. The Miracle Man was sixty-one years old. George Tweedy Stallings was survived by his wife, three sons, a stepdaughter, and two brothers.

Bill James (the author), in his book on baseball managers, has written that Stallings's alternating left-hand and right-hand-batting outfielders, depending on the opposition's pitcher, "had tremendous impact on other managers, almost revolutionary impact.... From 1915 to 1925, virtually every major team platooned at one or more positions."[2] It would, of course, remain for Casey Stengel to carry platooning—of both outfielders and infielders—to its ultimate effectiveness in directing the New York Yankees to ten pennants and seven World Series victories from 1949 to 1960.

But in a newspaper piece published in the winter of 1914–1915, in the afterglow of the Braves' pennant and World Series sweep, Stallings made a remark about himself that might well have served as his epitaph: "I have often said that if I go the wrong way after they finally call me out in this man's game, my worst punishment would be to manage an indifferent ball club, with a wild pitcher and a bone-headed catcher."[3]

At the end of the 1917 season, the Philadelphia Phillies released

Johnny Evers. The next year he joined the Knights of Columbus overseas aid mission and spent several months in Europe. The Trojan was out of baseball in 1919, then joined his old adversary John McGraw as a coach for the Giants. In 1921, Evers returned to Chicago for a second try as Cubs manager, resigning with a third of the season left and his team headed for seventh place. After two years as a coach for the Chicago White Sox, he managed that team to a last-place finish. Beginning in 1928, Evers was back with the Braves—for four years as coach and assistant manager, then two years as a scout. In 1935, at Albany in the International League, he managed still another last-place team.

After running an Albany sporting-goods store for a while, Evers tried his hand at the executive end of baseball, serving as vice president and general manager of the Albany club. That lasted one year, after which Evers took employment as superintendent of Albany's municipal stadium. In 1942 he had a stroke, which partially paralyzed him. For the next five years, he was mostly bedridden or wheelchair-bound, but in 1946 he received the pleasant news that, together with Joe Tinker (who had recently had a leg amputated) and the late Frank Chance, he had been elected to the National Baseball Hall of Fame. A second stroke took Evers's life on March 28, 1947, at the age of sixty-six. He never reconciled with his wife Helen, whose name is listed on his death certificate as Helen C. Fitzgibbons.

One way or another, **Rabbit Maranville** stayed connected to baseball for the rest of his life. After coming out of the navy, he continued to be the Braves' shortstop, until he was traded to Pittsburgh before the 1921 season. His first marriage having ended in divorce, Maranville married Helene Bertrand early in February 1921. With the Pirates, he added to his reputation for hijinks and nocturnal adventures, and continued to entertain crowds with his belt-buckle catches and run-ins with umpires. Playing in the so-called lively ball era, he batted better than he ever had and helped make the Pirates perennial contenders, although he was traded to the Cubs after the 1924 season and thus missed playing on the 1925 pennant and World Series winners. Following a poor year with the Cubs, Maranville drew his release, signed with Brooklyn, and had another poor season, although he no doubt enjoyed the easy-going atmosphere on Uncle Robbie's outfit. With Rochester in 1927, he again played for Stallings, until his old manager resigned during the season.

Having put in a solid year at Rochester, Rabbit returned to the majors with the St. Louis Cardinals. He played in 112 games on his second pennant-winner, but the following December, the Cardinals traded him to the Braves. There he remained, through bad seasons and a couple of decent ones, for the next eight years, although he missed all of 1934 after breaking his ankle in a spring-training game. Rabbit and Babe Ruth, eminently kindred spirits, were briefly teammates on the miserable 1935 Braves, until the Babe quit for good early in June.

Maranville spent several years managing in the New York–Pennsylvania, International, and Eastern Leagues. In 1936, at the age of forty-four, he played in 123 games for Class A Elmira and batted .323. For the last thirteen years of his life, he worked in youth baseball programs in Rochester, Detroit, and finally New York, where he ran clinics in the Polo Grounds and Yankee Stadium in the *Journal-American's* sandlot school. Future Yankees pitchers Whitey Ford and Bob Grim were among his protégés. On January 5, 1954, Rabbit died of heart disease at age sixty-two, only a few weeks before his election to baseball's Hall of Fame.

Sergeant Hank Gowdy added to his national acclaim, when he returned from France and refused an offer of $1,500 per week to go on the vaudeville circuit and talk about his war experiences. He remained with the Braves for the next four seasons, batting .317 in ninety-two games in 1922, his best mark so far. After he was traded to the Giants, his lively ball era batting averages were even better; in 1924 he played in his second World Series, against Washington. But in the bottom of the eleventh inning of game seven, with one out, Gowdy made one of the most egregious gaffes in Series history, when he went after a pop foul, stumbled on his catcher's mask, and missed the ball. A double, an infield error, and a bad-bounce single brought in the Series-winning run.

Released in mid-season 1925, Gowdy managed and played in the upper minors for three years before reuniting with Maranville and Evers on the Braves, working mainly as a coach but occasionally going behind the plate. Subsequently he coached for the Giants and Cincinnati, until World War II, when he reenlisted in the army. Given the rank of captain, he served as the athletic director at Fort Benning, Georgia, where, after the war, the baseball field was named for him. In the postwar years, Gowdy again held coaching positions with the Reds and Giants, before retiring to Columbus, Ohio, where in 1952 a complex of baseball fields (no longer in existence) was named for him. In 1966 he died in his home town at age seventy-six.

From 1913 to 1917, **Dick Rudolph** won ninety-four games for the Braves and pitched 1,368 innings. In 1918 arm trouble limited him to twenty starts and a 9–10 record, but he came back in 1919 to work 272 innings; and while his record with the sixth-place Braves was only 13–13, his 2.17 earned-run average was the lowest of his big-league career. The next season he started eighteen games, completed only three, and finished with a 4–8 record. From then on he pitched from time to time but worked mainly as a coach until 1928, when he and a partner purchased the Waterbury franchise in the Eastern League. After its team finished a distant last, Waterbury dropped from the league.

For a few years, Rudolph was in business with his brother in a funeral home in Nyack, New York; a job as supervisor of concessions in Yankee Stadium followed that. He also served as a volunteer coach for Fordham University's baseball team. On October 20, 1949, "Baldy," as teammates had called him, suffered a fatal heart attack at this home in the Bronx. He was sixty-two.

George "Lefty" Tyler won the second game of the 1918 World Series but lost the deciding sixth game, 2–1, both Boston Red Sox runs being unearned. Developing shoulder trouble the next year, he didn't pitch after mid-season. The medical wisdom of the time linked infected teeth to hurting shoulders, so in the offseason Tyler had nearly all his teeth extracted. That didn't help much; after going 11–12 in 1920, he was released early the next season. He pitched some for Stallings at Rochester in 1921, played in the New England and Eastern leagues, and umpired in the minors for a couple of years. After a period as an employee of the New England Power Company, he worked as a shoe-cutter in a mill in Haverhill, Massachusetts. At age sixty-three, Tyler died of a heart attack at his home in nearby Lowell.

Bill James served in the First World War, and after his unsuccessful trial with the Braves in 1919, was a coach for Sacramento in the Pacific Coast League. Later he drove a truck for an oil company and worked in the county tax assessor's office in Oroville. He died at seventy-nine in 1971. After quitting baseball at twenty-nine, **Charles "Butch" Schmidt** ran his Baltimore meat market for the next thirty-seven years. He also put on a great deal of weight, reaching three-hundred pounds at one point. On September 4, 1952, he was shopping for some beeves in the Union Stockyards when he succumbed to a heart attack. After **Joe Connolly** retired from professional baseball, he married, fathered three children, and became a prominent local citizen, winning elections to the North Smithfield, Rhode Island, town council and to both houses of the state legislature. In 1943 he was employed by the state board of milk control when he suffered a heart attack. He died at his home in Springfield, Rhode Island, at age fifty-five.

George "Possum" Whitted's big-league career ended in 1922 after one time at bat for Brooklyn. He managed in the minors at Toledo and Durham, eventually buying the Durham Bulls with his brother. Whitted died at seventy-two in a Wilmington, North Carolina, hospital. In 1962, at age sixty-eight, **Les Mann** was stricken with a fatal heart attack while driving his car in Pasadena, California. In October 1966, **James Carlisle "Red" Smith** was still actively employed at the age of seventy-six, working as a tax investigator in Atlanta, when he died from a stroke.

After he went from the Braves to Cincinnati, **Sherwood Magee** finally got his wish to play for a pennant-winner. He was in fifty-six games for the 1919 Reds, who outdistanced New York by nine lengths. In the World Series he singled in two pinch-hit appearances. In 1920, the man who had once slugged an umpire became one, and in 1928 he joined the National League's staff. His work was sufficiently impressive that he was reappointed for the following season, but in March 1929, with the teams in spring training, Magee died of pneumonia in his home in Philadelphia. He was forty-four. **Jim Gaffney** died four years later at sixty-three, of a stroke at a friend's home in East Hampton, Long Island. In 1920 he had considered buying the Brooklyn franchise, but after selling the Braves he never got back into baseball.

After finishing the 1915 season with Toronto and playing the next year with Kansas City, **Larry Gilbert** settled in his native New Orleans and became a fixture in the Southern Association. He led the league in batting in 1919 and continued to play the outfield until 1925. From 1923 to 1948 he managed the Pelicans, winning nine pennants over that span. Gilbert was seventy-three when he died in 1965. After he was sent down to Toledo, **Paul Strand** pitched and played the outfield for that and various other minor-league teams, eventually going to the outfield full time.

From 1921 to 1923, he was one of the foremost hitters in Pacific Coast League history. Playing his home games in the light air of Salt Lake City, Strand batted, successively, .314, .384, and .394; totaled eighty home runs; and drove in 420 runs. That got him back to the big leagues with Connie Mack's rebuilding Philadelphia Athletics, but it was a matter of different air and better pitchers. In forty-seven games, he batted .228 with no homers, before being sold to Toledo. Strand continued to pound minor-league pitching until he retired in 1928. He outlived the rest of his Braves teammates, dying at eighty in 1974.

* * *

At the beginning of June 1951, Strand was among several 1914 Braves who gathered in Boston on the seventy-fifth anniversary of the founding of the National League, of which Boston was a charter member. They had dinner together, and the next afternoon rode in vintage automobiles out to Braves Field for a Braves-Cubs game. Beforehand, some of the old Braves tossed the ball around the infield; Rabbit Maranville fielded grounders and made perfect pegs to Butch Schmidt at first base. Hank Gowdy threw one high in the air toward shortstop, where Maranville made his belt-buckle catch, to the delight of the modest-sized crowd. Rabbit had missed the dinner and also the parade, having just arrived after being flown from New York in Louis Perini's private aircraft. He thought the infield exhibition had been too short. "I was just getting warmed up when they made us stop," he complained.[4]

During the game (which the Cubs won, beating Warren Spahn), the *Boston Globe* reporter and cartoonist Gene Mack interviewed Bill James. At one point, with the bases loaded, the next Braves batter hit the first pitch into a double play. James remarked, "That's not Stallings baseball. He always said, 'Let the pitcher lick himself.'" Added Les Mann, "It's a different game now."[5]

Indeed, baseball in 1951 was a much different game from the game those aging men played, as it would be even more different sixty or sixty-five years later. It's doubtful that George Stallings would have recognized much about twenty-first-century baseball, with its continental expanse and reliance on air travel, thirty teams in six divisions, interleague play, a players' union far more powerful than anything in David Fultz's wildest dreams, free agency and staggering players' salaries, television rather than ticket sales as the biggest source of owners' revenue. Not to mention the Designated Hitter in one league but not in the other, barrages of home runs, obsessive pitching changes and the rarity of complete games, and umpires' calls second-guessed and sometimes changed by video replay.

It's also doubtful that more than a few of today's fans attending games in Turner Field in Atlanta or watching the Atlanta Braves on television would know anything about the ancestral Boston Braves. (For that matter, a dwindling number would know anything about the Atlanta Braves' most-immediate ancestors in Milwaukee.) The Braves of the George Stallings era belong to baseball's ever-more-distant past. But for a few years they were a remarkable team that, in 1914, did something seemingly miraculous. They will live in baseball history—if no longer in active memory—as the "Miracle Braves."

Chapter Notes

Prologue

1. *Boston Globe*, February 2, 1946, p. 2; February 17, 1944, p. 13. Kaese's *The Boston Braves* (New York: Putnam's, 1948) was revised and republished in 1953 and reprinted in paperback in 2002 (Boston: Northeastern University Press).

2. Boston teams also won major-league pennants in the Players' League in 1890 and in the American Association in 1891. So the city had three champions in three different leagues in two years.

3. Of course in 1904 there was no second World Series, because New York Giants owner John T. Brush and manager John McGraw infamously refused to play the upstart American Leaguers, thereby creating the only hiatus in Series competition until 1994.

4. Kaese, *Boston Braves*, p. 128.

5. Glenn Stout, *Fenway 1912: The Birth of a Ballpark, a Championship Season, and Fenway's Remarkable First Year* (Boston: Houghton Mifflin, 2011), p. 47.

6. *Sporting News*, April 4, 1912, p. 7.

7. Tyler could use that delivery, with the step toward first, because rule makers hadn't as yet required that the pitcher step forward as he threw the ball.

8. *Boston Globe*, August 1, 1912, p. 2.

9. The Braves also sent pitcher Billy Hogg to New Bedford in the Maranville deal. Hogg insisted he be paid the remaining $1,500 on his contract, so Maranville actually cost the franchise $4,000.

10. Unidentified newspaper clipping, Rabbit Maranville Collection, Giamatti Research Center, National Baseball Hall of Fame Library, Cooperstown, NY.

11. John Durant, *Baseball's Miracle Teams* (New York: Hastings House, 1975), p. 9; *Christian Science Monitor*, August 15, 1912, p. 3.

12. The 1912 Series lasted eight games because one game was a tie, called because of gathering darkness.

13. *Sporting News*, November 21, 1912, p. 1.

14. *Boston Globe*, May 14, 1929, p. 24; *New York Times*, October 10, 1927, p. 19; *Chicago Tribune*, December 21, 1954, p. B1.

Chapter 1

1. Information on Stallings's early life comes from his interview with Harvey T. Woodruff, *Chicago Tribune*, September 6, 1914, p. B4; and from Martin Kohout, "George Tweedy Stallings," Tom Simon, ed., *Dead Ball Stars of the National League* (Washington, D.C.: Brassey's, 2004), pp. 323–324. According to Kohout's research, much of what Stallings told Woodruff is incorrect.

2. Stallings did, though, have among his players at Philadelphia Napoleon Lajoie, who batted .361 in 1897, his rookie season, and went to become one of the great players in baseball history.

3. After the 1899 season, the National League cut back to eight teams, dropping Cleveland, Baltimore, Washington, and Louisville. All except Louisville eventually became members of the American League.

4. More famous is the conflict in the American League in 1901 and 1902 between Johnson and John McGraw, who insisted on bringing his rowdy ways from the Na-

tional League to Baltimore when that city became a member of the American League. In mid-season 1902, McGraw jumped from Johnson's league to become manager of the New York Giants, where he would make a great deal of baseball history.

5. Harold Seymour [and Dorothy Seymour Mills], *Baseball: The Golden Age* (New York: Oxford University Press, 1971), p. 54.

6. Lawrence S. Ritter, *The Glory of Their Times: The Story of the Early Days of Baseball Told by the Men Who Played It*, 2d ed. (New York: Vintage, 1985) p. 83.

7. Gowdy quoted in "Baseball's Greatest Teams," *Baseball Digest*, July 1949, in Stallings Collection; *St. Louis Post-Dispatch*, August 14, 1914, p. 8; Ritter, *Glory of Their Times*, p. 83.

8. William A. Phelon, "Who Will Win the 1913 Pennants?" *Baseball Magazine* 10 (May 1913), p. 14.

9. F. C. Lane, "The Gamest Player in Baseball," *Baseball Magazine* 11 (September 1913), pp. 51–61.

10. Rabbit Maranville, "Old or New, It's Still Baseball," *American Legion Magazine* 11 (October 1935), p. 55.

11. *Sporting Life*, March 8, 1913, p. 1.

12. *Sporting News*, March 13, 1913, p. 3.

13. William A. Phelon, "Ringing Up the Curtain on the 1913 Pennant Race," *Baseball Magazine* 11 (June 1913), p. 16.

14. After the 1911 season the Eastern League owners changed the organization's name to International League, in keeping with Toronto and Montreal as league members.

15. Dick Leyden, "Dick Rudolph," in Simon, ed., *Dead Ball Stars of the National League*, p. 328.

16. *Sporting Life*, June 14, 1913, p. 15; May 24, 1913, p. 5.

17. William A. Phelon, "The Baseball Campaign Up to Date," *Baseball* Magazine 11 (July 1913), p. 21; *St. Louis Post-Dispatch*, July 15, 1913, p. 9.

18. *St. Louis Post-Dispatch*, September 22, 1913, p. 12; *Chicago Tribune*, October 7, 1913, p. 28.

19. *Boston Globe*, September 7, 1913, p. 53.

Chapter 2

1. F. C. Lane, "The Sensational Evers Deal," *Baseball Magazine* 14 (August 1914), p. 12. See also C. P. Stack, "A Day with John Evers," *Baseball Magazine* 14 (February 1915), pp. 71–75.

2. *Boston Globe*, September 7, 1913, p. 53.

3. Ibid., May 20, 1913, p. 7.

4. Club owners in the minor leagues also put the reserve clause in players' contracts, but minor-league owners realized much of their income from selling their best players. Then there was also the provision by which players who had been in the minors for a certain number of years could be drafted by a major-league club for the specified draft price.

5. *Boston Globe*, February 11, 1914, p. 1; *Chicago Tribune*, February 11, 1914, p. 1.

6. Lane, "Sensational Evers Deal," p. 3

7. *Chicago Tribune*, February 11, 1914, p. 1.

8. Daniel R. Levitt, *The Battle That Forged Modern Baseball: The Federal League Challenge and Its Legacy* (Lanham, MD: Rowman & Littlefield, 2012), p. 84.

9. *Washington Post*, February 12, 1914, p. 8.

10. *Boston Globe*, February 23, 1914, p. 5.

11. The Murphy Theatre still stands on Main Street in Wilmington. Murphy died in Chicago in 1931.

12. Charles P. Stack, "Loyal John Evers," *Baseball Magazine* 12 (April 1914), p. 100; Lane, "Sensational Evers Deal," p. 114.

13. *St. Louis Post-Dispatch*, April 1, 1914, p. 10; *Christian Science Monitor*, April 13, 1914, p. 16; William A. Phelon, "The Big League Pennant Winners," *Baseball Magazine* 13 (May 1914), pp. 13–30; Frederick G. Lieb, "How Will They Finish Next October?" *Baseball Magazine* 12 (March 1914), p. 46 ; *Cincinnati Post*, March 10, 1914, p. 6; *Washington Post*, April 13, 1914, p. 9.

14. Whether the workers on Stallings's Haddock plantation were subjected to the contract labor laws isn't known.

15. Unidentified clipping, Rabbit

Maranville Collection, National Baseball Hall of Fame Library, Cooperstown, NY.

16. Bill Killefer, the Phillies' regular catcher and Alexander's favorite batterymate, signed a contract with the Chicago Federals for a big pay increase then jumped back to his old team for even more money.

17. *Cincinnati Post,* May 26, 1914, p. 6.

Chapter 3

1. Joann Ghio, "James Reveals Feud with Evers," *Baseball Digest* (October–November 1964), pp. 15–16, quoted in Gil Bogen, *Tinker, Evers, Chance: A Triple Biography* (Jefferson, NC: McFarland, 2008), p. 148.

2. *Cincinnati Post,* May 28, 1914, p. 6. Lee Magee, whose legal name was Leopold Christopher Hoernschmeyer, understandably chose to play professional baseball under a different name.

3. *Sporting Life,* June 6, 1914, p. 3.

4. Ibid., June 13, 1914, p. 7.

5. *Washington Post,* January 24, 1950, p. 13.

6. *St. Louis Post-Dispatch,* July 13, 1914, p. 8.

7. Unidentified clipping, George "Lefty" Tyler Collection, National Baseball Hall of Fame Library, Cooperstown, NY.

8. James Carlisle "Red" Smith Collection, National Baseball Hall of Fame Library, Cooperstown, NY.

9. *Cincinnati Post,* August 26, 1914, p. 2.

10. *Sporting Life,* August 6, 1914, p. 3.

11. Ibid., August 22, 1914, p. 3; *Washington Post,* August 24, 1914, p. 8; *St. Louis Post-Dispatch,* August 25, 1914, p. 14.

12. *Sporting Life,* August 6, 1914, p. 3.

13. Walter "Rabbit" Maranville, *Run, Rabbit, Run* (Cleveland: Society for American Baseball Research, 1991), p. 37; *New York Times,* August 27, 1914, p. 9. Maranville's account differs quite a lot from the contemporary report.

14. *St. Louis Post-Dispatch,* August 27, 1914, p. 16.

15. Three years earlier, Pittsburgh had paid St. Paul of the American Association a record $22,500 for O'Toole, who proved a big disappointment. His September 4 decision over Brooklyn was his twenty-third major-league victory and his last.

16. *Sporting News,* September 10, 1914, p. 4.

17. *New York Times,* September 8, 1914, p. 8.

18. Lawrence S. Ritter, *The Glory of Their Times: The Story of the Early Days of Baseball Told by the Men Who Played It,* 2d ed. (New York: Vintage, 1985), pp. 115.

19. Thomas L. Hughes, the pitcher in question, should be distinguished from Thomas James "Long Tom" Hughes, who won 113 games pitching for various major-league teams from 1900 to 1913. Thomas L. Hughes, at 6'2", was actually an inch taller than "Long Tom."

20. Harold Kaese, *The Boston Braves, 1875–1953* (rpt. Boston: Northeastern University Press, 2004), p. 158.

21. *St. Louis Post-Dispatch,* September 18, 1914, p. 19; "Editorials," *Baseball Magazine,* 13 (October 1914), p. 13.

22. Harold Seymour [and Dorothy Seymour Mills], *Baseball: The Golden Age* (New York: Oxford University Press, 1971), p. 159.

23. *Sporting Life,* October 3, 1914, p. 5.

24. Despite Fred Tyler's rigorous late-season trial, the next spring he was back in the minors.

25. *Boston Globe,* February 6, 1915, p. 4.

26. St. Louis's showing was the best for the city's National League entry since the city joined the league in 1892.

Chapter 4

1. William A. Phelon, "The Field against the Athletics," *Baseball Magazine* 14 (November 1914), pp. 30–31.

2. The National Commission, created as part of the 1903 peace settlement between the National and American leagues and empowered to be the ruling authority in professional baseball, consisted of the presi-

dents of the two leagues plus a third, supposedly neutral member. The third member was August "Garry" Herrmann, president of the Cincinnati Reds and a close friend of Johnson. Herrmann usually went along with whatever Johnson wanted to do.

3. Mack was a lean 6'1", the same height as Stallings. That made them the two tallest managers in the major leagues.

4. *Sporting Life*, October 17, 1914, p. 4; William Kashatus, *Money Pitcher: Chief Bender and the Tragedy of American Assimilation* (University Park: Penn State University Press, 2006), p. 112.

5. Walter "Rabbit" Maranville, *Run, Rabbit Run* (Cleveland: Society for American Baseball Research, 1991), p. 29.

6. Tom Swift, *Chief Bender's Burden: The Silent Struggle of a Baseball Star* (Lincoln: University of Nebraska Press, 2008), p. 40.

7. As late as the 1950s, before they had use of telescopic lens, photographers were allowed on the field during games.

8. *New York Times*, October 14, 1914, p. 8.

9. Since 1907, umpires had been stationed down the foul lines in the World Series, as well as on the bases.

10. *Washington Post*, October 14, 1914, p. 1.

11. In New York, St. Louis, and Chicago, the World Series shared press coverage with city series matching the Yankees and Giants, Browns and Cardinals, and White Sox and Cubs.

12. *Sporting Life*, October 24, 1914, p. 2.

13. Ibid., October 17, 1914, p. 3; F. C. Lane, "Where the Dope Went Wrong," *Baseball Magazine* 14 (December 1914), p. 15; *Boston Globe*, January 8, 1931, p. 22; Swift, *Chief Bender's Burden*, p. 228.

14. Lane, "Where the Dope Went Wrong," p. 16.

15. *Sporting News*, October 22, 1914, p. 6; Ring W. Lardner, "'Braves' Is Right," *American Magazine* 79 (March 1915), p. 70.

16. *New York Times*, November 11, 1915, p. S4.

17. *Sporting Life*, January 9, 1915, p. 3; Lane, "Where the Dope Went Wrong," p. 17.

Chapter 5

1. *Sporting News*, October 28, 1914, p. 4.

2. Ban Johnson certified Cobb as the American League batting champion, although various injuries had limited him to only 345 times at bat. Under present-day rules, Eddie Collins would have won the batting title.

3. Walter "Rabbit" Maranville, *Run, Rabbit, Run* (Cleveland: Society for American Baseball Research, 1991), p. 35.

4. *Sporting Life*, February 27, 1915, p. 6.

5. Ibid., October 31, 1914, p. 3.

6. F. C. Lane, "George Stallings, the Miracle Man," *Baseball Magazine* 14 (February 1915), p. 55.

7. Ibid., November 7, 1914, p. 3.

8. Ibid., November 14, 1914, p. 3; *Sporting News*, October 29, 1914, p. 4.

9. As the present writer did as a child in the school he attended in southeast Texas.

10. As bizarre as what Evers was doing might seem today, in that time the high-altitude, cold-weather treatment was widely prescribed for people with weak lungs and especially for those suffering from tuberculosis. Branch Rickey and Christy Mathewson spent winters at Lake Saranac, New York, battling tuberculosis, Rickey successfully, Mathewson unsuccessfully.

11. *Boston Globe*, December 13, 1914, p. 56.

12. Ibid., January 31, 1915, p. 39.

13. Tom Simon, "Sherwood Robert Magee," in Tom Simon, ed., *Deadball Stars of the National League* (Washington, D.C,: Brassey's, 2004), pp. 194–195.

14. Finneran lasted only two seasons in the National League. He resurfaced as an umpire in the Federal League.

15. Simon, "Sherwood Magee, p. 195.

16. *Boston Globe*, no date [December 1914], George T. Stallings Collection, National Baseball Hall of Fame Library, Cooperstown, NY.

17. William A. Phelon, "The Passing Show," *Baseball Magazine* 14 (February 1915), p. 17. In 1914, Quinn was pitching for

a third-place Baltimore team; for a seventh-place team in 1915 he would *lose* twenty-two games.

18. *Sporting Life*, February 20, 1915, p. 2; Eugene C. Murdock, *Ban Johnson: Czar of Baseball* (Westport, CT: Greenwood Press, 1982), p. 79.

19. *New York Times*, February 28, 1915, p. S3.

20. *Sporting Life*, March 13, 1915, p. 3; *Sporting News*, February 25, 1915, p. 2.

21. William A. Phelon, "Who Will Win the Pennants?" *Baseball Magazine* 15 (May 1915), p. 28.

Chapter 6

1. Lobert was nicknamed "Hans" because of his putative resemblance to Honus Wagner. The resemblance to the great Wagner ended there.

2. Cocreham wouldn't make it back to the majors. Luque would come back in 1918 with Cincinnati and pitch for the next eighteen years with the Reds, Brooklyn, and the Giants, finishing with 193 career victories. He would also become a legend as a pitcher and manager in Cuban baseball.

3. Harold Kaese, *The Boston Braves, 1871–1953* (rpt., Boston: Northeastern University Press, 2004), p. 158.

4. Gowdy quoted in "Baseball's Greatest Teams," *Baseball Digest*, July 1949, in George Tweedy Stallings Collection, Giamatti Research Center, National Baseball Hall of Fame Library, Cooperstown, NY.

5. *New York Morning Sun*, May 8, 1915, clipping in James Gaffney E. Collection, Giamatti Research Center, National Baseball Library, Cooperstown, NY.

6. *Sporting News*, July 1, 1915, p. 5.

7. Ibid., June 24, 1915, p. 5; William A. Phelon, "The Season's Game," *Baseball Magazine* 15 (August 1915), p. 21.

8. *Los Angeles Times*, July 7, 1915, p. III.

9. *Cincinnati Post*, July 7, 1915, p. 6. Fullerton would have been quoting either Garry Herrmann of Cincinnati, Charles Ebbets of Brooklyn, or Barney Dreyfuss of Pittsburgh, the only remaining National League club owners from 1901–1902.

10. *Sporting Life*, July 24, 1915, p. 7.

11. *Sporting News*, July 15, 1915, p. 5. Ty Cobb, Honus Wagner, and several other baseball notables had earlier appeared in *Sporting News* endorsements for Coca-Cola.

12. *Sporting Life*, July 24, 1915, p. 3.

13. Ibid., August 14, 1915, p.7; *St. Louis Post-Dispatch*, August 4, 1915, p. 7; August 5, 1915, p. 7.

14. My description of what happened has been pieced together from reports in *Sporting Life*, August 14, 1915, p. 7; *St. Louis Post-Dispatch*, August 4, 1915, p. 7; August 7, 1915, p. 8; and *Sporting News*, August 12, 1915, p. 1.

15. David Jones, "William Lawrence James," in Tom Simon, ed., *Deadball Stars of the National League* (Washington, D.C: Brassey's Inc., 2004), p. 326.

16. *Sporting Life*, August 14, 1915, pp. 7, 8; *St. Louis Post-Dispatch*, August 8, 1915, p. 18; *Cincinnati Post*, August 4, 1915, p. 6.

17. *Sporting News*, August 14, 1915, p. 7.

18. Bob Ruzzo, "Braves Field: An Imperfect History of the Perfect Ballpark," *Baseball Research Journal* 41 (Fall 2012), p. 53; F. C. Lane, "The World's Greatest Park," *Baseball Magazine* 15 (October 1915), 104.

19. *Sporting Life*, August 28, 1915, p. 6. For a professional game, perhaps, although the overflow in Fenway Park for the afternoon half of the September 7, 1914, doubleheader between the Braves and Giants may have been bigger. Also in 1914, a semipro championship game in the city park in Cleveland had attracted a throng estimated at 100,000.

20. "Pete Compton" was the ballplayer's *nom de jeux*, which was understandable, given that the legal name of the native of San Marcos, Texas, was Anna Sebastian Bash. Evidently his parents wanted a girl.

21. Although no fine accompanied Evers's suspension, given his $10,000 salary, the loss of five days' pay would have amounted to about $500, a very stiff penalty for that time.

22. Clarke went back to his farm and his

business holdings at Winfield, Kansas, although he would return to the Pirates as a coach in 1925 and become assistant manager and vice president the next year.

23. Boardman had made brief appearances for the Cardinals at the tail-end of the two previous seasons. The victory over Brooklyn was the only game he ever won in the majors.

24. *Sporting News*, September 23, 1915, p. 4; *Chicago Tribune*, September 26, 1915, p. B3.

25. *Sporting News*, October 7, 1915, pp. 1.

26. The older brother of the Philadelphia Athletics' Wally Schang, Bobby Schang had been traded to New York during the season by Pittsburgh. In four seasons (1914–1916 and 1927), he was never more than a fill-in catcher.

27. *Sporting News*, October 21, 1915, p. 1; October 7, 1915, p. 5; William A. Phelon, "Down the Home Stretch," *Baseball Magazine* 16 (November 1915), pp. 41f; Phelon, "The Season of 1915 in Retrospect," *Baseball Magazine* 16 (December 1915), pp. 75–81; Phelon, "The 'Ifs' of 1915," *Baseball Magazine* 16 (January 1916), pp. 81–86.

28. *Sporting Life*, October 23, 1915, p. 10.

29. The 1902 Giants did finish last, but McGraw only managed them the last sixty-three games of the season.

Chapter 7

1. Bob Ruzzo, "Fate and the Federal League," *Baseball Research Journal* 42 (Fall 2013), pp. 30–40.

2. Previous baseball "wars": 1882, National League versus American Association; 1884, National League and American Association versus Union Association; 1890, National League and American Association versus Players' League; 1891, National League versus American Association; 1901–1902, National League versus American League.

3. Branch Rickey, who had managed the Browns since late in the 1913 season, became Phil Ball's vice president and business manager. The two didn't get along;

in 1917 Rickey moved to the Cardinals. Roger Bresnahan, displaced by Tinker as Cubs manager, became manager and part-owner of the American Association team in Toledo, his home town.

4. *Sporting Life*, November 6, 1915, p. 3.

5. Philadelphia led the National League, tripling its 1914 attendance and drawing nearly 500,000, while the Giants actually drew about 20,000 more than in 1914, suggesting that New York fans may have found a last-place club refreshing.

6. Harold Kaese, *The Boston Braves, 1871–1953* (rpt., Boston: Northeastern University Press, 2004), pp. 174–175.

7. Ibid., p. 175; *Chicago Herald* quoted in *Boston Globe*, January 9, 1916, p. 1. Although "fans" was increasingly the common term for baseball-followers, the older terms "bugs," "cranks," or "kranks" were still occasionally used.

8. *Boston Globe*, February 14 1916, p. 6.

9. John J. Ward, "'Butch' Schmidt, the Player-Worker," *Baseball Magazine* 16 (March 1916), pp. 33ff.

10. *Cincinnati Post*, March 10, 1916, p. 7; *Sporting News*, March 9, 1916, p. 1.

11. *Sporting Life*, March 4, 1916, p. 1. Frederick W. Lieb would live to be ninety-three and have a distinguished career as a baseball reporter and prolific author of team histories. His judgment on Gowdy wasn't among his most prescient.

12. Ibid., March 18, 1916, p. 8.

13. David Jones, "William Lawrence James," Tom Simon, ed., *Deadball Stars of the National League* (Washington, D.C.: Brassey's Inc., 2004), p 326.

14. The Irish-American players on the Braves and other teams—at least those who were Catholic, which is to say the majority of them—might also have taken a strong interest in what was happening in Ireland that spring: the Easter Rebellion in Dublin raised by Irish nationalists against British rule, the failure of which was followed by the trials and executions of a number of its leaders. Anti-British feeling among Irish-American Catholics, already strong, reached a new intensity in the aftermath of the executions.

15. *Sporting Life*, April 1, 1916, p. 5.

16. Willam A. Phelon, "Who Will Win the Pennants?" *Baseball Magazine* 17 (May 1916), p. 14.

Chapter 8

1. *Sporting Life*, May 16, 1916, p. 3.

2. *Sporting Life*, May 16, 1916, p. 3; *Chicago Tribune*, May 5, 1916, p. 13.

3. *Boston Globe*, May 14, 1916, p. 23.

4. After winning three games and losing four, Dale was sold to Indianapolis. In 1920, while he was with Salt Lake City in the Pacific Coast League, Dale and other players in the league were accused of fixing games. Although he was cleared of criminal charges, the National Association, the minor leagues' governing body, expelled him from Organized Baseball.

5. *St. Louis Post-Dispatch*, May 21, 1916, p. 18; May 22, 1916, p. 16.

6. Charles C. Alexander, *Rogers Hornsby: A Biography* (New York: Henry Holt, 1995), p. 32.

7. Until 1931, hits that bounced into regular (versus temporary) seats were home runs.

8. *Sporting News*, July 7, 1915, p. 1.

9. *Boston Globe*, July 5, 1916, p. 7; *Sporting Life*, July 15, 1916, p. 7.

10. *Sporting Life*, July 15, 1916, p. 7; *St. Louis Post-Dispatch*, July 6, 1916, p.19.

11. Before the Braves left for Chicago, Stallings tried to sell Pete Compton and his .204 batting average to the American Association's Louisville club. That didn't work out, because one National League club (presumably Pittsburgh) refused to waive Compton. Although he didn't accompany the team west, he remained on the Boston roster until Stallings could sell him to Pittsburgh for the waiver price.

12. It should be recalled that the previous winter, facetiously or not, Stallings had said he would like to trade Maranville for Herzog.

13. Roush and McKechnie were both ex–Federal Leaguers, both with Indianapolis in 1915 and Newark in 1916.

14. Mathewson pitched and won one more game, in a matchup late that season with Mordecai "Three Finger" Brown, with whom he had battled many times in earlier years. After two seasons in the Federal League—as pitcher-manager with St. Louis, then as a seventeen-game winner for Chicago—Brown had stayed on with Charles Weeghman's and Joe Tinker's amalgamated Cubs for what would be his last season in the majors.

15. *St. Louis Post-Dispatch*, July 20, 1916, p. 10.

16. F. C. Lane, "The Greatest Pitching Staff in the National League," *Baseball Magazine* 17 (October 1916), pp. 42–43.

17. Harold Kaese, *The Boston Braves, 1871–1953* (rpt., Boston: Northeastern University Press, 2004), p. 178.

18. Rico caught one game and had a total of four at bats before Blackburn took over and Tragesser recovered.

19. Kaese, *Boston Braves*, p. 178; *Sporting Life*, August 12, 1916, p. 3.

20. *St. Louis Post-Dispatch*, August 13, 1916, p. 8.

21. Ibid., August 10, 1916, p. 15; *Sporting News*, August 17, 1916, p. 1; *Sporting Life*, August 27, 1916, p. 2.

22. *Sporting News*, August 17, 1916, p. 1; *Cincinnati Post*, August 19, 1916, p. 2; *Sporting Life*, September 9, 1916, p. 3; William A. Phelon, "Who Will Win the Pennants?" *Baseball Magazine* 17 (October 1916), p. 20.

23. *Sporting Life*, September 16, 1916, p.9.

24. *Sporting News*, September 28, 1916, p. 1. Some baseball writers still referred to the Brooklyn team as either the Superbas or the Dodgers.

25. Charles C. Alexander, *John McGraw* (New York: Viking, 1988), pp. 192–193; *Sporting News*, September 28, 1916, p. 1.

26. After his dismal showing in 1915 in the Federal League, Bender's 7-7 record in 1916 was better than might have been expected. He would do even better in 1917, ending his big-league career with an 8–2 mark.

27. *Los Angeles Times*, October 3, 1916, p. III (dispatch from New York bureau).

28. Alexander, *John McGraw*, p. 193.

29. In *Baseball: The Golden Age* (New York: Oxford University Press, 1971), Harold Seymour [and Dorothy Seymour Mills] used the term "piddling on my pennant" (p. 287). But as Jack Kavanagh and Norman Macht observed in *Uncle Robbie* (Cleveland: Society for American Baseball Research, 1999), "It is nicely alliterative, but the scholarly Dr. Seymour has undoubtedly softened Robinson's language" (p. 88). I agree.

Chapter 9

1. William A. Phelon, "The Greatest Race in Baseball History," *Baseball Magazine* 18 (November 1916), pp. 50–64.

2. *Sporting Life*, October 28, 1916, p. 8; November 11, 1916, p. 11.

3. *Chicago Tribune*, December 15, 1916, p. 13; *Christian Science Monitor*, December 15, 1916, p. 12.

4. *Boston Globe*, December 12, 1916, p. 1.

5. William A. Phelon, "Forecast and Recollections," *Baseball Magazine* 18 (January 1917), p. 16.

6. *Sporting News*, September 28, 1916, p. 1; William A. Phelon, "Who Will Win the Pennants?" *Baseball Magazine* 19 (May 1917), pp. 221ff.

7. Harold Kaese, *The Boston Braves, 1871–1953* (rpt., Boston: Northeastern University Press, 2004), p. 179.

8. John Evers, "Why I Am on the Bench," *Baseball Magazine* 19 (June 1917), p. 293.

9. William A. Phelon, "How Goes the Pennant Race?" *Baseball Magazine* 19 (July 1917), p. 395.

Epilogue

1. *Hartford Courant*, May 14, 1929, p. 13; *Chicago Tribune*, May 14, 1929, p. 31.

2. Bill James, *The Bill James Guide to Baseball Managers from 1870 to Today* (New York: Scribner's, 1997), p. 46.

3. *Boston Globe*, January 31, 1915, p. 39.

4. Ibid., June 3, 1951, p. C45.

5. Ibid.

Bibliography

Archival Resources

Files for the following were examined at the Giamatti Research Center, National Baseball Hall of Fame Library, Cooperstown, New York

Evers, John
Gaffney, James
Hughes, Thomas L.
James, William Lawrence
Konetchy, Edward
Magee, Sherwood
Maranville, Walter "Rabbit"
Rudolph, Richard
Schmidt, Charles "Butch"
Smith, James Carlisle "Red"
Stallings, George Tweedy
Tyler, George "Lefty"

Newspapers

Boston Globe, 1912–1952
Christian Science Monitor, 1913–1920
Cincinnati Post, 1913–1918
Hartford Courant, 1913–1917
Los Angeles Times, 1914–1916
New York Times, 1912–1929
St. Louis Post-Dispatch, 1913–1917
Sporting Life, 1911–1918
Sporting News, 1911–1918
Washington Post, 1913–1952

Internet Resources

George, Paul S. "One Hundred Years of Miami History."
http://baseballresearcher.blogspot.com.
http://www.historymiami.org/research-miami/topics/history-of-miami.
www.baseball-almanac.com.
www.baseball-reference.com.

Official Publications

Foster, John B., ed. *Spalding's Official Base Ball Guides.* New York: American Company, 1913, 1914, 1915, 1916, 1917, 1918.

Books

Adler, Rich. *Mack, McGraw, and the 1913 Season.* Jefferson, NC: McFarland, 2008.
Alexander, Charles C. *John McGraw.* New York: Viking, 1988; rpt. Lincoln: University of Nebraska Press, 1995.
Alexander, Charles C. *Rogers Hornsby: A Biography.* New York: Holt, 1995.
Alexander, Charles C. *Ty Cobb.* New York: Oxford University Press, 1982; rpt. Dallas: Southern Methodist University Press, 2006.
The Baseball Encyclopedia, 10th ed. New York: Macmillan, 1996.
Bogen, Gil. *Johnny Kling.* Jefferson, NC: McFarland, 2006.
_____. *Tinker, Evers, Chance: A Triple Biography.* Jefferson, NC: McFarland, 2003.
Browning, Reed. *Cy Young: A Baseball Life.* Amherst: University of Massachusetts Press, 2000.
Durant, John. *Baseball's Miracle Teams.* New York: Hastings House, 1975.
Grow, Nathaniel. *Baseball on Trial: The*

Origin of Baseball's Antitrust Exemption. Urbana: University of Illinois Press, 2014.

Huhn, Rick. *Eddie Collins: A Baseball Biography.* Jefferson, NC: McFarland, 2008.

James, Bill. *The Bill James Guide to Baseball Managers from 1870 to Today.* New York: Scribner's, 1997.

Jordan, David M. *The Athletics of Philadelphia: Connie Mack's White Elephants, 1901–1954.* Jefferson, NC: McFarland, 1999.

Kaese, Harold. *The Boston Braves, 1871–1953.* Rpt. Boston: Northeastern University Press, 2004.

Kashatus, William C. *Chief Bender and the Tragedy of Indian Assimilation.* University Park: Penn State University Press, 2006.

Kavanagh, Jack, and Norman Macht. *Uncle Robbie.* Cleveland: Society for American Baseball Research, 1999.

Kohout, Martin D. *Hal Chase: The Black Prince of Baseball.* Jefferson, NC: McFarland, 2001.

Kuklick, Bruce. *To Everything a Season: Shibe Park and Urban Philadelphia, 1909–1976.* Princeton: Princeton University Press, 1991.

Levitt, Daniel R. *The Battle That Shaped Baseball: The Federal League Challenge and Its Legacy.* Lanham, MD: Rowman & Littlefield, 2012.

Lowry, Philip J. *Green Cathedrals: The Ultimate Celebration of Major and Negro League Ballparks.* New York: Walker, 2006.

Macht, Norman. *Connie Mack and the Early Years of Baseball.* Lincoln: University of Nebraska Press, 2005.

Mack, Connie. *My 60 Years in the Big Leagues.* New York: Winston, 1950.

Mansch, Larry D. *Rube Marquard: The Life and Times of a Baseball Hall of Famer.* Jefferson, NC: McFarland, 1998.

Minor League Baseball Stars. Springfield, VA: Society for American Baseball Research, 1978.

Maranville, Walter "Rabbit." *Run, Rabbit, Run: The Hilarious and Mostly True Tales of Rabbit Maranville.* Cleveland: Society for American Baseball Research, 1991.

Murdock, Eugene C. *Ban Johnson: Czar of Baseball.* Westport, CT: Greenwood Press, 1982.

Nowlin, Bill, et al. *The Miracle Braves of 1914: Boston's Original Worst to First Champions.* Phoenix: Society for American Baseball Research, 2014.

Ritter, Lawrence S. *The Glory of Their Times: The Story of the Early Days of Baseball Told by the Men Who Played It,* 2d ed. New York: Vintage, 1985.

Seymour, Harold [and Dorothy Seymour Mills]. *Baseball: The Golden Years.* New York: Oxford University Press, 1971.

Simon, Tom, ed. *Deadball Stars of the National League.* Washington, D.C.: Brassey's, 2004.

Stout, Glenn. *Fenway 1912: The Birth of a Ballpark, a Championship Season, and Fenway's Remarkable First Year.* Boston: Houghton Mifflin, 2011.

Swift, Tom. *Chief Bender's Burden: The Silent Struggle of a Baseball Star.* Lincoln: University of Nebraska Press, 2007.

Thorn, John, et al. *Total Baseball: The Official Encyclopedia of Major League Baseball,* 7th ed. Kingston NY: Total Sports, 2001.

Young, William A. *John Tortes "Chief" Meyers: A Baseball Biography.* Jefferson, NC: McFarland, 2011.

Zinn, Paul G., and John G. *The Major League Pennant Races of 1916: "The Most Maddening Baseball Melee in History."* Jefferson, NC: McFarland, 2009.

Articles

Cary, J. B. "Charles Deal, the Man Who Made Good in the Pinch." *Baseball Magazine* 14 (February 1915), pp. 53–56.

Cotton, Joseph. "When 'Fat' Maranville Was an Amateur." *Baseball Magazine* 14 (February 1915), pp. 67–70.

Evers, John. "My Latest Move in Major Company." *Baseball Magazine* 19 (September 1917), pp. 490–491.

_____. "The Passing of Frank Chance." *Baseball Magazine* 10 (January 1913), pp. 24ff.

_____. "Why I Am on the Bench." *Baseball Magazine* 19 (June 1917), p. 293.

Farmer, Ted. "Hank Gowdy and the Call to Arms: Major League Baseball and World War I." *Nine* 5 (Spring 1997), pp. 265–287.

Hoefer, W. R. "'Red' Smith of the Braves." *Baseball Magazine* 19 (June 1917), pp. 301–302.

Lane, F. C. "The Gamest Player in Baseball." *Baseball Magazine* 11 (September 1913), pp. 51–61.

_____. "George Stallings, the Miracle Man." *Baseball Magazine* 14 (February 1915), pp. 57–65.

_____. "The Greatest of All Second Basemen," *Baseball Magazine* 10 (December 1912), pp. 33–44.

_____. "The Greatest Pitching Staff in the National League." *Baseball Magazine* 17 (October 1916), pp. 42–43.

_____. "The Sensational Evers Deal." *Baseball Magazine* 14 (August 1914), pp. 27–33ff.

_____. "The World's Greatest Ballpark." *Baseball Magazine* 15 (October 1915), p. 104.

Lardner, Ring W. "'Braves' Is Right." *American Magazine* 79 (March 1915), pp. 19ff.

Lieb, Frederick G. "How Will They Finish Next October?" *Baseball Magazine* 12 (March 1914), pp. 43–48.

Maranville, Rabbit. "Old and New, It's Still Baseball." *American Legion Magazine* 112 (October 1935), pp. 1–2ff.

Mason, Ward. "Vote for Hughes." *Baseball Magazine* 18 (November 1916), pp. 39–41.

Morse, Jacob C. "Where the Cubs Will Train." *Baseball Magazine* 6 (February 1911), pp. 12–14.

Phelon, William A. "The Baseball Campaign Up to Date." *Baseball Magazine* 11 (July 1913), pp. 19ff.

_____. "Baseball History in the Making." *Baseball Magazine* 19 (September 1917), pp. 498ff.

_____. "Baseball History Up to Date." *Baseball Magazine* 10 (February 1913), pp. 19ff.

_____. "The Field Against the Athletics." *Baseball Magazine* 14 (November 1914), pp. 30–31.

_____. "Forecast and Recollections." *Baseball Magazine* 18 (January 1917), pp. 16ff.

_____. "The Greatest Race in Baseball History," *Baseball Magazine* 18 (November 1916), pp. 50–64.

_____. "How Goes the Pennant Race?" *Baseball Magazine* 19 (June 1917), p. 395f.

_____. "Lining Up for 1916." *Baseball Magazine* (June 1916), pp. 13–18f.

_____. "The Opening Broadsides." *Baseball Magazine* 15 (June 1915), pp. 19–28f.

_____. "The Passing Show," *Baseball Magazine* 14 (February 1915), p. 17.

_____. "Ring Up the Curtain on the Pennant Race." *Baseball Magazine* 11 (June 1913), pp. 15–20.

_____. "The Season's Game." *Baseball Magazine* 15 (August 1915), pp. 17ff.

_____. "The Season of 1915 in Retrospect." *Baseball Magazine* 16 (December 1915), pp. 75–81.

_____. "Stirring Times in Baseball." *Baseball Magazine* 19 (August 1917), pp. 427ff.

_____. "Who Will Win the 1913 Pennants?" *Baseball Magazine* 10 (May 1913), pp. 12–24.

Ruzzo, Bob. "Braves Field: An Imperfect History of the Perfect Ballpark." *Baseball Research Journal* 41 (Fall 2012), pp. 50–60.

_____. "Fate and the Federal League."

Baseball Research Journal 42 (Fall 2013), pp. 30–40.

Stack, Charles P. "A Day with John Evers." *Baseball Magazine* 14 (February 1915), pp. 71–75.

_____. "Training Camps." *Baseball Magazine* 12 (March 1914), pp. 27ff.

Ward, John B. "Butch Schmidt, the Player Worker." *Baseball Magazine* 16 (March 1916), pp.33ff.

Ward, John V. "Youngsters Who Starred in 1913." *Baseball Magazine* 13 (May 1914), pp. 55ff.

Unpublished

Tootle, James R. Presentation on Hank Gowdy to Hank Gowdy Chapter, Society for American Baseball Research, Columbus, Ohio, January 26, 1913.

Index

Numbers in *bold italics* indicate pages with photographs.